Cambridge International
AS & A Level Mathematics:

Pure Mathematics 2 & 3

Practice Book

CAMBRIDGE
UNIVERSITY PRESS

University Printing House, Cambridge CB2 8BS, United Kingdom

One Liberty Plaza, 20th Floor, New York, NY 10006, USA

477 Williamstown Road, Port Melbourne, VIC 3207, Australia

314–321, 3rd Floor, Plot 3, Splendor Forum, Jasola District Centre, New Delhi – 110025, India

79 Anson Road, #06–04/06, Singapore 079906

Cambridge University Press is part of the University of Cambridge.

It furthers the University's mission by disseminating knowledge in the pursuit of education, learning and research at the highest international levels of excellence.

www.cambridge.org
Information on this title: www.cambridge.org/9781108457675

© Cambridge University Press 2018

First published 2018

20 19 18 17 16 15 14 13 12 11 10

Printed in Malaysia by Vivar Printing

A catalogue record for this publication is available from the British Library

ISBN 978-1-108-45767-5 Paperback

The questions, example answers, marks awarded and/or comments that appear in this book were written by the author(s). In examination, the way marks would be awarded to answers like these may be different.

This book has been compiled and authored by Muriel James, using some questions from:

Cambridge International AS and A Level Mathematics: Pure Mathematics 1 Coursebook (Revised edition) by Hugh Neill, Douglas Quadling and Julian Gilbey, that was originally published 2016.

Cambridge International AS and A Level Mathematics: Pure Mathematics 2 & 3 Coursebook (Revised edition) by Hugh Neill, Douglas Quadling and Julian Gilbey, that was originally published 2016.

A Level Mathematics for OCR A Student Book 1 (AS/Year 1) by Vesna Kadelburg, Ben Woolley, Paul Fannon and Stephen Ward

A Level Mathematics for OCR A Student Book 2 (Year 2) by Vesna Kadelburg, Ben Woolley, Paul Fannon and Stephen Ward

Cover image: Mint Images - Frans Lanting/Getty Images

....

Contents

How to use this book

Throughout this book you will notice particular features that are designed to help your learning. This section provides a brief overview of these features.

- Differentiate products and quotients.
- Use the derivatives of e^x, $\ln x$, $\sin x$, $\cos x$, $\tan x$, together with constant multiples, sums, differences and composites.
- Find and use the first derivative of a function which is defined parametrically or implicitly.

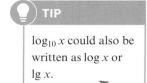

TIP

$\log_{10} x$ could also be written as $\log x$ or $\lg x$.

Learning objectives indicate the important concepts within each chapter and help you to navigate through the practice book.

Tip boxes contain helpful guidance about calculating or checking your answers.

END-OF-CHAPTER REVIEW EXERCISE 3

1 Find the exact solution of the following equations for $-\pi \leqslant \theta \leqslant \pi$.

  a i $\operatorname{cosec} \theta = -2$ ii $\operatorname{cosec} \theta = -1$

  b i $\cot \theta = \sqrt{3}$ ii $\cot \theta = 1$

  c i $\sec \theta = 1$ ii $\sec \theta = -\dfrac{2}{\sqrt{3}}$

  d i $\cot \theta = 0$ ii $\cot \theta = -1$

The **End-of-chapter review exercise** contains exam-style questions covering all topics in the chapter. You can use this to check your understanding of the topics you have covered.

WORKED EXAMPLE 2.2

On average, flaws occur in a roll of cloth at the rate of 3.6 per metre.

Assuming a Poisson distribution is appropriate, find the probability of:

  a exactly nine flaws in three metres of cloth

  b less than three flaws in half a metre of cloth.

Answer

  a $e^{-10.8}\dfrac{10.8^9}{9!} = 0.112$ Use the interval to determine the mean, λ. For three metres, $\lambda = 3 \times 3.6 = 10.8$.

  b $e^{-1.8}\left(1 + 1.8 + \dfrac{1.8^2}{2!}\right) = 0.731$ For half a metre, $\lambda = \dfrac{1}{2} \times 3.6 = 1.8$.

Worked examples provide step-by-step approaches to answering questions. The left side shows a fully worked solution, while the right side contains a commentary explaining each step in the working.

Throughout each chapter there are multiple exercises containing practice questions. The questions are coded:

PS   These questions focus on problem-solving.

P   These questions focus on proofs.

M   These questions focus on modelling.

🖩   You should not use a calculator for these questions.

🖩   You can use a calculator for these questions.

This book covers both Pure Mathematics 2 and Pure Mathematics 3. One topic (5.5 The trapezium rule) is only covered in Pure Mathematics 2 and this section is marked with the icon **P2**. Chapters 7–11 are only covered in Pure Mathematics 3 and these are marked with the icon **P3**. The icons appear in the Contents list and in the relevant sections of the book.

- Understand the meaning of $|x|$, sketch the graph of $y = |ax + b|$ and use relations such as $|a| = |b| \Leftrightarrow a^2 = b^2$ and $|x - a| < b \Leftrightarrow a - b < x < a + b$ in the course of solving equations and inequalities.
- Divide a polynomial, of degree not exceeding 4, by a linear or quadratic polynomial, and identify the quotient and remainder (which may be zero).
- Use the factor theorem and the remainder theorem.

1.1 The modulus function

WORKED EXAMPLE 1.1

Solve:

a $2|3x - 1| = \left| \dfrac{1}{2}x - 1 \right|$

b $x^2 - 5|x| + 4 = 0$

Answer

a $2|3x - 1| = \left| \dfrac{1}{2}x - 1 \right|$ $\qquad$ Split the equation into two parts.

$2(1 - 3x) = 1 - \dfrac{1}{2}x$ ------------------ (1)

$2(1 - 3x) = -\left(1 - \dfrac{1}{2}x\right)$ ---------- (2)

$2 - 6x = 1 - \dfrac{1}{2}x$ $\qquad$ Using equation (1), expand brackets.

$-5\dfrac{1}{2}x = -1$ $\qquad$ Solve.

$x = \dfrac{2}{11}$

$2 - 6x = -1 + \dfrac{1}{2}x$ $\qquad$ Solve using equation (2).

$-6\dfrac{1}{2}x = -3$

$x = \dfrac{6}{13}$

The solution is: $x = \dfrac{2}{11}$ or $x = \dfrac{6}{13}$.

b $x^2 - 5|x| + 4 = 0$ $\qquad$ Subtract $x^2 + 4$ from both sides.

$-5|x| = -x^2 - 4$ $\qquad$ Divide both sides by -5.

$|x| = \dfrac{1}{5}(x^2 + 4)$ $\qquad$ Split the equation into two parts.

$x = \dfrac{1}{5}(x^2 + 4)$ --------- (1)

$x = \dfrac{1}{5}(-x^2 - 4)$ -------- (2)

$$5x = x^2 + 4$$ $\quad\cdots\cdots\cdots\cdots$ Using equation (1), rearrange.
$$x^2 - 5x + 4 = 0$$
$$(x - 4)(x - 1) = 0$$ $\quad\cdots\cdots\cdots\cdots$ Factorise.
$$x = 4, 1$$

$$5x = -x^2 - 4$$ $\quad\cdots\cdots\cdots\cdots$ Using equation (2), rearrange.
$$x^2 + 5x + 4 = 0$$
$$(x + 4)(x + 1) = 0$$ $\quad\cdots\cdots\cdots\cdots$ Factorise.
$$x = -4, -1$$

The solutions are $x = \pm 1, \pm 4$

$$1^2 - 5|1| + 4 = 0$$ $\quad\cdots\cdots\cdots\cdots$ Check.
$$4^2 - 5|4| + 4 = 0$$
$$(-1)^2 - 5|-1| + 4 = 0$$
$$(-4)^2 - 5|-4| + 4 = 0$$

EXERCISE 1A

1 Solve:

a $|x + 2| = 5$ **b** $|x - 1| = 7$

c $|2x - 3| = 3$ **d** $|3x + 1| = 10$

e $|x + 1| = |2x - 3|$ **f** $|x - 3| = |3x + 1|$

g $|2x + 1| = |3x + 9|$ **h** $|5x + 1| = |11 - 2x|$

TIP

Remember:
$|a| = |b| \Leftrightarrow a^2 = b^2$

2 Solve these equations.

a $|x + 1| + |1 - x| = 2$ **b** $|x + 1| - |1 - x| = 2$

c $-|x + 1| + |1 - x| = 2$

3 Solve these equations.

a $|x| = |1 - x| + 1$ **b** $|x - 1| = |x| + 1$ **c** $|x - 1| + |x| = 1$

4 Solve these equations.

a $x + |2x - 1| = 3$ **b** $3 + |2x - 1| = x$

5 Solve:

a $|x^2 - 4| = 12$ **b** $|6 + x^2| = 5x$ **c** $|x^2 + 3x| = x + 1$

d $|x^2 - 4| = 4x + 1$ **e** $|3x^2 - 2x| = 1 - x$ **f** $|x^2 - 3x + 6| = 4 + 2x$

6 Solve the simultaneous equations.

a $\quad x + 2y = 4$ **b** $\quad 3x + y = 0$
$\quad |x + 2| + y = 5$ $\quad\quad y = |x^2 - 2x|$

7 Solve the equation $2|x - 1|^2 + 3|x - 1| - 2 = 0$.

8 a Solve the equation $x^2 - 5|x| + 6 = 0$.

   b Sketch the graph of $y = x^2 - 5|x| + 6$.

   c Write down the equation of the line of symmetry of the curve.

9 Solve the equation $|2x + 1| + |2x - 1| = 3$.

PS **10** Solve the equation $|3x - 2y + 10| + 2\sqrt{7 + 3x - 3y} = 0$.

1.2 Graphs of $y = |f(x)|$ where $f(x)$ is linear

WORKED EXAMPLE 1.2

a Sketch the graph of $y = \left|\dfrac{1}{3}x - 1\right|$, showing the points where the graph meets the axes.

   Use your graph to express $\left|\dfrac{1}{3}x - 1\right|$ in an alternative form.

b Use your answer to part **a** to solve graphically $\left|\dfrac{1}{3}x - 1\right| = 1$.

Answer

a

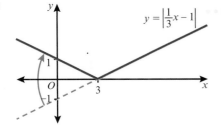

$y = \left|\dfrac{1}{3}x - 1\right|$

First sketch the graph of $y = \dfrac{1}{3}x - 1$.

Reflect in the x-axis the part of the line that is below the x-axis.

The line has gradient $\dfrac{1}{3}$ and a y-intercept of -1.

The graph shows that $\left|\dfrac{1}{3}x - 1\right|$ can be written as:

$$\left|\frac{1}{3}x - 1\right| = \begin{cases} \dfrac{1}{3}x - 1 & \text{if } x \geqslant 3 \\ -\left(\dfrac{1}{3}x - 1\right) & \text{if } x < 3 \end{cases}$$

3

b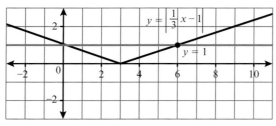

On the same axes, draw $y = 1$.

Find the points of intersection of the lines $y = \left|\dfrac{1}{3}x - 1\right|$ and $y = 1$.

There are two points of intersection of the lines $y = \left|\dfrac{1}{3}x - 1\right|$ and $y = 1$ so there are two roots.

The solutions to $\left|\dfrac{1}{3}x - 1\right| = 1$ are $x = 0$ and $x = 6$.

EXERCISE 1B

1   Sketch the graphs of each of the following functions showing the coordinates of the points where the graph meets the axes.

   a $y = |x - 4|$

   b $y = |5 - 2x|$

   c $y = \left|3 - \dfrac{1}{4}x\right|$

2   Sketch the following graphs.

   a $y = |x + 3|$

   b $y = |3x - 1|$

   c $y = |x - 5|$

   d $y = |3 - 2x|$

   e $y = 2|x + 1|$

   f $y = 3|x - 2|$

   g $y = -2|2x - 1|$

   h $y = 3|2 - 3x|$

   i $y = |x + 4| + |3 - x|$

   j $y = |6 - x| + |1 + x|$

   k $y = |x - 2| + |2x - 1|$

   l $y = 2|x - 1| - |2x + 3|$

3   Describe fully the transformation (or combination of transformations) that maps the graph of $y = |x|$ onto each of these functions.

   a $y = |x - 2| + 3$

   b $y = |x + 3| - 2$

   c $y = 1 - |x|$

   d $y = |3x| + 1$

   e $y = 2 - |x + 2|$

   f $y = 1 - 3|x|$

4   Sketch each of the following sets of graphs.

   a $y = x^2 - 2$ and $y = |x^2 - 2|$

   b $y = \sin x$ and $y = |\sin x|$

4

  c $y = (x - 1)(x - 2)(x - 3)$ and $y = |(x - 1)(x - 2)(x - 3)|$

  d $y = \cos 2x$ and $y = |\cos 2x|$ and $y = \cos |2x|$

  e $y = |x - 2|$ and $y = ||x| - 2|$

5 $f(x) = 3 - |2x - 3|$ for $-2 \leqslant x \leqslant 6$. Find the range of function f.

6 **a** Sketch the graph of $y = |2x - 3| + 1$ for $-2 < x < 6$, showing the coordinates of the vertex and the y-intercept.

  b On the same diagram, sketch the graph of $y = 5 - x$.

  c Use your graph to solve the equation $|2x - 3| + 1 = 5 - x$.

7 **a** Sketch the graph of $y = |2x - 1|$ for $-4 < x < 6$, showing the coordinates of the vertex and the y-intercept.

  b On the same diagram, sketch the graph of $y = |3 - x|$.

  c Use your graph to solve the equation $|2x - 1| = |3 - x|$.

8 **a** Sketch the graph of $y = |2x + 1| + |1 - x|$.

  b Use your graph to solve the equation $|2x + 1| + |1 - x| = 3$.

9 Write the equation of each graph in the form $y = |ax + b|$.

  a **i**
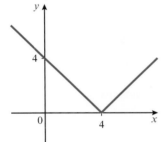

  ii
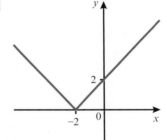

  b **i**
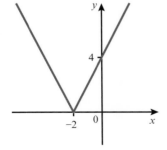

  ii
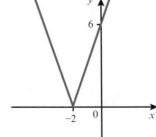

c i 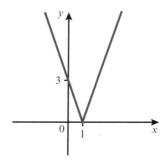　　　　ii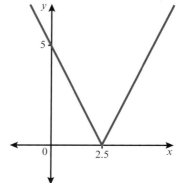

10 Sketch the graph of $y = x|x|$.

1.3 Solving modulus inequalities

WORKED EXAMPLE 1.3

Solve the inequality $|2x - 3| \leqslant |x - 2|$.

Answer

Method 1 ⋯⋯⋯⋯⋯⋯⋯⋯⋯⋯⋯⋯⋯ Use algebra.

$$|2x - 3| \leqslant |x - 2|$$ ⋯⋯⋯⋯⋯⋯⋯ Use $|a| \geqslant |b| \Leftrightarrow a^2 \geqslant b^2$.
$$(2x - 3)^2 \leqslant (x - 2)^2$$
$$4x^2 - 12x + 9 \leqslant x^2 - 4x + 4$$
$$3x^2 - 8x + 5 \leqslant 0$$ ⋯⋯⋯⋯⋯⋯⋯⋯⋯ Factorise.
$$(3x - 5)(x - 1) \leqslant 0$$

Critical values are $\dfrac{5}{3}$ and 1.

Hence, $1 \leqslant x \leqslant \dfrac{5}{3}$.

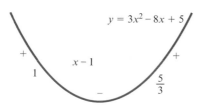

Method 2 $\cdots\cdots\cdots\cdots\cdots\cdots\cdots\cdots\cdots$ Use a graph.

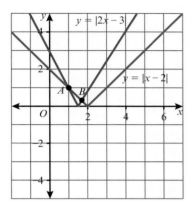

$\cdots\cdots\cdots\cdots\cdots\cdots$ The graphs of $y = |2x - 3|$ and $y = |x - 2|$ intersect at the points A and B.

$$|2x - 3| = \begin{cases} 2x - 3 & \text{if } x \geqslant \dfrac{3}{2} \\[2mm] -(2x - 3) & \text{if } x < \dfrac{3}{2} \end{cases}$$ $\cdots\cdots\cdots\cdots\cdots$ Find the points of intersection.

$$|x - 2| = \begin{cases} x - 2 & \text{if } x \geqslant 2 \\[1mm] -(x - 2) & \text{if } x < 2 \end{cases}$$

At A, the line $y = -(x - 2)$ intersects the line $y = -(2x - 3)$.

$-x + 2 = -2x + 3$

$\qquad x = 1$

At B, the line $y = 2x - 3$ intersects the line $y = -(x - 2)$.

$2x - 3 = -x + 2$

$\qquad 3x = 5$

$\qquad x = \dfrac{5}{3}$

To solve the inequality $|2x - 3| \leqslant |x - 2|$ find where the graph of the function $y = |2x - 3|$ is below the graph of $y = |x - 2|$.

Hence, $1 \leqslant x \leqslant \dfrac{5}{3}$.

1 Solve. (You may use either an algebraic method or a graphical method.)

a $|x + 2| < 1$

b $|x - 3| > 5$

c $|2x + 7| \leqslant 3$

d $|3x + 2| \geqslant 8$

e $|x + 2| < |3x + 1|$

f $|2x + 5| > |x + 2|$

g $|x| > |2x - 3|$

h $|4x + 1| \leqslant |4x - 1|$

TIP

When solving modulus inequalities use

$|a| \leqslant b \Leftrightarrow -b \leqslant a \leqslant b$
and $|a| \geqslant b \Leftrightarrow a \leqslant -b$
or $b \leqslant a$

2 a Sketch the graphs of $y = |x|$ and $y = 2|2x - 3|$ on the same axes.

   b Solve the inequality $|x| > 2|2x - 3|$.

3 a On the same axes sketch the graphs of $y = 1 - |x - 2|$ and $y = |2x - 3|$.

   b Solve the inequality $1 - |x - 2| > |2x - 3|$.

4 Rewrite the function $k(x)$ defined by $k(x) = |x + 3| + |4 - x|$ for the following three cases, without using the modulus in your answer.

   a $x > 4$

   b $-3 \leqslant x \leqslant 4$

   c $x < -3$

1.4 Division of polynomials

WORKED EXAMPLE 1.4

Find the remainder when $x^3 - 3x + 4$ is divided by $x + 3$.

Answer

There is no x^2 term in $x^3 - 3x + 4$ so we write it as $x^3 + 0x^2 - 3x + 4$.

$$
\begin{array}{r}
x^2 \\
x + 3 \overline{) x^3 + 0x^2 - 3x + 4} \\
\underline{x^3 + 3x^2} \\
-3x^2 - 3x
\end{array}
$$

Divide the first term of the polynomial by $x : x^3 \div x = x^2$

Multiply $(x + 3)$ by $x^2 : x^2(x + 3) = x^3 + 3x^2$

Subtract: $(x^3 + 0x^2) - (x^3 + 3x^2) = -3x^2$ and bring down the $-3x$ from the next column.

$$
\begin{array}{r}
x^2 - 3x \\
x + 3 \overline{) x^3 + 0x^2 - 3x + 4} \\
\underline{x^3 + 3x^2} \\
-3x^2 - 3x \\
\underline{-3x^2 - 9x} \\
6x + 4
\end{array}
$$

Repeat the process.

Divide $-3x^2$ by $x : -3x^2 \div x = -3x$

Multiply $(x + 3)$ by $-3x : -3x(x + 3) = -3x^2 - 9x$

Subtract: $(-3x^2 - 3x) - (-3x^2 - 9x) = 6x$ and bring down the 4 from the next column.

$$\begin{array}{r} x^2 - 3x + 6 \\ x + 3 \overline{\smash{\big)}\ x^3 + 0x^2 - 3x + 4} \\ \underline{x^2 + 3x^2} \\ -3x^2 - 3x \\ \underline{-3x^2 - 9x} \\ 6x + 4 \\ \underline{6x + 18} \\ -14 \end{array}$$

Repeat the process.

Divide $6x$ by x : $6x \div x = 6$

Multiply $(x + 3)$ by 6 : $6(x + 3) = 6x + 18$

Subtract: $(6x + 4) - (6x + 18) = -14$

The remainder is -14.

The calculation can be written as:

$$(x^3 - 3x + 4) = (x + 3) \times (x^2 - 3x + 6) - 14$$
$$\uparrow \qquad \uparrow \qquad \uparrow \qquad \uparrow$$
$$\text{dividend} \quad \text{divisor} \quad \text{quotient} \quad \text{remainder}$$

1 Find the quotient and the remainder when the first polynomial is divided by the second.

  a $x^3 + 2x^2 - 3x + 1$, $x + 2$

  b $x^3 - 3x^2 + 5x - 4$, $x - 5$

  c $2x^3 + 4x - 5$, $x + 3$

  d $5x^3 - 3x + 7$, $x - 4$

  e $2x^3 - x^2 - 3x - 7$, $2x + 1$

  f $6x^3 + 17x^2 - 17x + 5$, $3x - 2$

2 Use polynomial division to simplify the following expressions.

  a i $\dfrac{x^3 - 3x^2 - 13x - 30}{x^2 + 3x + 5}$

  ii $\dfrac{x^3 + 5x^2 - 5x + 63}{x^2 - 2x + 9}$

  b i $\dfrac{x^4 + 7x^3 + 13x^2 + 2x - 2}{x^2 + 3x - 1}$

  ii $\dfrac{x^4 + 3x^3 - 32x^2 - 17x + 3}{x^2 - 4x - 3}$

3 **a** Use algebraic division to show that $x - 3$ is a factor of $2x^3 - 5x^2 - x - 6$.

  b Hence show that there is only one real root for the equation $2x^3 - 5x^2 - x - 6 = 0$

4 Use algebraic division to show that $x + 2$ is a factor of $x^3 + 8$.

5 Use algebraic division to find the remainder when $(1 + x)^4$ is divided by $x + 2$.

1.5 The factor theorem

WORKED EXAMPLE 1.5

a Factorise $f(x) = 2x^3 - 7x^2 + 4x - 3$.

b Hence, solve $2x^3 - 7x^2 + 4x - 3 = 0$, stating the number of real roots of the equation.

Answer

a Let $f(x) = 2x^3 - 7x^2 + 4x - 3$

$f(1) = 2(1)^3 - 7(1)^2 + 4(1) - 3 = -4$,
so $x - 1$ is not a factor of $f(x)$.

$f(-1) = 2(-1)^3 - 7(-1)^2$
$\quad\quad + 4(-1) - 3 = -16$,
so $x + 1$ is not a factor of $f(x)$.

$f(3) = 2(3)^3 - 7(3)^2 + 4(3) - 3 = 0$,
so $x - 3$ is a factor of $f(x)$.

If $x - c$ is a factor, then c can only be $\pm 1, \pm 3$ because the positive and negative factors of 3 are $\pm 1, \pm 3$.

The other factors of $f(x)$ can be found by any of the following methods.

Method 1

Substitution.

Substitute the other factors of 3 into $f(x) = 2x^3 - 7x^2 + 4x - 3$.

This (in other questions) could lead to a long method and may not yield further results.

Method 2

Long division (generally a shorter method).

$$
\begin{array}{r}
2x^2 - x + 1 \\
x - 3 \overline{\smash{\big)}\, 2x^3 - 7x^2 + 4x - 3} \\
\underline{2x^3 - 6x^2} \\
-x^2 + 4x \\
\underline{-x^2 + 3x} \\
x - 3 \\
\underline{x - 3} \\
0
\end{array}
$$

$f(x) \equiv (x - 3)(2x^2 - x + 1)$

Hence, $f(x) = (x - 3)(2x^2 - x + 1)$

$(2x^2 - x + 1)$ will not factorise further.

Method 3

Equate coefficients.

Since $x - 3$ is a factor,
$2x^3 - 7x^2 + 4x - 3$ can be written as
$2x^3 - 7x^2 + 4x - 3$
$= (x - 3)(ax^2 + bx + c)$

$2x^3 - 7x^2 + 4x - 3$
$= (x - 3)(2x^2 + bx + 1)$

Coefficient of x^3 is 2, so $a = 2$

Constant term is -3, so $c = 1$ since
$-3 \times 1 = -3$.

$-7 = b - 6$, so $b = -1$

Equate the coefficients of x^2.

$4 = 1 - 3b$, so $b = -1$.

Equate the coefficients of x.

Hence, $f(x) \equiv (x - 3)(2x^2 - x + 1)$

b $2x^3 - 7x^2 + 4x - 3 = 0$

Factorise.

$(x - 3)(2x^2 - x + 1) = 0$

Either $(x - 3) = 0$

Solve.

$x = 3$

Or $2x^2 - x + 1 = 0$

Use the quadratic formula $a = 2$,
$b = -1$, $c = 1$

$x = \dfrac{-(-1) \pm \sqrt{(-1)^2 - 4(2)(1)}}{2(2)}$

No solutions.

There is only one real solution to
the equation, which is $x = 3$.

EXERCISE 1E

1   Decide whether each of the following expressions is a factor of $2x^3 - 3x^2 - 3x + 2$.

  a   **i** $x - 1$ **ii** $x + 1$

  b   **i** $x - 2$ **ii** $x + 2$

  c   **i** $x - \dfrac{1}{2}$ **ii** $x + \dfrac{1}{2}$

  d   **i** $2x - 1$ **ii** $2x + 1$

  e   **i** $3x - 1$ **ii** $3x + 2$

2 Fully factorise the following expressions.

a i $x^3 + 2x^2 - x - 2$ ii $x^3 + x^2 - 4x - 4$

b i $x^3 - 7x^2 + 16x - 12$ ii $x^3 + 6x^2 + 12x + 8$

c i $x^3 - 3x^2 + 12x - 10$ ii $x^3 - 2x^2 + 2x - 15$

d i $6x^3 - 11x^2 + 6x - 1$ ii $12x^3 + 13x^2 - 37x - 30$

3 Solve the following equations.

a i $x^3 + 12 = 2x^2 + 11x$ ii $x^3 - x^2 - 17x = 15$

b i $x^3 - 5x^2 + 7x - 2 = 0$ ii $x^3 - 6x^2 + 7x - 2 = 0$

4 Find the roots of the following equations.

a i $x^3 - 6x^2 + 11x = 6$ ii $x^3 - 2x^2 + 6 = 5x$

b i $x^3 + x^2 - x - 1 = 0$ ii $x^3 - 3x^2 - 10x + 24 = 0$

5 a Show that $(x - 2)$ is a factor of $p(x) = x^3 - 3x^2 - 10x + 24$.

     b Hence express $p(x)$ as the product of three linear factors and solve $p(x) = 0$.

P

6 a Show that $(x - 3)$ is a factor of $p(x) = x^3 - x^2 - 2x - 12$.

     b Hence show that $p(x) = 0$ only has one real root.

7 $x^3 + 7x^2 + cx + d$ has factors $(x + 1)$ and $(x + 2)$. Find the values of c and d.

8 $f(x) = x^3 - ax^2 - bx + 168$ has factors $(x - 7)$ and $(x - 3)$.

     a Find a and b.

     b Find the remaining factor of $f(x)$.

9 The polynomial $x^2 + kx - 8k$ has a factor $(x - k)$. Find the possible values of k.

10 The polynomial $x^2 - (k + 1)x - 3$ has a factor $(x - k + 1)$. Find k.

PS

11 The polynomial $x^2 - 5x + 6$ is a factor of $2x^3 - 15x^2 + ax + b$. Find the values of a and b.

12 Use the factor theorem to factorise the following quartic polynomials $p(x)$. In each case, write down the real roots of the equation $p(x) = 0$.

a $x^4 - x^3 - 7x^2 + x + 6$ b $x^4 + 4x^3 - x^2 - 16x - 12$

c $2x^4 - 3x^3 - 12x^2 + 7x + 6$ d $6x^4 + x^3 - 17x^2 - 16x - 4$

e $x^4 - 2x^3 + 2x - 1$ f $4x^4 - 12x^3 + x^2 + 12x + 4$

1.6 The remainder theorem

WORKED EXAMPLE 1.6

Use the remainder theorem to find the remainder when
$3x^3 - 4x^2 + 3x - 1$ is divided by $2x - 1$.

Answer

Let $f(x) = 3x^3 - 4x^2 + 3x - 1$

Remainder $= f\left(\dfrac{1}{2}\right)$

$= 3\left(\dfrac{1}{2}\right)^3 - 4\left(\dfrac{1}{2}\right)^2 + 3\left(\dfrac{1}{2}\right) - 1$

$= \dfrac{3}{8} - 1 + \dfrac{3}{2} - 1$

$= -\dfrac{1}{8}$

 TIP

If a polynomial $P(x)$ is divided by $x - c$, the remainder is $P(c)$.

If a polynomial $P(x)$ is divided by $ax - b$, the remainder is $P\left(\dfrac{b}{a}\right)$.

EXERCISE 1F

1   When $3x^3 - 2x^2 + ax + b$ is divided by $x - 1$, the remainder is 3. When divided by $x + 1$ the remainder is -13. Find the values of a and b.

2   When $x^3 + ax^2 + bx + 5$ is divided by $x - 2$, the remainder is 23. When divided by $x + 1$ the remainder is 11. Find the values of a and b.

3   When $x^3 + ax^2 + bx - 5$ is divided by $x - 1$, the remainder is -1. When divided by $x + 1$ the remainder is -5. Find the values of a and b.

4   When $2x^3 - x^2 + ax + b$ is divided by $x - 2$, the remainder is 25. When divided by $x + 1$ the remainder is -5. Find the values of a and b.

5   Find the values of a and b if $ax^4 + bx^3 - 8x^2 + 6$ has a remainder $2x + 1$ when divided by $x^2 - 1$.

6   The expression $px^4 + qx^3 + 3x^2 - 2x + 3$ has a remainder $x + 1$ when divided by $x^2 - 3x + 2$. Find the values of p and q.

7   The expression $ax^2 + bx + c$ is divisible by $x - 1$. It leaves a remainder 2 when divided by $x + 1$, and has a remainder 8 when divided by $x - 2$. Find the values of a, b and c.

P   8   The cubic polynomial $x^3 + x^2 + Ax + B$, where A and B are constants, is denoted by $f(x)$. When $f(x)$ is divided by $x - 1$ the remainder is 4, and when $f(x)$ is divided by $x + 2$ the remainder is 10. Prove that $x + 3$ is a factor of $f(x)$.

1 Given that $k > 0$, find in terms of k the solution of the inequality $|x - k| \leqslant |2x - k|$.

PS 2 Solve the equation $|x + k| = |x| + k$, where $k > 0$.

3 a State the sequence of three transformations that transform the graph of $y = |x|$ to the graph of $y = 5 - 3|x|$. Hence sketch the graph of $y = 5 - 3|x|$.

   b Solve the equation $|2x - 1| = 5 - 3|x|$.

   c Write down the solution of the inequality $|2x - 1| \leqslant 5 - 3|x|$.

4 Solve the equation $x|x| = x^2$.

5 Sketch the graph of $y = x + |x|$.

6 Show that $\dfrac{x^3 + 2x^2 - 3x - 6}{x + 2} = x^2 + bx + c$ where b and c are integers to be found.

PS 7 The polynomial $x^2 - 4x + 3$ is a factor of the polynomial $x^3 + ax^2 + 27x + b$. Find the values of a and b.

P 8 The cubic polynomial $x^3 + x^2 + Ax + B$, where A and B are constants, is denoted by $f(x)$. When $f(x)$ is divided by $x - 1$ the remainder is 4, and when $f(x)$ is divided by $x + 2$ the remainder is 10. Prove that $x + 3$ is a factor of $f(x)$.

PS 9 The diagram shows the graph with equation $y = ax^4 + bx^3 + cx^2 + dx + e$. Find the values of a, b, c, d and e.

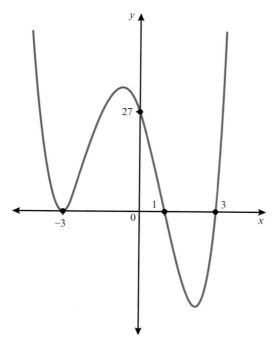

PS 10 Given $f(x) = 8x^3 - x^2 + 7$, the remainder when $f(x)$ is divided by $x - a$ is eight times the remainder when $f(x)$ is divided by $2x - a$. Find the two possible values of the constant a.

14

Chapter 2
Logarithmic and exponential functions

- Understand the relationship between logarithms and indices, and use the laws of logarithms (excluding change of base).
- Understand the definition and properties of e^x and $\ln x$, including their relationship as inverse functions and their graphs.
- Use logarithms to solve equations and inequalities in which the unknown appears in indices.
- Use logarithms to transform a given relationship to linear form, and hence determine unknown constants by considering the gradient and/or intercept.

2.1 Logarithms to base 10

WORKED EXAMPLE 2.1

a Solve $10^x = 45$, giving your answer correct to 3 significant figures.

b Solve $\log_{10} x = 1.2$, giving your answer correct to 3 significant figures.

Answer

a
$$10^x = 45$$

Take logs to base 10 of both sides.

$$\log_{10} 10^x = \log_{10} 45$$
$$x = \log_{10} 45$$

$\log_{10} 10^x = x$ for $x \in \mathbb{R}$

$$x = 1.6532\ldots$$
$$x = 1.65 \ (3 \text{ significant figures})$$

b
$$\log_{10} x = 1.2$$

Write each side as an exponent of 10.

$$10^{\log_{10} x} = 10^{1.2}$$

$10^{\log_{10} x} = x$ for $x > 0$

$$x = 10^{1.2}$$

$$x = 15.84\ldots$$
$$x = 15.8 \ (3 \text{ significant figures})$$

EXERCISE 2A

1 Convert from exponential form to logarithmic form.

   a $10^3 = 1000$ **b** $10^x = 500$ **c** $10^x = 0.02$

2 Solve each of these equations, giving your answers correct to 3 significant figures.

   a $10^x = 12$ **b** $10^x = 4.24$ **c** $10^x = 0.69$

3 Convert from logarithmic form to exponential form.

   a $\log_{10} 100000 = 5$ **b** $\log_{10} x = 1.03$ **c** $\log_{10} x = -0.2$

4 Solve each of these equations, giving your answers correct to 3 significant figures.

   a $\log_{10} x = 1.33$ **b** $\log_{10} x = 3.76$ **c** $\log_{10} x = -1.6$

> **TIP**
>
> $\log_{10} x$ could also be written as $\log x$ or $\lg x$.

 5 Without using a calculator, find the value of:

   a $\log 10000$ **b** $\log 0.00001$ **c** $\log \left(100\sqrt{10} \right)$

   d $\lg \left(\sqrt[4]{10} \right)$ **e** $\lg \left(100\sqrt[4]{10} \right)$ **f** $\lg \left(\dfrac{10000}{\sqrt{1000}} \right)$

6 Solve the equation $\log_{10} (3x + 1) = 2$.

7 Given that the function f is defined as $f : x \mapsto 10^{2x} + 5$ for $x \in \mathbb{R}$, find an expression for $f^{-1}(x)$.

 8 Solve the simultaneous equations $(\log_{10} x)^2 - (\log_{10} y)^2 = 6$ and $\log_{10} x + \log_{10} y = 4$, giving your answers to 3 significant figures.

2.2 Logarithms to base a

WORKED EXAMPLE 2.2

   a Find the value of $\log_4 64$.

   b Simplify $\log_x \left(\dfrac{x^2}{\sqrt[3]{x^2}} \right)$.

Answer

   a $\begin{aligned} \log_4 64 &= \log_4 4^3 \\ &= 3 \end{aligned}$ Write 64 as a power of 4, $64 = 4^3$

   b $\begin{aligned} \log_x \left(\dfrac{x^2}{\sqrt[3]{x^2}} \right) &= \log_x \left(x^{2-\frac{2}{3}} \right) \\ &= \dfrac{4}{3} \end{aligned}$ Write $\dfrac{x^2}{\sqrt[3]{x^2}}$ as a power of x.

EXERCISE 2B

1   Convert from exponential form to logarithmic form.

    a $5^3 = 125$ b $2^6 = 64$ c $3^{-3} = \dfrac{1}{27}$

    d $2^{-7} = \dfrac{1}{128}$ e $3^x = 17$ f $x^y = 5$

    g $a^{2b} = c$ h $x^{3y} = 0.5$

2   Convert from logarithmic form to exponential form.

    a $\log_2 32 = 5$ b $\log_3 243 = 5$ c $\log_2 1 = 0$

    d $\log_{64} 4 = \dfrac{1}{3}$ e $\log_3 \dfrac{1}{27} = -3$ f $\log_2 y = 6$

    g $\log_x 1 = 0$ h $\log_x 6 = 2y$

3   Solve:

    a $\log_3 (x + 5) = 2$ b $\log_2 (3x - 1) = 5$ c $\log_y (7 - 2x) = 0$

4   Without using a calculator, find the value of:

    a $\log_3 \dfrac{1}{3}$ b $\log_6 216$ c $\log_5 25$

    d $\log_5 0.04$ e $\log_2 \left(\dfrac{1}{16}\right)$ f $\log_3 \left(3\sqrt{3}\right)$

    g $\log_3 \left(\dfrac{\sqrt[4]{3}}{3}\right)$ h $\log_5 \left(\dfrac{\sqrt[3]{5}}{5}\right)^3$

5   Simplify:

    a $\log_x x^4$ b $\log_x \sqrt[4]{x}$ c $\log_x \left(x^5 \sqrt{x}\right)$

    d $\log_x \dfrac{1}{x^2}$ e $\log_x \left(\dfrac{1}{x^3}\right)^4$ f $\log_x \left(\sqrt{x^3}\right)$

    g $\log_x \left(\dfrac{x^3}{\sqrt[3]{x}}\right)$ h $\log_x \left(\dfrac{x^2}{\sqrt{x}}\right)^4$

6   Given that the function f is defined as $f : x \mapsto 3 + \log_3 (x + 1)$ for $x \in \mathbb{R}, \ x > -1$, find an expression for $f^{-1}(x)$.

7   Solve:

    a $\log_4 (\log_2 x) = 1$ b $\log_3 9^{1.5-x} = x^2$

8   Find the value of y in each of the following.

    a $\log_y 49 = 2$ b $\log_4 y = -3$ c $\log_3 81 = y$

    d $\log_{10} y = -1$ e $\log_2 y = 2.5$ f $\log_y 1296 = 4$

    g $\log_{\frac{1}{2}} y = 8$ h $\log_{\frac{1}{2}} 1024 = y$ i $\log_y 27 = -6$

> **TIP**
>
> If $y = a^x$ then
> $x = \log_a y$
>
> $\log_a a = 1$
> $\log_a 1 = 0$
> $\log_a a^x = x$
> $a^{\log_a x} = x$
>
> The conditions for $\log_a x$ to be defined are:
>
> • $a > 0$ and $a \neq 1$
> • $x > 0$

2.3 The laws of logarithms

Use the laws of logarithms to simplify these expressions.

a $\quad \log_3 8 - \log_3 4 + 2\log_3 2$

b $\quad \dfrac{\lg 0.1}{2\lg 100}$

Answer

a $\quad \log_3 8 - \log_3 4 + 2\log_3 2$

$\quad = \log_3 \dfrac{8}{4} + 2\log_3 2$

$\quad = \log_3 2 + 2\log_3 2$

$\quad = 3\log_3 2 \ (\text{or } \log_3 8)$

b $\quad \dfrac{\lg 0.1}{2\lg 100}$

$\quad = \dfrac{\lg 10^{-1}}{2\lg 10^2}$

$\quad = \dfrac{-\lg 10}{4\lg 10}$

$\quad = -\dfrac{1}{4}$

💡 **TIP**

If x and y are both positive and $a > 0$ and $a \neq 1$:

$\log_a (xy) = \log_a x + \log_a y$

$\log_a \left(\dfrac{x}{y}\right) = \log_a x - \log_a y$

$\log_a (x)^m = m \log_a x$

$\log_a \left(\dfrac{1}{x}\right) = -\log_a x$

EXERCISE 2C

1 Without using a calculator and by showing your working,

simplify $\dfrac{\log_5 125}{2\log_5 25}$.

2 Find an equivalent form for each of the following expressions:

a i $7\log x - 2\log x$ **ii** $2\log x + 3\log x$

b i $(\log x - 1)(\log y + 3)$ **ii** $(\log x + 2)^2$

c i $\dfrac{\log a + \log b}{\log a \log b}$ **ii** $\dfrac{(\log a)^2 - 1}{\log a - 1}$

3 Make x the subject of the following:

a i $\log_3 x = y$ **ii** $\log_4 x = 2y$

b i $\log_a x = 1 + y$ **ii** $\log_a x = y^2$

c i $\log_x 3y = 3$ **ii** $\log_x y = 2$

d i $y = 2 + \ln x$ **ii** $\ln y = \ln x - 2$

4 Write each of the following in terms of $\log p$, $\log q$ and $\log r$. The logarithms have base 10.

a $\log pqr$ **b** $\log pq^2 r^3$ **c** $\log 100pr^5$

d $\log\sqrt{\dfrac{p}{q^2 r}}$ **e** $\log\dfrac{pq}{r^2}$ **f** $\log\dfrac{1}{pqr}$

g $\log\dfrac{p}{\sqrt{r}}$ **h** $\log\dfrac{pr^7 q}{10}$ **i** $\log\sqrt{\dfrac{10p^{10}r}{q}}$

5 Given $b > 0$, simplify each of the following:

a i $\log_b b^4$ **ii** $\log_b \sqrt{b}$

b i $\log_{\sqrt{b}} b^3$ **ii** $\log_b b^2 - \log_b \sqrt{b}$

6 If $x = \log a$, $y = \log b$ and $z = \log c$, express the following in terms of x, y and z:

a i $\log b^7$ **ii** $\log a^2 b$

b i $\log\left(\dfrac{ab^2}{c}\right)$ **ii** $\log\left(\dfrac{a^2}{bc^3}\right)$

c i $\log\left(\dfrac{100}{bc^5}\right)$ **ii** $\log(5b) + \log(2c^2)$

d i $\log a^3 - 2\log ab^2$ **ii** $\log(4b) + 2\log(5ac)$

7 If $x = \log a$, $y = \log b$ and $z = \log c$ express the following in terms of x, y and z:

a $\log(a^2 b)$ **b** $\log\left(\dfrac{100a}{\sqrt{c}}\right)$

> **TIP**
>
> Be careful! $\dfrac{\log_x 8}{\log_x 2}$ is
>
> not $\dfrac{8}{2}$ nor $\log_x 4$
>
> Write $\dfrac{\log_x 8}{\log_x 2}$ as
>
> $\dfrac{\log_x 2^3}{\log_x 2}$ then $\dfrac{3\log_x 2}{\log_x 2}$
>
> which is 3.

2.4 Solving logarithmic equations

WORKED EXAMPLE 2.4

Solve:

    a $\log_3 (x - 8) + \log_3 x = 2$ **b** $(\log_3 x)^2 - 9\log_3 x + 14 = 0$

Answer

    a $\log_3 x(x - 8) = 2$ The multiplication law has been used.

              $x(x - 8) = 3^2$

               $x^2 - 8x = 9$

            $x^2 - 8x - 9 = 0$

          $(x - 9)(x + 1) = 0$

           $x = 9$ or $x = -1$

      $\log_3 (9 - 8) + \log_3 9 = 2$ is defined   Check when $x = 9$.

      $\log_3 1 + \log_3 9 = 2$ is defined

      $\log_3 9 = 2$ is defined

      So $x = 9$ is a solution, since both sides of the equation are defined and equivalent in value.

      $\log_3 (-1 - 8) + \log_3 (-1) = 2$ is not defined.   Check when $x = -1$.

      So $x = -1$ is not a solution of the original equation.

      Hence, the solution is $x = 9$.

    b $(\log_3 x)^2 - 9 \log_3 x + 14 = 0$ Let $y = \log_3 x$.

               $y^2 - 9y + 14 = 0$ Factorise.

            $(y - 7)(y - 2) = 0$

                 $y = 7$ or 2

      $\log_3 x = 7$ or $\log_3 x = 2$

      $x = 3^7$ or $x = 3^2$

      $x = 2187$ or $x = 9$

      $(\log_3 2187)^2 - 9 \log_3 2187 + 14 = 0$ Check when $x = 2187$.

      $7^2 - 9(7) + 14 = 0$ is defined.

      $(\log_3 9)^2 - 9 \log_3 9 + 14 = 0$ Check when $x = 9$.

      $2^2 - 9(2) + 14 = 0$ is defined.

      $x = 9$ or $x = 2187$ satisfy the original equation.

      Hence, the solutions are $x = 9$ or $x = 2187$

EXERCISE 2D

1   Solve the equation $\log_{10}(9x + 1) = 3$.

2   Solve the equation $\log_8 \sqrt{1 - x} = \dfrac{1}{3}$.

3   Solve the equation $3(1 + \log x) = 6 + \log x$.

4   Find all values of x that satisfy $(\log_3 x)^2 = 4$.

 5   Solve the simultaneous equations:

$\log_3 x + \log_5 y = 6$ $\qquad$ $\log_3 x - \log_5 y = 2$

6   Solve the following for x:

   a i $\quad \log_3 \left(\dfrac{2 + x}{2 - x} \right) = 1$ $\qquad\qquad$ ii $\log_2 (7x + 4) = 5$

   b i $\quad \log_3 x - \log_3 (x - 6) = 1$ $\qquad\qquad$ ii $\log_8 x - 2 \log_8 \left(\dfrac{1}{x} \right) = 1$

   c i $\quad \log_3 (x - 7) + \log_3 (x + 1) = 2$ $\quad$ ii $2 \log (x - 2) - \log (x) = 0$

7   Find the value of x, for which $3 \log_b x = \log_b 64$.

8   Solve the equation $\log (3x + 6) = \log (3) + 1$.

9   Solve the equation $\log (x + 5) - 1 = \log (x - 1)$.

10 Solve the equation $\log_2 (x + 2) = 3 - \log_2 x$.

2.5 Solving exponential equations

WORKED EXAMPLE 2.5

Solve, giving your answers correct to 3 significant figures:

   a $\quad 5^{4x-1} = 7^{x+2}$ $\qquad\qquad\qquad\qquad$ b $\quad 2(2^{2x}) - 11(2^x) + 5 = 0$

Answer

   a $\qquad 5^{4x-1} = 7^{x+2}$ $\qquad\qquad\qquad\qquad\qquad$ Take logs to base 10 of both sides.
   $\qquad \log 5^{4x-1} = \log 7^{x+2}$

   $\qquad\qquad\qquad\qquad\qquad\qquad\qquad\qquad\qquad\qquad$ Use the power rule.

   $\qquad (4x - 1) \log 5 = (x + 2) \log 7$ $\qquad\qquad\quad$ Expand the brackets.

   $\qquad 4x \log 5 - \log 5 = x \log 7 + 2 \log 7$
   $\qquad 4x \log 5 - x \log 7 = 2 \log 7 + \log 5$
   $\qquad x(4 \log 5 - \log 7) = 2 \log 7 + \log 5$ $\qquad\qquad$ Rearrange to find x.

21

$$x = \frac{2\log 7 + \log 5}{4\log 5 - \log 7}$$

$x = 1.22$ to 3 significant figures

b $2(2^{2x}) - 11(2^x) + 5 = 0$ .... Use the substitution $y = 2^x$.

$2y^2 - 11y + 5 = 0$ ....

$(2y - 1)(y - 5) = 0$ .... Factorise.

$y = 0.5$ or $y = 5$

When $y = 0.5$

$2^x = 0.5$ .... Take logs of both sides.

$x \log 2 = \log 0.5$

$$x = \frac{\log 0.5}{\log 2}$$

$x = -1$

When $y = 5$ .... Take logs of both sides.

$2^x = 5$

$x \log 2 = \log 5$

$$x = \frac{\log 5}{\log 2}$$

$x = 2.321$ ....

Hence, the solutions are $x = -1$ and

$x = 2.32$ to 3 significant figures.

EXERCISE 2E

1 Solve for x, giving your answers correct to 3 significant figures.

 a i $3 \times 4^x = 90$ ii $1000 \times 1.02^x = 10\,000$

 b i $6 \times 7^{x+1} = 1.2$ ii $5 \times 2^{2x-5} = 94$

 c i $3^{2x} = 4^{x-1}$ ii $5^x = 6^{x-1}$

 d i $3 \times 2^{3x} = 7 \times 3^{3x-2}$ ii $4 \times 8^{x-1} = 3 \times 5^{2x+1}$

2 Solve the equation $5^{4x+3} = 28$, giving your answer correct to 3 significant figures.

3 Find the exact solution of the equation $4 \times 3^{x-5} = 1$.

4 Find the exact solution of the equation $10^x = 5 \times 2^{3x}$, giving your answer in the form $x = \dfrac{\log p}{q + \log r}$, where p, q and r are integers.

5 Solve the equation $2^{3x-1} = 5^{2-x}$ giving your answer in the form $x = \dfrac{\log a}{\log b}$ where a and b are integers.

6 Find the exact solution(s) of each equation.

a i $4^x - 5 \times 2^x + 6 = 0$ ii $9^x - 6 \times 3^x + 8 = 0$

b i $9^x - 8 \times 3^x = 9$ ii $25^x - 5^x = 6$

c i $25^x - 15 \times 5^x + 50 = 0$ ii $4^x - 7 \times 2^x + 12 = 0$

d i $\log_4 x = (\log_4 x^2)^2$ ii $(\log_3 x)^2 - 3\log_3 x + 2 = 0$

7 Find exact solutions of the equation $4^x - 10 \times 2^x + 16 = 0$.

2.6 Solving exponential inequalities

WORKED EXAMPLE 2.6

Solve the inequality $3 \times 2^{3x+1} > 7$ giving your answer in terms of base 10 logarithms.

Answer

$3 \times 2^{3x+1} > 7$ .... Divide both sides by 3.

$2^{3x+1} > \dfrac{7}{3}$ .... Take log to base 10 of both sides and use the power rule.

$(3x+1)\log 2 > \log \dfrac{7}{3}$ .... Expand brackets.

$(3\log 2)x + \log 2 > \log \dfrac{7}{3}$ ...... Rearrange.

$x > \dfrac{\log \dfrac{7}{3} - \log 2}{3\log 2}$ .... Simplify.

$x > \dfrac{\log \dfrac{7}{6}}{\log 8}$

EXERCISE 2F

1 Solve the following inequalities, giving your answers correct to 3 significant figures if not exact.

a $3^x > 8$ b $5^x < 10$ c $7^{2x+5} \leqslant 24$

d $0.5^x < 0.001$ e $0.4^x < 0.0004$ f $0.2^x > 25$

g $4^x \times 4^{3-2x} \leqslant 1024$ h $0.8^{2x+5} \geqslant 4$ i $0.8^{1-3x} \geqslant 10$

2 A radioactive isotope decays so that after t days an amount 0.82^t units remains. How many days does it take for the amount to fall to less than 0.15 units?

PS **3** A biological culture contains 500 000 bacteria at 12 noon on Monday. The culture increases by 10% every hour. At what time will the culture exceed 4 million bacteria?

P **4** Prove that the solution to the inequality $2^{3x+1} \times 3^{1-x} \leqslant 4$ is $x \leqslant -\dfrac{\log \dfrac{3}{2}}{\log \dfrac{8}{3}}$

2.7 Natural logarithms

WORKED EXAMPLE 2.7

Solve $0.5^{3+x} < 12$ giving your answer to 3 significant figures.

Answer

$0.5^{3+x} < 12$ .... Take logs to base 10 of both sides and use the power rule.

$(3 + x) \log 0.5 < \log 12$ .... Expand brackets.

$3 \log 0.5 + x\log 0.5 < \log 12$ ..... Rearrange.

$x > \dfrac{\log 12 - 3 \log 0.5}{\log 0.5}$

$x > -6.58$ (3 significant figures)

> **TIP**
>
> Be careful! Since $\log 0.5$ is negative, the inequality sign needs to be reversed when dividing.

EXERCISE 2G

1 Use a calculator to evaluate correct to 3 significant figures:

   a e^2 **b** $e^{0.5}$ **c** $e^{1.8}$ **d** e^{-3}

2 Use a calculator to evaluate correct to 3 significant figures:

   a $\ln 1$ **b** $\ln 0.5$ **c** $\ln(-1)$ **d** $\ln 0.1$

 3 Without using a calculator, find the value of:

   a $e^{\ln 2^2}$ **b** $e^{\frac{1}{2}\ln 4}$ **c** $3e^{\ln 4}$ **d** $e^{-\ln\frac{1}{4}}$

> **TIP**
>
> $\ln e^x = x$
> $e^{\ln x} = x$

> **TIP**
>
> If $y = e^x$ then
> $x = \ln y$
>
> $\ln y$ can be written as $\log_e y$.

24

4 Solve:

   a $e^{\ln x} = 1$ **b** $\ln e^x = 1$

   c $e^{2\ln x} = 16$ **d** $e^{-\ln x} = 2$

5 Solve, giving your answers correct to 3 significant figures.

   a $e^x = 1$ **b** $e^{2x} = 16$

   c $e^{x+4} = 10$ **d** $e^{2x-3} = 23$

6 Solve, giving your answers in terms of natural logarithms.

   a $e^x = 11$ **b** $e^{4x} = 7$

   c $e^{2x-1} = 8$ **d** $e^{\frac{1}{2}x+3} = 2$

7 Solve, giving your answers in terms of natural logarithms.

   a $e^x > 9$ **b** $e^{4x-2} \leqslant 3$ **c** $2 \times e^{3x+2} < 1$

8 Solve, giving your answers correct to 3 significant figures.

   a $\ln x = 2$ **b** $\ln x = -2$

   c $\ln(x - 3) = 8$ **d** $\ln(3x + 1) = -1$

25

9 Solve, giving your answers correct to 3 significant figures.

   a $\ln(4 - x^2) = \ln x$ **b** $\ln(x + 4) - \ln x = \ln(3x + 1)$

   c $3\ln(x + 1) = -\ln(2x - 1)$ **d** $\ln(x + 1) = \ln x + 2\ln 3$

   e $\ln(x + 3) - \ln x = 4$ **f** $\ln(1 + x^2) = 1 + 2\ln x$

10 Express y in terms of x for each of these equations.

   a $\ln y = -0.5 - 5\ln x$ **b** $\ln y = 0.7 + 2\ln x$

11 Solve, giving your answers correct in exact form.

   a $e^{2x} - 16e^x + 15 = 0$ **b** $e^{2x} - 6e^x + 8 = 0$

   c $e^{2x} - 6e^x + 5 = 0$ **d** $6e^{1-x} = 24e^x$

12 Solve the following pairs of simultaneous equations.

   a $\ln(x + 3) = 2y + 1$ **b** $8^y = 4^{2x+3}$

          $e^{2y} = x - 2$ $\ln y - \ln x = 4$

2.8 Transforming a relationship to linear form

Convert $\dfrac{1}{y} = a^3 e^{-x}$, where a is a constant, into the form $Y = mX + c$.

Answer

$\dfrac{1}{y} = a^3 e^{-x}$ .... Take natural logarithms of both sides.

$\ln \dfrac{1}{y} = \ln (a^3 e^{-x})$

$\ln 1 - \ln y = \ln a^3 + \ln e^{-x}$

$\quad - \ln y = 3 \ln a - x$

$\quad\quad \ln y = x - 3 \ln a$ .... Now compare $\ln y = x - 3 \ln a$ with $Y = mX + c$.

$\begin{array}{cccc} \boxed{\ln y} = & \boxed{x} & - & 3\ln a \\ \uparrow & \uparrow\ \uparrow & & \uparrow \\ Y\ =\ & m\ X & + & c \end{array}$

So, $Y = mX + c$, where
$Y = \ln y,\ X = x,$
$m = 1$ and $c = -3 \ln a$

---

1 Given that a and b are constants, use logarithms to change each of these non-linear equations into the form $Y = mX + c$. State what the variables X and Y and the constants m and c represent. (**Note:** there may be more than one method to do this.)

    a $y = d + cx^2$ **b** $y = a + b\sqrt{x}$ **c** $y = ax + \dfrac{x^2}{b}$

    d $y = px^q$ **e** $e^y = kb^x$ **f** $ke^y = x^2 - bx$

2 The variables x and y satisfy the equation $y = kx^n$, where k and n are constants. The graph of $\ln y$ against $\ln x$ is a straight line passing through the points $(0.48, 0.21)$ and $(0.70, 1.10)$ as shown in the diagram. Find the value of k and the value of n correct to 2 significant figures.

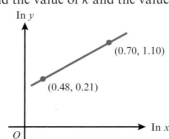

3 The variables x and y satisfy the equation $y = ka^x$, where k is a constant. The graph of $\ln y$ against x is a straight line passing through the points (2, 1.91) and (8, 1.72) as shown in the diagram. Find the value of k and the value of a correct to 2 significant figures.

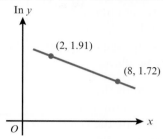

4 The table shows experimental values of the variables x and y.

x	0.4	0.9	1.2	.2.3	3.8
y	8.35	13.47	17.94	51.32	215.20

a By plotting a suitable straight line graph, show that x and y are related by the equation $y = a \times b^x$, where a and b are constants.

b Use your graph to estimate the value of a and the value of b correct to 2 significant figures.

5 The data below fits a law of the form $y = ae^{kx}$, where a and k are constants. The table below shows experimental values of y and x.

y	0.285	0.841	5.21	173.2	1181
x	5.3	9.8	17.4	32.0	40.0

By drawing a graph of $\ln y$ against x, estimate the value of a and k, giving your answers to 2 significant figures.

6 The figure shows part of a straight line drawn to represent the equation $xy = ax^2 + b$.

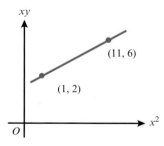

Find the values of a and b.

7   The variables p and q are related by an equation of the form $q = kp^z$, where k and z are constants. The diagram shows the graph of $\ln q$ against $\ln p$. The graph is a straight line, and it passes through the points $A(1.61, 2.82)$ and $B(3.22, 3.62)$. Find the values of k and z, giving the answers correct to 1 decimal place.

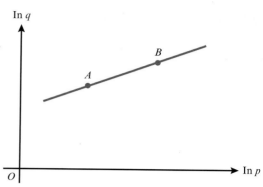

8   The variables x and y are related by the equation $2^y = 3^{1-x}$. Show that the graph of y against x is a straight line, and state the values of the gradient and the intercept on the y-axis.

M 9   A student is investigating the number of friends people have on a large social networking site. He collects some data on the percentage (P) of people who have n friends and plots the graph shown here.

The student proposes two possible models for the relationship between n and P.

Model 1: $P = ak^{-n}$

Model 2: $P = an^{-k}$

To check which model is a better fit, he plots the graph of y against x, where $y = \log P$ and $x = \log n$.

The graph is approximately a straight line with equation $y = 1.2 - 2.6x$.

a   Is Model 1 or Model 2 a better fit for the data? Explain your answer.

b   Find the values of a and k.

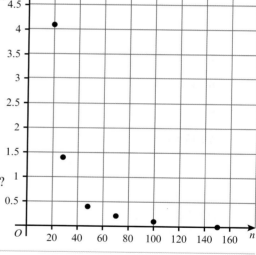

END-OF-CHAPTER REVIEW EXERCISE 2

1 Solve the equation $\log(x^2 + 1) = 1 + 2\log(x)$.

2 Solve the equation $2e^{2x} - 9e^x + 4 = 0$ giving your answers in the form $k\ln 2$.

3 Solve the equation $5^{2x+1} - 14 \times 5^x - 3 = 0$.

4 **a** Sketch the graphs of $y = 2\ln(x)$ and $y = \ln(x+3)$ on the same graph.

   b Find the exact solution of the equation $2\ln(x) = \ln(x+3)$.

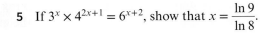 5 If $3^x \times 4^{2x+1} = 6^{x+2}$, show that $x = \dfrac{\ln 9}{\ln 8}$.

6 Solve the simultaneous equations:

   $\ln x + \ln y^2 = 8$

   $\ln x^2 + \ln y = 6$

7 If $y = \ln x - \ln(x+2) + \ln(4 - x^2)$, express x in terms of y.

8 Find the values of x for which $(\log_3 x)^2 = \log_3 x^3 - 2$.

9 Solve the inequality $2 \times 3^{3x+1} < 8$.

10 Given $f(x) = 1 + e^{2x-3}$

   a find the inverse function $f^{-1}(x)$

   b state the geometrical relationship between the graph of $f(x)$ and $f^{-1}(x)$.

11 The graph of $y = e^{2x} - 3$ can be obtained from the graph of $y = e^x$ using two transformations. Describe these transformations.

> **TIP**
>
> For any base $a > 0$,
> $\log_a a = 1$ and
> $\log_a 1 = 0$

29

- Understand the relationship of the secant, cosecant and cotangent functions to cosine, sine and tangent, and use properties and graphs of all six trigonometric functions for angles of any magnitude.
- Use trigonometrical identities for the simplification and exact evaluation of expressions and in the course of solving equations, and select an identity or identities appropriate to the context, showing familiarity in particular with the use of:
  - $\sec^2 \theta \equiv 1 + \tan^2 \theta$ and $\operatorname{cosec}^2 \theta \equiv 1 + \cot^2 \theta$
  - the expansion of $\sin (A \pm B)$, $\cos (A \pm B)$ and $\tan (A \pm B)$
  - the formulae for $\sin 2A$, $\cos 2A$ and $\tan 2A$
  - the expression of $a \sin \theta + b \cos \theta$ in the forms $R \sin (\theta \pm \alpha)$ and $R \cos (\theta \pm \alpha)$.

3.1 The cosecant, secant and cotangent ratios

WORKED EXAMPLE 3.1

Solve $5 \cot^2 x - 2 \operatorname{cosec} x + 2 = 0$ for $0 \leqslant x \leqslant 2\pi$.

Answer

$5(\operatorname{cosec}^2 x - 1) - 2 \operatorname{cosec} x + 2 = 0$ Use $1 + \cot^2 x \equiv \operatorname{cosec}^2 x$.

$5 \operatorname{cosec}^2 x - 5 - 2 \operatorname{cosec} x + 2 = 0$

$5 \operatorname{cosec}^2 x - 2 \operatorname{cosec} x - 3 = 0$ At this stage you could factorise, but it may be easier to turn your equation into one with $\sin x$ since most calculators do not have $\operatorname{cosec} x$ programmed into them.

$\dfrac{5}{\sin^2 x} - \dfrac{2}{\sin x} - 3 = 0$

$3 \sin^2 x + 2 \sin x - 5 = 0$ Factorise.

$(3 \sin x + 5)(\sin x - 1) = 0$

$\sin x = -\dfrac{5}{3}$ or $\sin x = 1$

$\sin x = -\dfrac{5}{3}$ No solutions.

$\sin x = 1 \Rightarrow x = \dfrac{\pi}{2}$

The only solution in the range is $x = \dfrac{\pi}{2}$.

1 Find, giving your answers to 3 decimal places:

   a $\cot 304°$ **b** $\sec (-48)°$ **c** $\operatorname{cosec} 62°$

2 Simplify the following.

   a $\sec\left(\dfrac{1}{2}\pi - x\right)$ **b** $\dfrac{\cos x}{\sin x}$ **c** $\sec (-x)$

   d $1 + \tan^2 x$ **e** $\cot (\pi + x)$ **f** $\operatorname{cosec} (\pi + x)$

3 Find the exact values of:

   a $\sec \dfrac{1}{4}\pi$ **b** $\operatorname{cosec} \dfrac{1}{2}\pi$

   c $\cot \dfrac{5}{6}\pi$ **d** $\operatorname{cosec}\left(-\dfrac{3}{4}\pi\right)$

   e $\cot\left(-\dfrac{1}{3}\pi\right)$ **f** $\sec \dfrac{13}{6}\pi$

   g $\cot\left(-\dfrac{11}{2}\pi\right)$ **h** $\sec \dfrac{7}{6}\pi$

4 Given that $\sin A = \dfrac{3}{5}$, where A is acute, and $\cos B = -\dfrac{1}{2}$, where B is obtuse, find the exact values of:

   a $\sec A$ **b** $\cot A$ **c** $\cot B$ **d** $\operatorname{cosec} B$

5 Given that $\operatorname{cosec} C = 7$, $\sin^2 D = \dfrac{1}{2}$ and $\tan^2 E = 4$, find the possible values of $\cot C$, $\sec D$ and $\operatorname{cosec} E$, giving your answers in exact form.

6 Simplify the following.

   a $\sqrt{\sec^2 \phi - 1}$ **b** $\dfrac{\tan \phi}{1 + \tan^2 \phi}$

   c $\dfrac{\tan \phi}{\sec^2 \phi - 1}$ **d** $\dfrac{1}{\sqrt{1 + \cot^2 \phi}}$

   e $\dfrac{1}{\sqrt{\operatorname{cosec}^2 \phi - 1}}$ **f** $(\operatorname{cosec} \phi - 1)(\operatorname{cosec} \phi + 1)$

7 **a** Express $3 \tan^2 \theta - \sec \theta$ in terms of $\sec \theta$.

   b Hence solve the equation $3 \tan^2 \phi - \sec \phi = 1$ for $0 \leqslant \phi \leqslant 2\pi$.

8 Use an algebraic method to find the solution for $0 \leqslant x \leqslant 2\pi$ to the equation $5 \cot x + 2 \operatorname{cosec}^2 x = 5$.

9 Find, in exact form, all the roots of the equation $2 \sin^2 t + \operatorname{cosec}^2 t = 3$ which lie between 0 and 2π.

31

10 Prove that $\operatorname{cosec} A + \cot A \equiv \dfrac{1}{\operatorname{cosec} A - \cot A}$ provided that $\operatorname{cosec} A \neq \cot A$.

11 Prove that $\dfrac{\sec \theta - 1}{\tan \theta} \equiv \dfrac{\tan \theta}{\sec \theta + 1}$ provided that $\tan \theta \neq 0$.

3.2 Compound angle formulae

WORKED EXAMPLE 3.2

Find the value of $\tan x$ given that $\sin (x + 30°) - 2 \cos (x - 30°) = 0$.

Answer

$$\sin (x + 30°) - 2 \cos (x - 30°) = 0$$

Use the addition formulae.

$$\sin x \cos 30° + \cos x \sin 30° - 2(\cos x \cos 30° + \sin x \sin 30°) = 0$$

$$\sin x \cos 30° + \cos x \sin 30° - 2 \cos x \cos 30° - 2 \sin x \sin 30° = 0$$

$$\sin x \cos 30° - 2 \sin x \sin 30° = 2 \cos x \cos 30° - \cos x \sin 30°$$

Move all $\sin x$ terms to the left and all $\cos x$ terms to the right of the equation. Then factorise.

$$\sin x (\cos 30° - 2 \sin 30°) = \cos x (2 \cos 30° - \sin 30°)$$

$$\frac{\sin x}{\cos x} = \frac{(2 \cos 30° - \sin 30°)}{(\cos 30° - 2 \sin 30°)}$$

$$\tan x = \frac{2\left(\frac{\sqrt{3}}{2}\right) - \frac{1}{2}}{\frac{\sqrt{3}}{2} - 2\left(\frac{1}{2}\right)}$$

Divide by $\cos x$.

$$\tan x = \frac{2\sqrt{3} - 1}{\sqrt{3} - 2}$$

$$\tan x = -3\sqrt{3} - 4$$

EXERCISE 3B

1 Express the following in the form $A \sin x + B \cos x$, giving exact values of A and B.

   a $\sin \left(x + \dfrac{\pi}{3}\right)$ **b** $\sin \left(x - \dfrac{\pi}{4}\right)$

   c $\cos \left(x + \dfrac{3\pi}{4}\right)$ **d** $\cos \left(x - \dfrac{3\pi}{2}\right)$

TIP

Remember: the notation $\sin^2 x$ means $(\sin x)^2$. This is not the same as $\sin (x^2)$.

32

2 Given that $\cos A = \dfrac{3}{5}$ and $\cos B = \dfrac{24}{25}$, where A and B are acute, find the exact values of:

   a $\tan A$ **b** $\sin B$

   c $\cos(A - B)$ **d** $\tan(A + B)$

3 Given that $\sin A = \dfrac{3}{5}$ and $\cos B = \dfrac{24}{25}$, where A is obtuse and B is acute, find the exact values of $\cos(A + B)$ and $\cot(A - B)$.

P   **4** Prove that $\cos(A + B) - \cos(A - B) = -2\sin A \sin B$.

5 **a**   Express $\tan\left(\theta - \dfrac{\pi}{4}\right)$ in terms of $\tan\theta$.

    b   Given that $\tan\left(\theta - \dfrac{\pi}{4}\right) = 6\tan\theta$, find two possible values of $\tan\theta$.

    c   Hence solve the equation $\tan\left(\theta - \dfrac{\pi}{4}\right) = 6\tan\theta$ for $0 < \theta < \pi$.

6 **a**   Show that $\sin(A + B) + \sin(A - B) = 2\sin A\cos B$.

    b   Hence solve the equation $\sin\left(x + \dfrac{\pi}{6}\right) + \sin\left(x - \dfrac{\pi}{6}\right) = 3\cos x$ for $0 \leqslant x \leqslant \pi$.

P   **7** Prove that $\tan 15° = 2 - \sqrt{3}$

8 Solve the equation $2\sin(30° + x) + 2\cos(60° + x) = \sqrt{3}$ for $-180° \leqslant x \leqslant 180°$.

P   **9** Prove the following identities:

   a $\sin(x + 90°) = \cos x$

   b $\sin(A + B)\sin(A - B) = \sin^2 A - \sin^2 B$

   c $\dfrac{\sin(A + B)}{\cos(A - B)} + 1 = \dfrac{(1 + \tan B)(1 + \cot A)}{\cot A + \tan B}$

10 Given that $\tan(A + B) = 5$ and $\tan B = 2$, find the value of $\tan A$.

3.3 Double angle formulae

WORKED EXAMPLE 3.3

a Solve the equation $2 \sin 2x = \sin x$ for $0 \leqslant x \leqslant 360°$. (Give your answers to 3 significant figures if not exact.)

b Prove that $\dfrac{\sin 2\theta}{1 + \cos 2\theta} \equiv \tan \theta$.

Answer

a

$$2 \sin 2x = \sin x$$
$$4 \sin x \cos x = \sin x$$
$$4 \sin x \cos x - \sin x = 0$$
$$\sin x \,(4 \cos x - 1) = 0$$
$$\sin x = 0$$
$$x = 0°, \ 180°, \ 360°$$
$$4 \cos x - 1 = 0$$
$$\cos x = 0.25$$
$$x = 75.5°, \ 284°$$

Solutions are
$0°, 75.5°, 180°, 284°, 360°$

Use the identity
$\sin 2A \equiv 2 \sin A \cos A$.

Factorise.

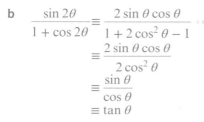

b

$$\frac{\sin 2\theta}{1 + \cos 2\theta} \equiv \frac{2 \sin \theta \cos \theta}{1 + 2\cos^2 \theta - 1}$$
$$\equiv \frac{2 \sin \theta \cos \theta}{2 \cos^2 \theta}$$
$$\equiv \frac{\sin \theta}{\cos \theta}$$
$$\equiv \tan \theta$$

Start with the left hand side.

Use $\sin 2A \equiv 2 \sin A \cos A$ and $\cos 2A \equiv 2\cos^2 A - 1$

TIP

There are three identities for $\cos 2\theta$ which you could have used but only $\cos 2\theta \equiv 2\cos^2 \theta - 1$ results in a single term in the denominator.

EXERCISE 3C

1 a i Given that $\cos \theta = -\dfrac{1}{4}$, find the exact value of $\cos 2\theta$.

ii Given that $\sin A = -\dfrac{2}{3}$, find the exact value of $\cos 2A$.

b i Given that $\sin x = \dfrac{1}{3}$ and $0 < x < \dfrac{\pi}{2}$, find the exact value of $\cos x$.

ii Given that $\sin x = \dfrac{3}{5}$ and $0 < x < \dfrac{\pi}{2}$, find the exact value of $\cos x$.

c i Given that $\sin x = \dfrac{1}{3}$ and $0 < x < \dfrac{\pi}{2}$, find the exact value of $\sin 2x$.

ii Given that $\sin x = \dfrac{3}{5}$ and $0 < x < \dfrac{\pi}{2}$, find the exact value of $\sin 2x$.

2 Simplify using a double angle identity:

   a $2\cos^2(3A) - 1$ **b** $4\sin 5x \cos 5x$

   c $3 - 6\sin^2\left(\dfrac{b}{2}\right)$ **d** $5\sin\left(\dfrac{x}{3}\right)\cos\left(\dfrac{x}{3}\right)$

3 Use double angle identities to solve the following equations.

   a $\sin 2x = 3\sin x$ for $0 \leqslant x \leqslant 2\pi$ **b** $\cos 2x - \sin^2 x = -2$ for $0° \leqslant x \leqslant 180°$

   c $5\sin 2x = 3\cos x$ for $-\pi < x < \pi$ **d** $\tan 2x - \tan x = 0$ for $0° \leqslant x \leqslant 360°$

P   **4** Prove these identities:

   a $(\sin x + \cos x)^2 \equiv 1 + \sin 2x$ **b** $\cos^4\theta - \sin^4\theta \equiv \cos 2\theta$

   c $\tan 2A - \tan A = \dfrac{\tan A}{\cos 2A}$ **d** $\tan\alpha - \dfrac{1}{\tan\alpha} = -\dfrac{2}{\tan 2\alpha}$

5 If $\tan 2A = 1$, find the possible values of $\tan A$. Hence state the exact value of $\tan 22\frac{1}{2}°$.

6 If $\sin A = \dfrac{2}{3}$ and A is obtuse, find the exact values of $\cos A$, $\sin 2A$ and $\tan 2A$.

P   **7** Prove that $4\sin\left(x + \dfrac{1}{6}\pi\right)\sin\left(x - \dfrac{1}{6}\pi\right) \equiv 3 - 4\cos^2 x$.

P   **8**   **a**   Show that:

      i $\cos^2\left(\dfrac{1}{2}x\right) = \dfrac{1}{2}(1 + \cos x)$ **ii** $\sin^2\left(\dfrac{1}{2}x\right) = \dfrac{1}{2}(1 - \cos x)$

   b   Express $\tan^2\left(\dfrac{1}{2}x\right)$ in terms of $\cos x$.

9 Solve these equations for values of A between 0 and 2π inclusive. Give your answers to 3 significant figures if not exact.

   a $\cos 2A + 3 + 4\cos A = 0$ **b** $2\cos 2A + 1 + \sin A = 0$ **c** $\tan 2A + 5\tan A = 0$

10 The polynomial $f(x)$ is defined by $f(x) = 9x^3 - 7x - 2$.

   a   Use the factor theorem to show that $(3x + 1)$ is a factor of $f(x)$.

   b   Hence express $f(x)$ as a product of three linear factors.

   c   **i**   Show that the equation $9\cos 2\theta \sin\theta + 5\sin\theta + 4 = 0$ can be written as $9x^3 - 7x - 2 = 0$, where $x = \sin\theta$.

      ii   Hence find all solutions of the equation $2\cos 2\theta \sin\theta + 9\sin\theta + 3 = 0$ in the interval $0° < \theta < 360°$, giving your solutions to the nearest degree.

3.4 Further trigonometric identities

WORKED EXAMPLE 3.4

Prove that $\operatorname{cosec} x + \cot x \equiv \cot \dfrac{1}{2}x$.

Answer

$$\operatorname{cosec} x + \cot x \equiv \frac{1}{\sin x} + \frac{\cos x}{\sin x}$$

Write everything on the left hand side in terms of sines and cosines.

$$\equiv \frac{1 + \cos x}{\sin x}$$

$$\equiv \frac{1 + \left(2\cos^2 \dfrac{1}{2}x - 1 \right)}{2\sin \dfrac{1}{2}x \cos \dfrac{1}{2}x}$$

Use the identities
$\cos 2A \equiv 2\cos^2 A - 1$
and $\sin 2A \equiv 2\sin A \cos A$.

$$\equiv \frac{2\cos^2 \dfrac{1}{2}x}{2\sin \dfrac{1}{2}x \cos \dfrac{1}{2}x}$$

$$\equiv \frac{\cos \dfrac{1}{2}x}{\sin \dfrac{1}{2}x}$$

$$\equiv \cot \dfrac{1}{2}x$$

Proven.

TIP

As $\cos 2A \equiv 2\cos^2 A - 1$
So $\cos A \equiv 2\cos^2 \dfrac{1}{2}A - 1$
As $\sin 2A \equiv 2\sin A \cos A$
So $\sin A \equiv 2\sin \dfrac{1}{2}A \cos \dfrac{1}{2}A$ etc.

EXERCISE 3D

1   Show that $\dfrac{1 - \cos 2\theta}{1 + \cos 2\theta} \equiv \tan^2 \theta$.

2   **a**   Given that $\tan \alpha \tan 2\alpha = 6$, find the possible values of $\tan \alpha$.

    b   Solve the equation $\tan \alpha \tan 2\alpha = 1$ for $0 \leqslant \alpha \leqslant \pi$, giving your answer in terms of π.

3 **a** Express $\cos 3A$ in terms of $\cos A$.   **b** Express $\tan 3A$ in terms of $\tan A$.

4 Express $\cos 4\theta$ in terms of:

   a $\cos \theta$ **b** $\sin \theta$

5 Given that $a \sin 4x = b \sin 2x$ and $0 < x < \dfrac{\pi}{2}$, express $\sin^2 x$ in terms of a and b.

P **6** Prove that $\operatorname{cosec} 2x \equiv \dfrac{\sec x \, \operatorname{cosec} x}{2}$.

P **7** Prove that $\cot 2x \equiv \dfrac{\cot^2 x - 1}{2 \cot x}$.

8 **a** Show that $\sin 3x \equiv 3 \sin x - 4 \sin^3 x$.

   b Hence, solve the equation $1 - \sin 3x = 2 \sin x (2 \sin x - 1)$ for $0° \leqslant x \leqslant 360°$.

9 **a** Show that $\cos 3x \equiv 4 \cos^3 x - 3 \cos x$.

   b Hence, solve the equation $1 + \cos 3x = \cos x (1 + \cos x)$ for $0° \leqslant x \leqslant 360°$.

P **10** Prove each of the following identities.

   a $\cot A - \tan A \equiv 2 \cot 2A$

   b $\dfrac{\sin A}{\sin B} - \dfrac{\cos A}{\cos B} \equiv \dfrac{2 \sin (A - B)}{\sin 2B}$

   c $\dfrac{\cos A}{\sin B} - \dfrac{\sin A}{\cos B} \equiv \dfrac{2 \cos (A + B)}{\sin 2B}$

   d $\dfrac{\sin 2A}{1 - \cos 2A} \equiv \cot A$

3.5 Expressing $a \sin \theta + b \cos \theta$ in the form $R \sin (\theta \pm \alpha)$ or $R \cos (\theta \pm \alpha)$

WORKED EXAMPLE 3.5

Given the function $f(\theta) = \dfrac{1}{3 + \sin \theta - 2 \cos \theta}$, find:

   a its minimum value   **b** its maximum value.

Answer

a $\sin \theta - 2 \cos \theta = R \sin (\theta - \alpha)$

   $\therefore \sin \theta - 2 \cos \theta = R \sin \theta \cos \alpha - R \cos \theta \sin \alpha$

   $R \cos \alpha = 1 \text{ -------(1)}$ ⟶ Equate the coefficients of $\sin \theta$.

   $R \sin \alpha = 2 \text{ -------(2)}$ ⟶ Equate the coefficients of $\cos \theta$.

   $\tan \alpha = 2 \Rightarrow \alpha = 63.4°$ ⟶ $(2) \div (1)$

   $1^2 + 2^2 = R^2 \Rightarrow R = \sqrt{5}$ ⟶ Square equations (1) and (2) and then add them.

$$\therefore \sin \theta - 2 \cos \theta = \sqrt{5}\sin (\theta - 63.4°)$$

$$f(\theta) = \frac{1}{3 + \sin \theta - 2 \cos \theta}$$

$$f(\theta) = \frac{1}{3 + \sqrt{5}\sin (\theta - 63.4°)}$$
$$\therefore \theta - 63.4° = 90°$$
$$\theta = 153.4°$$

The minimum value of $f(\theta)$ is when the denominator is the maximum value.

This occurs when $\sin(\theta - 63.4°) = 1$.

$$f(\theta) = \frac{1}{3 + \sqrt{5} \sin (\theta - 63.4°)}$$

$$f(\theta) = \frac{1}{3 + \sqrt{5}}$$

The minimum value of
$$f(\theta) = \frac{1}{3 + \sin \theta - 2 \cos \theta} \text{ is } \frac{1}{3 + \sqrt{5}} \text{ when}$$
$$\theta = 153.4°$$

b
$$f(\theta) = \frac{1}{3 + \sqrt{5}\sin (\theta - 63.4°)}$$
$$\therefore \theta - 63.4° = 270°$$
$$\theta = 333.4°$$

The maximum value of $f(\theta)$ is when the denominator is the minimum value.

This occurs when $\sin(\theta - 63.4°) = -1$

$$f(\theta) = \frac{1}{3 + \sqrt{5}\sin (\theta - 63.4°)}$$

$$f(\theta) = \frac{1}{3 - \sqrt{5}}$$

The maximum value of
$$f(\theta) = \frac{1}{3 + \sin \theta - 2 \cos \theta} \text{ is } \frac{1}{3 - \sqrt{5}} \text{ when}$$
$$\theta = 333.4°$$

EXERCISE 3E

1 Express in the form $r \sin (\theta - a)$ where $r > 0$ and $0° < a < 90°$:

   a $2 \sin \theta - 2 \cos \theta$ b $\sin \theta - \sqrt{3} \cos \theta$

2 Express in the form $r \cos (x + \theta)$ where $r > 0$ and $0 < \theta < \dfrac{\pi}{2}$:

   a $\sqrt{6} \cos x - \sqrt{2} \sin x$ b $5 \cos x - 5 \sin x$

3 a   Express $\sqrt{3} \sin x + \cos x$ in the form $R \cos (x - \theta)$.

   b   Hence find the coordinates of the minimum and maximum points on the graph of $y = \sqrt{3} \sin x + \cos x$ for $0 \leqslant x \leqslant 2\pi$

4   Find, to 3 significant figures, all values of x in the interval $0 \leqslant x \leqslant 2\pi$ for which $2 \sin x - \cos x = 2$.

5   Express $5 \cos \theta + 6 \sin \theta$ in the form $R \cos (\theta - \beta)$ where $R > 0$ and $0 < \beta < \frac{1}{2}\pi$. State:

   a   the maximum value of $5 \cos \theta + 6 \sin \theta$ and the least positive value of θ which gives this maximum

   b   the minimum value of $5 \cos \theta + 6 \sin \theta$ and the least positive value of θ which gives this minimum.

6   Express $8 \sin x + 6 \cos x$ in the form $R \sin (x + \phi)$, where $R > 0$ and $0° < \phi < 90°$. Deduce the number of roots for $0° < x < 180°$ of the following equations.

   a $8 \sin x + 6 \cos x = 5$ b $8 \sin x + 6 \cos x = 12$

7   Find the greatest and least values of each of the following expressions, and state, correct to one decimal place, the smallest non-negative value for which this occurs, given that $0° \leqslant x \leqslant 360°$.

   a $2 \cos x + \sin x$ b $7 + 3 \sin x - 4 \cos x$

   c $\dfrac{1}{\sin x + \cos x + 2}$ d $\dfrac{3}{16 + 5 \cos x - 12 \sin x}$

8   By expressing $\sin 2x + \cos 2x$ in the form $R \sin (2x + a)$, solve the equation $\sin 2x + \cos 2x = 1$ for $-\pi \leqslant x \leqslant \pi$.

9   a   Express $\sqrt{5} \sin x + \sqrt{7} \cos x$ in the form $R \sin (x + \alpha)$, where $0 < \alpha < \frac{\pi}{2}$. Give the value of α correct to three decimal places.

   b   Hence find the minimum value of $\dfrac{48}{2 - (\sqrt{5} \sin x + \sqrt{7} \cos x)}$. Give your answer in the form $a + b\sqrt{3}$.

10 a   Show that the equation $2 \sec \theta - \tan \theta = 3$ can be expressed in the form $R \cos (\theta - \alpha) = 2$, where the values of R and α are to be found and $0° < \alpha < 90°$.

   b   Hence solve the equation $2 \sec \theta - \tan \theta = 3$, giving all values of θ such that $0° < \alpha < 360°$.

1 Find the exact solution of the following equations for $-\pi \leqslant \theta \leqslant \pi$.

   a i $\operatorname{cosec} \theta = -2$ ii $\operatorname{cosec} \theta = -1$

   b i $\cot \theta = \sqrt{3}$ ii $\cot \theta = 1$

   c i $\sec \theta = 1$ ii $\sec \theta = -\dfrac{2}{\sqrt{3}}$

   d i $\cot \theta = 0$ ii $\cot \theta = -1$

(P) 2 Prove that $\dfrac{\sin \theta}{1 - \cos \theta} - \dfrac{\sin \theta}{1 + \cos \theta} \equiv 2 \cot \theta$.

3 a Given that $\sec^2 x - 3 \tan x + 1 = 0$, show that $\tan^2 x - 3 \tan x + 2 = 0$.

   b Find the possible values of $\tan x$.

   c Hence solve the equation $\sec^2 x - 3 \tan x + 1 = 0$ for $0 \leqslant x \leqslant 2\pi$.

4 a Express $5 \sin x + 12 \cos x$ in the form $R \sin (x + \theta)$.

   b Hence give details of two successive transformations which transform the graph of $y = \sin x$ into the graph of $y = 5 \sin x + 12 \cos x$.

5 a Express $3 \sin x - 7 \cos x$ in the form $R \sin (x - \theta)$.

   b Hence find the range of the function $f(x) = 3 \sin x - 7 \cos x$.

6 Write each of the following as a single trigonometric function, and hence find the maximum value of each expression, and the smallest positive value of x for which it occurs.

   a $\sin x \cos \dfrac{\pi}{4} + \cos x \sin \dfrac{\pi}{4}$ b $2 \cos x \cos 25° + 2 \sin x \sin 25°$

7 a Show that $\cos (x + y) + \cos (x - y) = 2 \cos x \cos y$.

   b Hence solve the equation $\cos 3x + \cos x = 3 \cos 2x$ for $0 \leqslant x \leqslant 2\pi$.

(PS) 8 a Find the value of $\tan^{-1} \sqrt{3} + \tan^{-1} \left(-\dfrac{1}{\sqrt{3}} \right)$.

   b If $x = \tan^{-1} A$ and $y = \tan^{-1} B$, find $\tan (A + B)$ in terms of x and y.

9 If $A = \sin^{-1} x$, where $x > 0$:

   a show that $\cos A = \sqrt{1 - x^2}$

   b find expressions in terms of x for $\operatorname{cosec} A$ and $\cos 2A$.

10 a Write $\cos\left(x + \dfrac{\pi}{3}\right)$ in the form $a\cos x + b\sin x$ for $-2\pi \leqslant x \leqslant 2\pi$.

b Hence find the exact values of x for which $\cos\left(x + \dfrac{\pi}{3}\right) = \cos\left(x - \dfrac{\pi}{3}\right)$.

11 A water wave has the profile shown in the graph, where y represents the height of the wave in metres, and x is the horizontal distance, also in metres.

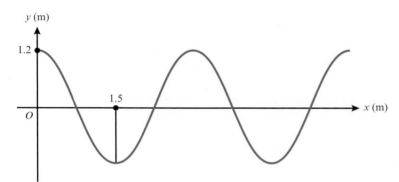

a Given that the equation of the wave can be written as $y_1 = a\cos(px)$, find the values of a and p.

b A second wave has the profile given by the equation $y_2 = 0.9\sin\left(\dfrac{2\pi}{3}x\right)$. Write down the amplitude and the period of the second wave.

When the two waves combine, a new wave is formed with the profile given by $y = y_1 + y_2$.

c Write the equation for y in the form $R\sin(kx + \alpha)$ for a suitable value of α, where $R > 0$ and $0 < \alpha < \dfrac{\pi}{2}$.

d State the amplitude and the period of the combined wave.

e Find the smallest positive value of x for which the height of the combined wave is zero.

f Find the first two positive values of x for which the height of the combined wave is 1.3 m.

12 a Show that the equation $3\cosec^2\theta + 5\cot\theta = 5$ can be written in the form $a\cot^2\theta + b\cot\theta + c = 0$. State the values of the constants a, b and c.

b Hence solve the equation $3\cosec^2\theta + 5\cot\theta = 5$ for $0° \leqslant \theta \leqslant 360°$, giving your answers to the nearest degree.

41

- Differentiate products and quotients.
- Use the derivatives of e^x, $\ln x$, $\sin x$, $\cos x$, $\tan x$, together with constant multiples, sums, differences and composites.
- Find and use the first derivative of a function which is defined parametrically or implicitly.

4.1 The product rule

42

 TIP

Use the product rule:
If u and v are functions of x and if $y = uv$, then: $\dfrac{d}{dx}(uv) = u\dfrac{dv}{dx} + v\dfrac{du}{dx}$

WORKED EXAMPLE 4.1

a Find $f'(x)$ when $f(x) = x^2(2x^2 - 5)^3$, writing your answer in a fully factorised form.

b Hence find the equation of the tangent at the point where $x = 1$ on the curve $f(x) = x^2(2x^2 - 5)^3$.

Answer

a $f(x) = x^2(2x^2 - 5)^3$

This is a product, so use the product rule.

$f'(x) = \underbrace{x^2}_{\text{first}} \underbrace{\dfrac{d}{dx}\left[(2x^2 - 5)^3\right]}_{\substack{\text{differentiate} \\ \text{second}}} + \underbrace{(2x^2 - 5)^3}_{\text{second}} \underbrace{\dfrac{d}{dx}(x^2)}_{\substack{\text{differentiate} \\ \text{first}}}$

Use the chain rule for differentiating $(2x^2 - 5)^3$.

$= x^2\underbrace{\left[3(2x^2 - 5)^2(4x)\right]}_{\text{chain rule}} + (2x^2 - 5)^3(2x)$

$= 12x^3(2x^2 - 5)^2 + 2x(2x^2 - 5)^3$

Factorise.

$= 2x(2x^2 - 5)^2\left[6x^2 + (2x^2 - 5)\right]$

Simplify.

$f'(x) = 2x(2x^2 - 5)^2(8x^2 - 5)$

b $f'(x) = 2x(2x^2 - 5)^2(8x^2 - 5)$
$f'(1) = 2(1)(2(1)^2 - 5)^2(8(1)^2 - 5)$
$f'(1) = 54$

Substitute $x = 1$ into the gradient function.

$f(1) = (1)^2(2(1)^2 - 5)^3$
$f(1) = -27$

Having substituted $x = 1$ into the original function.

$-27 = 54(1) + c$
$c = -81$

Having used $y = mx + c$, $x = 1$, $y = -27$, $m = 54$.

The equation of the tangent is $y = 54x - 81$.

EXERCISE 4A

1   Find f′(x) and fully factorise each answer.

   a i $f(x) = (x + 1)^4(x - 2)^5$ ii $f(x) = (x - 3)^7(x + 5)^4$

   b i $f(x) = (2x - 1)^4(1 - 3x)^3$ ii $f(x) = (1 - x)^5(4x + 1)^2$

2   Differentiate the following:

   a $x\sqrt{x + 1}$ b $2x\sqrt{3 - x}$ c $x^2\sqrt{3 - 4x}$

   d $(1 - 3x)\sqrt{2x + 5}$ e $(3x + 5)^2\sqrt{x - 2}$ f $\sqrt{x}(5x - 4)^3$

3   Find the equation of the tangent to the curve $y = x^2(x + 1)^4$ at the point (1, 16).

4   Find the coordinates of the stationary point on the curve $y = x\sqrt{2x + 3}$.

PS 5   A rectangle is drawn inside a semicircle of radius 6 cm as in the diagram.

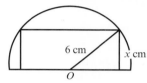

6 cm x cm

O

Given that the width of the rectangle is x cm, show that the area of the rectangle is $2x\sqrt{36 - x^2}$. Calculate the maximum value for this area and the value of x for which it occurs.

6   Find the exact values of the x-coordinates of the stationary points on the curve $y = (3x + 1)^5(3 - x)^3$.

7   The volume, V, of a solid is given by the equation $V = x^2\sqrt{8 - x}$. Use calculus to find the maximum value of V and the value of x at which it occurs.

8   Given that $f(x) = x^2\sqrt{1 + x}$ show that $f'(x) = \dfrac{x(a + bx)}{2\sqrt{1 + x}}$, where a and b are constants to be found.

PS 9   a   If $a < b$ and p and q are positive integers, find the x-coordinate of the stationary point of the curve $y = (x - a)^p(x - b)^q$ in the domain $a < x < b$.

   b   Sketch the graph in the case when $p = 2$ and $q = 3$.

   c   By considering the graph, or otherwise, identify a condition involving p and/or q to determine when this stationary point is a local minimum.

10   The equation of a curve is $y = \sin x \sin 2x$.

   a   Show that $\dfrac{dy}{dx}$ may be written in the form $2 \sin x(3 \cos^2 x - 1)$.

   b   Hence show that the value of y at any stationary point on the curve is either 0 or $\pm \dfrac{4}{3\sqrt{3}}$.

43

4.2 The quotient rule

Find the derivative of $y = \dfrac{(3x+1)^3}{\sqrt{2x-1}}$.

Answer

$$y = \frac{(3x+1)^3}{\sqrt{2x-1}}$$

$$\frac{dy}{dx} = \frac{\overbrace{\sqrt{2x-1}}^{\text{denominator}} \times \overbrace{\dfrac{d}{dx}\left[(3x+1)^3\right]}^{\substack{\text{differentiate} \\ \text{numerator}}} - \overbrace{(3x+1)^3}^{\text{numerator}} \times \overbrace{\dfrac{d}{dx}\left[\sqrt{2x-1}\right]}^{\substack{\text{differentiate} \\ \text{denominator}}}}{\underbrace{(\sqrt{2x-1})^2}_{\text{denominator squared}}}$$

$$= \frac{(\sqrt{2x-1})\left[3(3x+1)^2(3)\right] - (3x+1)^3\left[\dfrac{1}{2}(2x-1)^{-\frac{1}{2}}(2)\right]}{2x-1}$$

$$= \frac{9(3x+1)^2\sqrt{2x-1} - \dfrac{(3x+1)^3}{\sqrt{2x-1}}}{2x-1}$$

Multiply numerator and denominator by $\sqrt{2x-1}$.

$$= \frac{9(3x+1)^2(2x-1) - (3x+1)^3}{(2x-1)\sqrt{2x-1}}$$

Factorise the numerator.

$$= \frac{(3x+1)^2\left[9(2x-1) - (3x+1)\right]}{(2x-1)^{\frac{3}{2}}}$$

$$= \frac{5(3x+1)^2(3x-2)}{(2x-1)^{\frac{3}{2}}}$$

💡 **TIP**

Use the quotient rule: If u and v are functions of x and if $y = \dfrac{u}{v}$, then:

$$\frac{d}{dx}\left(\frac{u}{v}\right) = \frac{v\dfrac{du}{dx} - u\dfrac{dv}{dx}}{v^2}$$

EXERCISE 4B

1 Differentiate the following using the quotient rule:

a i $y = \dfrac{x - 1}{x + 1}$

   ii $y = \dfrac{x + 2}{x - 3}$

b i $y = \dfrac{\sqrt{2x + 1}}{x}$

   ii $y = \dfrac{x^2}{\sqrt{x - 1}}$

c i $y = \dfrac{1 - 2x}{x^2 + 2}$

   ii $y = \dfrac{4 - x^2}{1 + x}$

2 Differentiate with respect to x.

a $\dfrac{x}{\sqrt{x + 1}}$

b $\dfrac{\sqrt{x - 5}}{x}$

c $\dfrac{\sqrt{3x + 2}}{2x}$

3 Find the coordinates of the stationary points on the graph of $y = \dfrac{x^2}{2x - 1}$.

4 The graph of $y = \dfrac{x - a}{x + 2}$ has gradient 1 at the point $(a, 0)$ and $a \neq -2$. Find the value of a.

5 Find the equation of the normal to the curve $y = \dfrac{2x - 1}{x(x - 3)}$ at the point on the curve where $x = 2$.

6 Find the turning points of the curve $y = \dfrac{x^2 + 4}{2x - x^2}$.

7 a If $f(x) = \dfrac{x^2 - 3x}{x + 1}$, find $f'(x)$.

  b Find the values of x for which $f(x)$ is decreasing.

8 Find the range of values of x for which the function $f(x) = \dfrac{x^2}{1 - x}$ is increasing.

9 Given that $y = \dfrac{x^2}{\sqrt{x + 1}}$, show that $\dfrac{dy}{dx} = \dfrac{x(ax + b)}{2(x + 1)^p}$, stating clearly the value of the constants a, b and p.

P 10 Show that if the curve $y = f(x)$ has a maximum stationary point at $x = a$ then the curve $y = \dfrac{1}{f(x)}$ has a minimum stationary point at $x = a$ as long as $f(a) \neq 0$.

TIP

A question such as: 'Differentiate $y = \dfrac{2x}{(x + 3)^2}$ with respect to x' can be approached using the quotient rule or written as $y = 2x(x + 3)^{-2}$ and the product rule then used.

4.3 Derivatives of exponential functions

Differentiate with respect to x.

a $\quad -3\dfrac{x}{e^{\sqrt{x}}}$ $\qquad\qquad$ **b** $\quad 3xe^{2x^2}$ $\qquad\qquad\qquad$ **c** $\quad (e^{2x} - \sqrt{x})^2$

Answer

a $\qquad -3\dfrac{x}{e^{\sqrt{x}}} = \dfrac{-3x}{e^{x^{\frac{1}{2}}}} = -3xe^{-x^{\frac{1}{2}}}$ $\quad$ .... Use the quotient rule or the product rule.

$$\dfrac{d}{dx}\left(\dfrac{-3x}{e^{x^{\frac{1}{2}}}}\right) = \dfrac{e^{x^{\frac{1}{2}}} \times \dfrac{d}{dx}(-3x) - (-3x) \times \dfrac{d}{dx}\left(e^{x^{\frac{1}{2}}}\right)}{e^{2x^{\frac{1}{2}}}}$$

Quotient rule (plus the chain rule for $\dfrac{d}{dx}\left(e^{x^{\frac{1}{2}}}\right)$).

$$= \dfrac{e^{x^{\frac{1}{2}}} \times (-3) - (-3x) \times \left(\frac{1}{2}x^{-\frac{1}{2}}\right)e^{x^{\frac{1}{2}}}}{e^{2x^{\frac{1}{2}}}}$$

Rewrite.

Be careful! $e^{\sqrt{x}} \times e^{\sqrt{x}} = e^{2\sqrt{x}}$

$$= \dfrac{-3e^{\sqrt{x}} + \dfrac{3xe^{\sqrt{x}}}{2\sqrt{x}}}{e^{2\sqrt{x}}}$$

Multiply top and bottom by $2\sqrt{x}$.

$$= \dfrac{-6\sqrt{x}e^{\sqrt{x}} + 3xe^{\sqrt{x}}}{2\sqrt{x}e^{2\sqrt{x}}}$$

$$= \dfrac{-3\sqrt{x}e^{\sqrt{x}}(2 - \sqrt{x})}{2\sqrt{x}e^{2\sqrt{x}}}$$

Be careful! $e^{2\sqrt{x}} \div e^{\sqrt{x}} = e^{\sqrt{x}}$

$$= \dfrac{3(\sqrt{x} - 2)}{2e^{\sqrt{x}}}$$

b $\quad \dfrac{d}{dx}\left(3xe^{2x^2}\right) = 3x \times \dfrac{d}{dx}\left(e^{2x^2}\right) + e^{2x^2} \times \dfrac{d}{dx}(3x)$ $\quad$ ...... Use the product rule.

$$= 3x \times \left(4xe^{2x^2}\right) + e^{2x^2} \times (3)$$

$$= 12x^2e^{2x^2} + 3e^{2x^2}$$

$$= 3e^{2x^2}(4x^2 + 1)$$

c $\quad \dfrac{d}{dx}\left(e^{2x} - \sqrt{x}\right)^2$ .... Expand brackets (or alternatively use the chain rule*).

$= \dfrac{d}{dx}\left(e^{4x} - 2e^{2x}\sqrt{x} + x\right)$ .... Use the product rule.

$= 4e^{4x} - \left(4e^{2x}\sqrt{x} + 2e^{2x} \times \dfrac{1}{2}x^{-\frac{1}{2}}\right) + 1$ .... Simplify.

$= 4e^{4x} - 4e^{2x}\sqrt{x} - 2e^{2x} \times \dfrac{1}{2}x^{-\frac{1}{2}} + 1$

$= 4e^{4x} - 4e^{2x}\sqrt{x} - \dfrac{e^{2x}}{\sqrt{x}} + 1$

Note: The alternative method of using the chain rule (not involving expanding the brackets) gives the answer $2\left(2e^{2x} - \dfrac{1}{2\sqrt{x}}\right)\left(e^{2x} - \sqrt{x}\right)$. This would be a preferred method if stationary points were required to be found or if the brackets were raised to a higher power.

EXERCISE 4C

1   Differentiate with respect to x.

a $\quad e^{3x}$

b $\quad 3e^{\frac{x}{2}}$

c $\quad 4e^{\sqrt{x}}$

d $\quad e^{\frac{2}{x}}$

e $\quad e^{3x-2}$

f $\quad e^{3x^2+1}$

g $\quad \dfrac{2}{e^{x^3}}$

h $\quad (2 + e^{2x})^2$

i $\quad \dfrac{1}{e^x + 2}$

j $\quad \sqrt{1 - 3e^{4x}}$

k $\quad (1 + e^{x^3})^3$

l $\quad e^x\sqrt{1 - 4x}$

m $\quad \dfrac{x^2 - 2xe^x}{1 + e^x}$

n $\quad \dfrac{e^{5x}}{2e^{\sqrt{x}}}$

o $\quad e^{3x}(1 - e^x)^2$

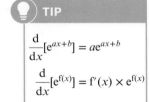

TIP

$\dfrac{d}{dx}[e^{ax+b}] = ae^{ax+b}$

$\dfrac{d}{dx}[e^{f(x)}] = f'(x) \times e^{f(x)}$

2   The graph of $y = xe^{-kx}$ has a stationary point when $x = \dfrac{2}{5}$. Find the value of k.

3   Sketch the graph of $y = x^2e^x$, indicating clearly the coordinates of any stationary points on the curve and of any points where the curve cuts the axes.

4 a Find the equations of the tangents to the curve $y = xe^x$ at the points $x = 1$ and $x = -1$.

b Find the x-coordinate of the intersection of these two tangents, writing your answer as an exact value.

5 Find the value of x where the gradient of $f(x) = 5 - 2e^x$ is -6.

6 Find the equation of the tangent to the curve $y = e^x + x$ which is parallel to $y = 3x$.

7 Find the range of the function f: $x \mapsto e^x - 4x + 2$.

8 Differentiate $y = (3x^2 - x + 2)e^{2x}$, giving your answer in the form $P(x)e^{2x}$ where $P(x)$ is a polynomial.

9 Find the x-coordinates of the stationary points on the curve $y = (2x + 1)^5 e^{-2x}$.

PS 10 A radioactive isotope is decaying according to the formula $m = 600 + 80e^{-0.004t}$ where m is the mass in grams and t is the time in years from the first observation.

a Find the value of t when $m = 630$.

b Find the rate at which the isotope will be decreasing when $t = 120$. Give your answer to 3 significant figures.

PS 11 A circular oil patch has an area $A\,m^2$ where $A = 2e^{0.5t}$ and t is the time in minutes after the first observation.

a Find the rate at which the oil patch is increasing per minute when $t = 3$ minutes.

b Find how long (to the nearest minute) after the first observation the oil patch will reach an area of $65\,m^2$.

12 Find the equation of the normal to the curve $y = 3e^x$ at the point $x = \ln 3$. Give your answer in the form $x + ky = p + \ln q$ where k, p and q are integers.

4.4 Derivatives of natural logarithmic functions

WORKED EXAMPLE 4.4

Differentiate with respect to x.

a $3x^2 \ln(1-4x)$ **b** $\dfrac{\ln 3x}{(x+2)^3}$

Answer

a $\dfrac{\mathrm{d}}{\mathrm{d}x}\left[3x^2 \ln(1-4x)\right]$

$= 3x^2 \times \dfrac{\mathrm{d}}{\mathrm{d}x}\ln(1-4x) + \ln(1-4x) \times \dfrac{\mathrm{d}}{\mathrm{d}x}(3x^2)$

$= 3x^2 \times \dfrac{-4}{1-4x} + \ln(1-4x) \times 6x$

$= -\dfrac{12x^2}{1-4x} + 6x\ln(1-4x)$

$= \dfrac{12x^2}{4x-1} + 6x\ln(1-4x)$

Use the product rule.

b $\dfrac{\mathrm{d}}{\mathrm{d}x}\left(\dfrac{\ln 3x}{(x+2)^3}\right)$

$= \dfrac{(x+2)^3 \times \frac{\mathrm{d}}{\mathrm{d}x}(\ln 3x) - \ln 3x \times \frac{\mathrm{d}}{\mathrm{d}x}((x+2)^3)}{((x+2)^3)^2}$

$= \dfrac{(x+2)^3 \times \frac{3}{3x} - \ln 3x \times 3(x+2)^2}{(x+2)^6}$

$= \dfrac{(x+2)^3 - 3x(x+2)^2 \ln 3x}{x(x+2)^6}$

$= \dfrac{(x+2)^2(x+2-3x\ln 3x)}{x(x+2)^6}$

$= \dfrac{(x+2-3x\ln 3x)}{x(x+2)^4}$

Use the quotient rule.

TIP

$\dfrac{\mathrm{d}}{\mathrm{d}x}(\ln x) = \dfrac{1}{x}$

$\dfrac{\mathrm{d}}{\mathrm{d}x}\left[\ln(f(x))\right] = \dfrac{f'(x)}{f(x)}$

49

EXERCISE 4D

1 Differentiate each of the following functions with respect to x.

a $\ln 2x$

b $\ln(2x - 1)$

c $\ln(1 - 2x)$

d $\ln x^2$

e $\ln(a + bx)$

f $\ln\dfrac{1}{x}$

g $\ln\dfrac{1}{3x + 1}$

h $\ln\dfrac{2x + 1}{3x - 1}$

i $3\ln x^{-2}$

j $\ln(x(x + 1))$

k $\ln(x^2(x - 1))$

l $\ln(x^2 + x - 2)$

m $\dfrac{\ln 3x}{x}$

n $\dfrac{\ln 2x}{x^2}$

2 Find the exact coordinates of the stationary point on the curve $y = \dfrac{\ln x}{x}$ and determine its nature.

3 Find any stationary values of the following curves and determine whether they are maxima or minima. Sketch the curves.

a $y = x - \ln x$

b $y = \dfrac{1}{2}x^2 - \ln 2x$

c $y = x^2 - \ln x^2$

d $y = x^n - \ln x^n$, for $n \geqslant 1$

4 Find the equation of the normal to the curve $y = 2e^{-x}$ at the point where $x = \ln 3$. Give your answer in the form $ax + by = p\ln q + c$, where a, b, c, p and q are integers.

5 Let $f(x) = \ln(x - 2) + \ln(x - 6)$. Write down the natural domain of $f(x)$. Find $f'(x)$ and hence find the intervals for which $f'(x)$ is:

a positive

b negative.

Sketch the curve $y = f(x)$.

6 Differentiate the following with respect to x, and simplify your answers as much as possible.

a $x^2 \ln x$

b $\dfrac{\ln x}{x^2}$

c $\dfrac{e^x}{x^2 e^x + 1}$

d xe^{x^2}

7 Let $f(x) = e^{2x}$. Find the inverse function $f^{-1}(x)$, and sketch the graphs of both $y = f(x)$ and $y = f^{-1}(x)$ on the same set of axes. How is the graph of $y = f^{-1}(x)$ related to the graph of $y = \ln x$?

 8 Given that $x = \ln(y^2 - 4)$, find an expression for $\dfrac{dy}{dx}$ in terms of y.

9 Show that the function $f(x) = \ln x + \dfrac{1}{x^k}$ has a stationary point with y-coordinate $\dfrac{\ln k + 1}{k}$.

10 Find the exact value of the gradient of the graph $f(x) = e^x - \dfrac{\ln x}{2}$ when $x = \ln 3$.

11 a Sketch the graph $y = \ln x$.

  b The tangent to this graph at the point $(p, \ln p)$ passes through the origin. Find the value of p.

  c For what range of values of k does $\ln x = kx$ have two solutions?

4.5 Derivatives of trigonometric functions

WORKED EXAMPLE 4.5

a Differentiate $6\cos^2 4x$ with respect to x.

b Show that $\dfrac{d}{dx}\ln(\tan x) = 2\operatorname{cosec} 2x$.

Answer

a $\dfrac{d}{dx}(6\cos^2 4x) = 6\dfrac{d}{dx}(\cos^2 4x)$

$= 6 \times 2 \times 4 \times \cos 4x \times (-\sin 4x)$

$= -48\cos 4x \sin 4x$

$= -24\sin 8x$

b $\dfrac{d}{dx}\ln(\tan x) = \dfrac{1}{\tan x} \times \sec^2 x$ Use the chain rule.

$= \dfrac{\cos x}{\sin x} \times \dfrac{1}{\cos^2 x}$

$= \dfrac{1}{\sin x \cos x}$

$= \dfrac{1}{\frac{1}{2}\sin 2x}$

$= 2\operatorname{cosec} 2x$ Shown.

 TIP

$\dfrac{d}{dx}(\sin x) = \cos x$

$\dfrac{d}{dx}(\cos x) = -\sin x$

$\dfrac{d}{dx}(\tan x) = \sec^2 x$

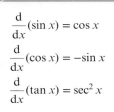 TIP

Remember to fully simplify your answers using trigonometric identities where possible.

51

EXERCISE 4E

1 Differentiate the following with respect to x.

  a $-\sin x$ **b** $-\cos x$ **c** $\sin 4x$

  d $2\cos 3x$ **e** $\sin\frac{1}{2}\pi x$ **f** $\cos 3\pi x$

  g $\cos(2x-1)$ **h** $5\sin\left(3x+\frac{1}{4}\pi\right)$ **i** $\cos\left(\frac{1}{2}\pi - 5x\right)$

  j $-\sin\left(\frac{1}{4}\pi - 2x\right)$ **k** $-\cos\left(\frac{1}{2}\pi + 2x\right)$ **l** $\sin\left(\frac{1}{2}\pi(1+2x)\right)$

2 Differentiate the following with respect to x.

a $\sin^2 x$ b $\cos^2 x$ c $\cos^3 x$

d $5 \sin^2 \dfrac{1}{2}x$ e $\cos^4 2x$ f $\sin x^2$

g $7 \cos 2x^3$ h $\sin^2 \left(\dfrac{1}{2}x - \dfrac{1}{3}\pi \right)$ i $\cos^3 2\pi x$

j $\sin^3 x^2$ k $\sin^2 x^2 + \cos^2 x^2$ l $\cos^2 \dfrac{1}{2}x$

TIP

It is important to remember that, in calculus, all angles are measured in radians unless a question tells you otherwise.

3 Show that $\dfrac{d}{dx} \ln \operatorname{cosec} x = -\cot x$ and $\dfrac{d}{dx} \ln \cos x = -\tan x$. Use these and other similar results to differentiate the following with respect to x.

a $\ln \sin 2x$ b $\ln \cos 3x$

c $\ln \sin^2 x$ d $\ln \cos^3 2x$

4 Differentiate the following with respect to x.

a $e^{\sin x}$ b $e^{\cos 3x}$ c $5e^{\sin^2 x}$

5 Find any stationary points in the interval $0 \leqslant x < 2\pi$ on each of the following curves, and find out whether they are maxima, minima or neither.

a $y = \sin x + \cos x$ b $y = x + \sin x$ c $y = \sin^2 x + 2 \cos x$

d $y = \cos 2x + x$ e $y = \cos 2x - 2 \sin x$

6 Find the equations of the tangent and the normal to the graph of $y = 3\tan x - 2\sqrt{2}\sin x$ at $x = \dfrac{\pi}{4}$. Give all the coefficients in an exact form.

7 Given that $y = \dfrac{1}{4} \tan x + \dfrac{1}{x^2}$ for $0 < x \leqslant 2\pi$, solve the equation $\dfrac{dy}{dx} = 1 - \dfrac{2}{x^3}$.

8 Find the exact coordinates of the minimum point of the curve $y = e^{-x}\cos x$, $0 \leqslant x \leqslant \pi$.

9 The volume of water in millions of litres (V) in a tidal lake is modelled by $V = 60 \cos t + 100$, where t is the time in days after a hydroelectric plant is switched on.

a   What is the smallest volume of the lake?

b   A hydroelectric plant produces an amount of electricity proportional to the rate of flow of water through a tidal dam. Assuming all flow is through the dam, find the time in the first 6 days when the plant is producing maximum electricity.

PS **10 a** Express $\sec^2 x$ in terms of $\tan x$.

b Let $y = \tan^{-1} x$. By first expressing x in terms of y, prove that
$\dfrac{dy}{dx} = \dfrac{1}{1 + x^2}$.

c Find the equation of the normal to the curve $y = \tan^{-1}(3x)$ at
the point where $x = \dfrac{1}{\sqrt{3}}$.

11 A function is defined by $f(x) = 2x + \dfrac{1}{2}\sin 2x - \tan x$ for $-\dfrac{\pi}{2} \leqslant x \leqslant \dfrac{\pi}{2}$.

a Find $f'(x)$.

b Show that the stationary points of $f(x)$ satisfy the equation
$2\cos^4 x + \cos^2 x - 1 = 0$.

c Hence show that the function has two stationary points.

4.6 Implicit differentiation

WORKED EXAMPLE 4.6

Find the gradients of the normals to the curve $x^2 + 3xy + 2y^2 = 10$ at the points where $x = -1$.

Answer

$x^2 + 3xy + 2y^2 = 10$	Find the y-coordinates on the curve where $x = -1$.
$(-1)^2 + 3(-1)y + 2y^2 = 10$	Substitute $x = -1$ into the curve equation.
$1 - 3y + 2y^2 = 10$	
$2y^2 - 3y - 9 = 0$	Factorise
$(2y + 3)(y - 3) = 0$	
$y = -\dfrac{3}{2}, \, 3$	
The two points on the curve are $\left(-1, -\dfrac{3}{2}\right)$ and $(-1, 3)$	
$x^2 + 3xy + 2y^2 = 0$	Differentiate with respect to x.
$\dfrac{d}{dx}(x^2) + \dfrac{d}{dx}(3xy) + \dfrac{d}{dx}(2y^2) = 0$	Use the product rule for $\dfrac{d}{dx}(3xy)$.
$2x + 3x\dfrac{d}{dx}(y) + y\dfrac{d}{dx}(3x) + \dfrac{d}{dy}(2y^2) = 0$	

$$2x + 3x\frac{dy}{dx} + 3y + 4y\frac{dy}{dx} = 0 \quad \cdots\cdots\cdots\cdots \text{Rearrange terms.}$$

$$3x\frac{dy}{dx} + 4y\frac{dy}{dx} = -2x - 3y \quad \cdots\cdots \text{Factorise.}$$

$$(3x + 4y)\frac{dy}{dx} = -2x - 3y \quad \cdots\cdots\cdots\cdots \text{Rearrange.}$$

$$\frac{dy}{dx} = \frac{-2x - 3y}{3x + 4y}$$

When $x = -1$ and $y = -\frac{3}{2}$, $\quad \cdots\cdots\cdots\cdots$ Find the gradient of the curve at the point $\left(-1, -\frac{3}{2}\right)$.

$$\frac{dy}{dx} = \frac{-2(-1) - 3\left(-\frac{3}{2}\right)}{3(-1) + 4\left(-\frac{3}{2}\right)} = -\frac{13}{18}$$

$\therefore$ Gradient of the normal is $\dfrac{18}{13}$.

When $x = -1$ and $y = 3$, $\quad \cdots\cdots\cdots\cdots$ Find the gradient of the curve at the point $(-1, 3)$.

$$\frac{dy}{dx} = \frac{-2(-1) - 3(3)}{3(-1) + 4(3)} = -\frac{7}{9}$$

Gradient of the curve at the point $(-1, 3)$ is $-\dfrac{7}{9}$.

$\therefore$ Gradient of the normal is $\dfrac{9}{7}$.

The gradients of the normals are $\dfrac{18}{13}$ and $\dfrac{9}{7}$.

EXERCISE 4F

1 Find the gradient of each curve at the given point:

  a **i** $x^2 + 3y^2 = 7$ at $(2, -1)$

  ii $2x^3 - y^3 = -6$ at $(1, 2)$

  b **i** $\cos x + \sin y = 0$ at $(0, \pi)$

  ii $\tan x + \tan y = 2$ at $\left(\dfrac{\pi}{4}, \dfrac{\pi}{4}\right)$

  c **i** $x^2 + 3xy + y^2 = 20$ at $(2, 2)$

  ii $3x^2 - xy^2 + 3y = 21$ at $(-1, 3)$

  d **i** $xe^y + ye^x = 2e$ at $(1, 1)$

  ii $x\ln y - \dfrac{x}{y} = 2$ at $(-1, 1)$

2 Find $\dfrac{dy}{dx}$ in terms of x and y:

   a **i** $3x^2 - y^3 = 15$ **ii** $x^4 + 3y^2 = 20$

   b **i** $xy^2 - 4x^2y = 6$ **ii** $y^2 - xy = 7$

   c **i** $\dfrac{x+y}{x-y} = 2y$ **ii** $\dfrac{y^2}{xy+1} = 1$

   d **i** $xe^y - 4\ln y = x^2$ **ii** $3x \sin y + 2 \cos y = \sin x$

3 Find the coordinates of stationary points on the curves given by these implicit equations:

   a $-x^2 + 3xy + y^2 = 13$ **b** $2x^2 - xy + y^2 = 28$

4 A curve has equation $3x^2 - y^2 = 8$. Point A has coordinates $(-2, 2)$.

   a Show that point A lies on the curve.

   b Find the equation of the normal to the curve at A.

5 Find the equation of the tangent to the curve with equation $4x^2 - 3xy - y^2 = 25$ at the point $(2, -3)$.

6 Find the points on the curve $4x^2 + 2xy - 3y^2 = 39$ at which the tangent is parallel to one of the axes.

7 Find the coordinates of the stationary point on the curve given by $e^x + ye^{-x} = 2e^2$.

8 The line L is tangent to the curve C which has the equation $y^2 = x^3$ when $x = 4$ and $y > 0$.

   a Find the equation of L.

   b Show that L meets C again at the point P with an x-coordinate which satisfies the equation $x^3 - 9x^2 + 24x - 16 = 0$.

   c Find the coordinates of the point P.

9 **a** Find the equation of the normal to the curve $xy + y^2 = 2x$ at the point $(1, 1)$.

   b Find the coordinates of the point where the normal meets the curve again.

P 10 A curve is defined by the implicit equation $x^2 - \dfrac{1}{2}y^2 + 2xy + 5 = 0$.

   a Find an expression for $\dfrac{dy}{dx}$ in terms of x and y.

   b Hence prove that the curve has no tangents parallel to the y-axis.

4.7 Parametric differentiation

Find and determine the nature of the stationary point on the curve defined by the parametric equations $x = 3 - t^3$, $y = t^2 - 2t$.

Answer

$$x = 3 - t^3 \Rightarrow \frac{dx}{dt} = -3t^2$$

$$y = t^2 - 2t \Rightarrow \frac{dy}{dt} = 2t - 2$$

$$\frac{dy}{dx} = \frac{dy}{dt} \times \frac{dt}{dx}$$
Use the chain rule.

$$= (2t - 2) \times \frac{1}{-3t^2}$$

$$= -\frac{2t - 2}{3t^2}$$

$$= \frac{2 - 2t}{3t^2}$$

$$\frac{2 - 2t}{3t^2} = 0$$
At a stationary point $\frac{dy}{dx} = 0$

$$2 - 2t = 0$$
$$t = 1$$
Substitute $t = 1$ into $x = 3 - t^3$ and $y = t^2 - 2t$.

$$x = 3 - 1^3$$
$$x = 2$$

$$y = 1^2 - 2$$
$$y = -1$$
The stationary point is at $(2, -1)$.

Now find $\frac{d^2y}{dx^2}$ to determine its nature

$$\frac{dy}{dx} = \frac{2 - 2t}{3t^2}$$
Differentiate using the quotient rule.

$$\frac{d^2y}{dx^2} = \frac{d}{dx}\left(\frac{2 - 2t}{3t^2}\right)$$

$$= \frac{d}{dt}\left(\frac{2 - 2t}{3t^2}\right)\frac{dt}{dx}$$

$$= \frac{(3t^2)(-2) - (2 - 2t)(6t)}{9t^4} \times \frac{dt}{dx}$$
$$\frac{dt}{dx} = -\frac{1}{3t^2}$$

$$\frac{d^2y}{dx^2} = \frac{-6t^2 - 12t + 12t^2}{9t^4} \times \left(-\frac{1}{3t^2}\right)$$

$$\frac{d^2y}{dx^2} = -\frac{6t(t + 2 - 2t)}{9t^4}\left(-\frac{1}{3t^2}\right)$$

$$\frac{d^2y}{dx^2} = \frac{2(2 - t)}{9t^5}$$ .... At the stationary point $t = 1$.

$$\frac{d^2y}{dx^2} = \frac{2(2 - 1)}{9(1)^5}$$

$$\frac{d^2y}{dx^2} = \frac{2}{9}$$

$$\frac{d^2y}{dx^2} > 0 \text{ as } \frac{2}{9} > 0$$

So the stationary point at $(2, -1)$ is a minimum.

57

TIP

An alternative method for finding $\dfrac{d^2y}{dx^2}$ is to convert the parametric equations into a Cartesian equation by eliminating the parameter. Two of the most common ways of doing this are by substitution, or by using a trigonometric identity. This method has not been used in this example since substitution leads to a complicated Cartesian equation.

EXERCISE 4G

1 Find the expression for $\dfrac{dy}{dx}$ in terms of t or θ for the following parametric curves.

   a **i** $x = 3t^2$, $y = 2t$ **ii** $x = 5t^2$, $y = 2 - t$

   b **i** $x = 2\cos(2\theta)$, $y = \cos\theta$ **ii** $x = \cos(2\theta)$, $y = 3\sin\theta$

   c **i** $x = \tan\theta$, $y = \sec\theta$ **ii** $x = 3\sec\theta$, $y = 2\tan\theta$

TIP

You can check your answers by using a calculator or graphing software which can plot parametric equations.

2 Find Cartesian equations for curves with these parametric equations.

   a $x = t^2$, $y = \dfrac{1}{t}$ **b** $x = 3t^2$, $y = 6t$

   c $x = 2\cos t$, $y = 2\sin t$

3 Find Cartesian equations for curves with these parametric equations.

    a $x = \cos^2 t,\ y = \sin^2 t$ b $x = \cos^3 t,\ y = \sin^3 t$

    c $x = 1 - \dfrac{1}{t},\ y = 1 + \dfrac{1}{t}$ d $x = 3t^2,\ y = 2t^3$

4 The tangent to the curve with parametric equations $x = t^2,\ y = e^{-t}$ at the point $\left(1, \dfrac{1}{e}\right)$ crosses the coordinate axes at the points M and N. Find the exact area of triangle OMN.

5 a   Find the equation of the normal to the curve with equation $x = 4t,\ y = \dfrac{4}{t}$ at the point $(16, 1)$.

    b   Find the coordinates of the point where the normal crosses the curve again.

P 6 Prove that the curve with parametric equations $x = t^3 - 3t^2 + 7t,\ y = 5t^2 + 1$ has no tangent parallel to the y-axis.

P 7 Let P be the point on the curve $x = t^2,\ y = \dfrac{1}{t}$ with coordinates $\left(p^2, \dfrac{1}{p}\right)$. The tangent to the curve at P meets the x-axis at point A and the y-axis at point B. Prove that $PA = 2PB$.

P 8 Point $Q(aq^2, 2aq)$ lies on the parabola with parametric equations $x = at^2,\ y = 2at$.

    a   Let M be the point where the normal to the parabola at Q crosses the x-axis. Find, in terms of a and q, the coordinates of M.

    b N is the perpendicular from Q in the x-axis. Prove that the distance $MN = 2a$.

PS 9 A curve has parametric equations $x = 3t^2 + 2t,\ y = 2t^2 + 3t$. Find the coordinates of the point where the tangent has gradient $\dfrac{3}{4}$.

P 10 The parametric equations of a curve are $x = 2\theta + \cos \theta,\ y = \theta + \sin \theta$, where $0 \leqslant \theta \leqslant 2\pi$.

    a   Find $\dfrac{dy}{dx}$ in terms of θ.

    b   Show that, at points on the curve where the gradient is $\dfrac{3}{4}$, the parameter θ satisfies an equation of the form $5 \sin(\theta + \alpha) = 2$, where the value of α is to be stated.

    c   Solve the equation in part **b** to find the two possible values of θ.

 TIP

At a point where the tangent is parallel to the x-axis, $\dfrac{dy}{dt} = 0$.

At a point where the tangent is parallel to the y-axis, $\dfrac{dx}{dt} = 0$.

END-OF-CHAPTER REVIEW EXERCISE 4

1 Find the exact coordinates of the stationary point on the curve with equation $ye^x = 3x - 6$.

2 A function is defined by $g(x) = 3x + \ln(2x)$ for $x > 0$.

    a Find $g'(x)$ and hence prove that $g(x)$ has an inverse function.

    b Find the gradient of $g'(x)$ at the point where $x = 3$.

3 A curve is given by the implicit equation $x^2 - xy + y^2 = 12$.

    a Find the coordinates of the stationary points on the curve.

    b Show that at the stationary points, $(x - 2y)\dfrac{d^2y}{dx^2} = 2$.

    c Hence determine the nature of the stationary points.

PS 4 A chain hangs from two posts. Its height h above the ground satisfies the equation

$h = e^x + \dfrac{1}{e^{2x}}$, $-1 \leqslant x \leqslant 2$. The left post is positioned at $x = -1$, and the right post is positioned at $x = 2$.

    a State, with reasons, which post is taller.

    b Show that the minimum height occurs when $x = \dfrac{1}{3}\ln 2$.

    c Find the exact value of the minimum height of the chain.

5 The function f is defined by $f : x \mapsto \ln(x^2 - 35)$ for $|x| \geqslant 6$. For what values of x does the graph of this function have gradient 1?

6 **a** Solve the equation $\sin 2x = \sin x$ for $0 \leqslant x \leqslant 2\pi$, giving your answers in terms of π.

    b Find the coordinates of the stationary points of the curve $y = \sin 2x - \sin x$ for $0 \leqslant x \leqslant 2\pi$, giving your answers correct to three significant figures.

    c Hence sketch the curve $y = \sin 2x - \sin x$ for $0 \leqslant x \leqslant 2\pi$.

7 **a** Let $y = e^{3x^2 - 6x}$. Find $\dfrac{dy}{dx}$.

    b Find the coordinates of the stationary point on the curve $y = e^{3x^2 - 6x}$, and decide whether it is a maximum or a minimum.

    c Find the equation of the normal to the curve $y = e^{3x^2 - 6x}$ at the point where $x = 2$.

P 8 P is a point on the parabola given parametrically by $x = at^2$, $y = 2at$, where a is a constant. Let S be the point $(a, 0)$, Q be the point $(-a, 2at)$ and T be the point where the tangent at P to the parabola crosses the axis of symmetry of the parabola.

    a Show that $SP = PQ = QT = ST = at^2 + a$.

    b Prove that angle QPT is equal to angle $S\hat{P}T$.

    c If PM is parallel to the axis of the parabola, with M to the right of P, and PN is the normal to the parabola at P, show that angle MPN is equal to angle NPS.

9 a Show that $\dfrac{d}{dx}(\operatorname{cosec} x) = -\operatorname{cosec} x \cot x$.

    b Find the coordinates of the points on the curve $y = \operatorname{cosec} x$ $(0 \leqslant x \leqslant \pi)$ where the gradient is equal to $2\sqrt{3}$.

 10 a Find $\dfrac{d}{dx}\ln y$ in terms of y and $\dfrac{dy}{dx}$.

    b If $y = \dfrac{x^4}{(2+5x)\sqrt{x^2+1}}$ find and simplify an expression for $\ln y$.

    c Hence find the derivative of $y = \dfrac{x^4}{(2+5x)\sqrt{x^2+1}}$.

- Extend the idea of 'reverse differentiation' to include the integration of e^{ax+b}, $\dfrac{1}{ax+b}$, $\sin(ax+b)$, $\cos(ax+b)$ and $\sec^2(ax+b)$.
- Use trigonometrical relationships in carrying out integration.
- Understand and use the trapezium rule to estimate the value of a definite integral.

5.1 Integration of exponential functions

WORKED EXAMPLE 5.1

Find $\displaystyle\int_1^2 (9e^{-2x+1} + 4e^{-x})\,dx$.

Answer

$$\int_1^2 (9e^{-2x+1} + 4e^{-x})\,dx = \left[\frac{9}{-2}e^{-2x+1} + \frac{4}{-1}e^{-x}\right]_1^2$$

$$= \left[-\frac{9}{2}e^{-2x+1} - 4e^{-x}\right]_1^2$$

$$= \left(-\frac{9}{2}e^{-2(2)+1} - 4e^{-2}\right) - \left(-\frac{9}{2}e^{-2(1)+1} - 4e^{-1}\right)$$

$$= -\frac{9}{2}e^{-3} - 4e^{-2} + \frac{9}{2}e^{-1} + 4e^{-1}$$

$$= -\frac{9}{2}e^{-3} - 4e^{-2} + \frac{17}{2}e^{-1}$$

61

EXERCISE 5A

1 Find the following integrals:

a i $\displaystyle\int 3e^{3x}\,dx$ 　　　　ii $\displaystyle\int e^{2x+5}\,dx$

b i $\displaystyle\int 4e^{\frac{2x-1}{3}}\,dx$ 　　　　ii $\displaystyle\int e^{\frac{1}{2}x}\,dx$

c i $\displaystyle\int -6e^{-3x}\,dx$ 　　　　ii $\displaystyle\int \frac{1}{e^{4x}}\,dx$

d i $\displaystyle\int \frac{-2}{e^{\frac{x}{4}}}\,dx$ 　　　　ii $\displaystyle\int e^{-\frac{2}{3}x}\,dx$

2 Find:

a $\displaystyle\int e^{2x}(1 + e^{-2x})\,dx$

b $\displaystyle\int e^{-x}(1 + e^{-2x})\,dx$

c $\displaystyle\int e^{x}(e^{x} + 3)^{2}\,dx$

d $\displaystyle\int \frac{1 - e^{2x}}{e^{-2x}}\,dx$

e $\displaystyle\int \frac{9 - e^{2x}}{e^{2x}}\,dx$

f $\displaystyle\int (e^{-3x})^{4}\,dx$

3 Evaluate:

a $\displaystyle\int_{0}^{5} e^{4x}\,dx$

b $\displaystyle\int_{0}^{\frac{1}{2}} e^{2x}\,dx$

c $\displaystyle\int_{0}^{\ln 2} 2e^{-3x}\,dx$

d $\displaystyle\int_{0}^{4} e^{1-3x}\,dx$

e $\displaystyle\int_{0}^{1} \frac{2}{e^{3x+2}}\,dx$

f $\displaystyle\int_{0}^{2} (e^{x} + 2)^{2}\,dx$

g $\displaystyle\int_{0}^{2} (e^{x} + e^{3x})^{2}\,dx$

h $\displaystyle\int_{0}^{2} (3e^{3x})^{3}\,dx$

i $\displaystyle\int_{0}^{1} \frac{(e^{-x})^{2}}{e^{3x}}\,dx$

4 A curve is such that $\dfrac{d^{2}y}{dx^{2}} = 2e^{-x}$. Given that $\dfrac{dy}{dx} = 1$ when $x = 0$ and that the curve passes through the point $\left(1, \dfrac{2}{e} + 4\right)$, find the equation of the curve.

5 Find the exact area of the region bounded by the curve $y = 4e^{-3x} + 3e^{-x}$, and the x-axis from $x = 0$ and $x = 1$.

6 Find the exact area of the shaded region.

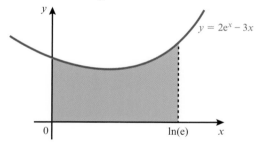

$y = 2e^{x} - 3x$

ln(e)

7 a Find $\displaystyle\int_{0}^{a} (2e^{-2x} + 3e^{-x})\,dx$, where a is a positive constant.

b Hence find the value of $\displaystyle\int_{0}^{\infty} (2e^{-2x} + 3e^{-x})\,dx$.

PS **8**

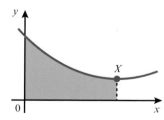

The diagram shows the curve $y = e^{x} + 3e^{-2x}$ and its minimum point X. Find the area of the shaded region, giving your answer to 3 significant figures.

P 9

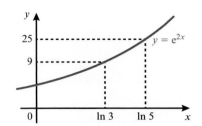

The diagram shows the graph of $y = e^{2x}$. The points $(\ln 3, 9)$ and $(\ln 5, 25)$ lie on the curve.

a   Find the value of $\displaystyle\int_{\ln 3}^{\ln 5} e^{2x}\,dx$.

b   Hence show that $\displaystyle\int_{3}^{5} \ln y\,dy = \ln\left(\frac{3125}{27e^2}\right)$.

10 The diagram shows the curves with equations $y = 3e^x - 3$ and $y = 13 - 5e^{-x}$.

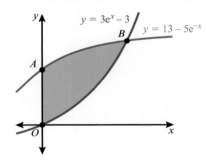

a   Write down the coordinates of point A.

b   The curves intersect at the point B.

   i   Show that the x-coordinate of B satisfies the equation $3e^{2x} - 16e^x + 5 = 0$.

   ii   Hence find the exact coordinates of B.

c   Find the exact value of the shaded area.

63

5.2 Integration of $\dfrac{1}{ax+b}$

Find the value of:

a $\displaystyle\int_1^2 \frac{1}{5-2x}\,dx$

b $\displaystyle\int_3^4 \frac{1}{5-2x}\,dx$

Answer

a $\displaystyle\int_1^2 \frac{1}{5-2x}\,dx = \left[\left(\frac{1}{-2}\right)\ln|5-2x|\right]_1^2$ .... Substitute limits.

$= \left(-\frac{1}{2}\ln|1|\right) - \left(-\frac{1}{2}\ln|3|\right)$

$= -\frac{1}{2}\ln 1 + \frac{1}{2}\ln 3$ .... Simplify.

$= \frac{1}{2}\ln 3$

b $\displaystyle\int_3^4 \frac{1}{5-2x}\,dx = \left[\left(\frac{1}{-2}\right)\ln|5-2x|\right]_3^4$ .... Substitute limits.

$= \left(-\frac{1}{2}\ln|-3|\right) - \left(-\frac{1}{2}\ln|-1|\right)$

$= -\frac{1}{2}\ln 3 + \frac{1}{2}\ln 1$ .... Simplify.

$= -\frac{1}{2}\ln 3$

> **TIP**
>
> In this example, $\ln|-3|$ and $\ln|-1|$ must be used since $\ln x$ is only defined for $x > 0$.
>
> It is normal practice to include the modulus sign only when finding definite integrals. Use technology to interpret your answers to parts **a** and **b**.

1 Find:

a i $\displaystyle\int \frac{1}{x+4}\,dx$ **ii** $\displaystyle\int \frac{5}{5x-2}\,dx$

b i $\displaystyle\int \frac{2}{3x+4}\,dx$ **ii** $\displaystyle\int \frac{-8}{2x-5}\,dx$

c i $\displaystyle\int \frac{-3}{1-4x}\,dx$ **ii** $\displaystyle\int \frac{1}{7-2x}\,dx$

d i $\displaystyle\int 1 - \frac{3}{5-x}\,dx$ **ii** $\displaystyle\int 3 + \frac{1}{3-x}\,dx$

2 Evaluate:

a $\displaystyle\int_0^3 \frac{1}{x+4}\,dx$ **b** $\displaystyle\int_1^2 \frac{1}{3x+1}\,dx$ **c** $\displaystyle\int_0^4 \frac{1}{5x+5}\,dx$

d $\displaystyle\int_0^1 \frac{2}{4x+1}\,dx$ **e** $\displaystyle\int_0^1 \frac{4}{2x-5}\,dx$ **f** $\displaystyle\int_0^1 \frac{2}{4-x}\,dx$

3 Evaluate:

a $\displaystyle\int_4^5\left(1+\frac{3}{3-x}\right)$

b $\displaystyle\int_1^2\left(\frac{3}{2x}-\frac{2}{2x-1}\right)dx$

c $\displaystyle\int_{-1}^0\left(x-1+\frac{1}{2x-1}\right)dx$

4 a Given that $\dfrac{2x}{x-1}\equiv 2+\dfrac{A}{x-1}$, find the value of the constant A.

b Hence show that $\displaystyle\int_2^4\frac{2x}{2x-1}dx=4+\ln 9$.

5 a Find the quotient and remainder when $6x^2+5x$ is divided by $2x-1$.

b Hence work out $\displaystyle\int_1^2\frac{6x^2+5x}{2x-1}dx$, giving your answer in the form $a+b\ln c$.

PS 6 The diagram shows part of the curve $y=\dfrac{3}{2x-1}$. Given that the shaded region has area $\dfrac{3}{2}\ln 3$, find the value of k.

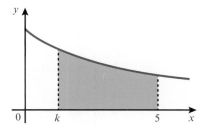

7 Given that $\dfrac{dy}{dx}=\dfrac{3}{2x+1}$ and the graph of y against x passes through the point $(1, 0)$, find y in terms of x.

8 A curve has the property that $\dfrac{dy}{dx}=\dfrac{8}{4x-3}$ and it passes through $(1, 2)$. Find its equation.

5.3 Integration of $\sin(ax+b)$, $\cos(ax+b)$ and $\sec^2(ax+b)$

WORKED EXAMPLE 5.3

Find:

a $\displaystyle\int\sin\frac{1}{2}x\,dx$

b $\displaystyle\int\cos\left(4-\frac{1}{2}x\right)dx$

c $\displaystyle\int_0^{\frac{\pi}{3}}\left(\sin 2x+\frac{1}{3}\pi\right)dx$

Answer

a $\displaystyle\int\sin\frac{1}{2}x\,dx=-2\cos\frac{1}{2}x+c$

b $\displaystyle\int\cos\left(4-\frac{1}{2}x\right)dx=-2\sin\left(4-\frac{1}{2}x\right)+c$

$$\text{c} \quad \int_0^{\frac{\pi}{3}} \left(\sin 2x + \frac{1}{3}\pi \right) dx = \left[-\frac{1}{2}\cos(2x) + \frac{1}{3}\pi x \right]_0^{\frac{\pi}{3}} \quad \cdots \quad \text{Substitute limits.}$$

$$= \left(-\frac{1}{2}\cos\frac{2\pi}{3} + \frac{\pi^2}{9} \right) - \left(-\frac{1}{2}\cos 0 + 0 \right)$$

$$= \frac{1}{4} + \frac{\pi^2}{9} + \frac{1}{2}$$

$$= \frac{3}{4} + \frac{\pi^2}{9}$$

> **TIP**
>
> Remember that the formulae for differentiating and integrating these trigonometric functions only apply when x is measured in **radians**.

EXERCISE 5C

1 Evaluate the following.

a $\displaystyle\int_0^{\frac{1}{2}\pi} \sin x \, dx$

b $\displaystyle\int_0^{\frac{1}{4}\pi} \cos x \, dx$

c $\displaystyle\int_0^{\frac{1}{4}\pi} \sin 2x \, dx$

d $\displaystyle\int_{\frac{1}{4}\pi}^{\frac{1}{3}\pi} \cos 3x \, dx$

e $\displaystyle\int_{-\frac{1}{6}\pi}^{\frac{1}{3}\pi} \sin\left(3x + \frac{1}{6}\pi \right) dx$

f $\displaystyle\int_0^{\frac{1}{2}\pi} \sin\left(\frac{1}{4}\pi - x \right) dx$

g $\displaystyle\int_0^1 \cos(1-x) \, dx$

h $\displaystyle\int_0^{\frac{1}{2}\pi} \sin\left(\frac{1}{2}x + 1 \right) dx$

i $\displaystyle\int_0^{2\pi} \sin\frac{1}{2}x \, dx$

2 Find the exact value of $\displaystyle\int_0^{\frac{\pi}{3}} 2\sin(5x) \, dx$.

3 Find:

a $\displaystyle\int \sec^2 3x \, dx$

b $\displaystyle\int 3\sec^2(7x-2) \, dx$

c $\displaystyle\int \frac{1}{\cos^2(4x+1)} \, dx$

4 Evaluate:

a $\displaystyle\int_0^{\frac{1}{12}\pi} \sec^2 4x \, dx$

b $\displaystyle\int_{-\frac{1}{6}\pi}^{\frac{1}{6}\pi} (1 - 3\sec^2 x) \, dx$

c $\displaystyle\int_{\frac{1}{4}\pi}^{\frac{1}{3}\pi} \sec^2 3x \, dx$

5 **a** Find $\dfrac{d}{dx}(2\tan 3x)$.

    b Hence find the exact value of $\displaystyle\int_{-\frac{1}{12}\pi}^{\frac{1}{12}\pi} 3\sec^2 3x \, dx$.

6 A curve is such that $f'(x) = x^2 - 4\cos x$. Given that $f(0) = 3$, find the equation of the curve.

7 A curve is such that $\dfrac{dy}{dx} = 2\cos x - 3\sin x$. Given that $y\left(\dfrac{\pi}{4}\right) = \dfrac{1}{\sqrt{2}}$, find the equation of the curve.

8 Find the area enclosed by the curve $y = \cos 2x$ $\left(0 \leqslant x \leqslant \dfrac{\pi}{4} \right)$, the x-axis and the y-axis.

9 A curve is such that $\dfrac{d^2y}{dx^2} = -18\sin 3x + 2\cos x$. Given that $\dfrac{dy}{dx} = 2$ when $x = \dfrac{\pi}{2}$ and that the curve passes through the point $(0, 2\pi - 3)$, find the equation of the curve.

PS **10** The diagram shows part of the graph of

$y = \dfrac{3}{2}\cos\left(2x - \dfrac{\pi}{3}\right)$ between the points A and

B whose coordinates need to be determined.

Find the exact area of the shaded region.

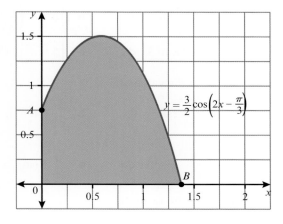

$y = \dfrac{3}{2}\cos\left(2x - \dfrac{\pi}{3}\right)$

5.4 Further integration of trigonometric functions

WORKED EXAMPLE 5.4

Find $\displaystyle\int \cos^4 x \, dx$.

Answer

$\cos^4 x = (\cos^2 x)^2$ · · · · · · Use $\cos^2 x \equiv \dfrac{1}{2}(\cos 2x + 1)$.

$\qquad = \left[\dfrac{1}{2}(\cos 2x + 1)\right]^2$ · · · · · · Expand.

$\qquad = \dfrac{1}{4}(\cos^2 2x + 2\cos 2x + 1)$

$\displaystyle\int \cos^4 x \, dx = \int \dfrac{1}{4}(\cos^2 2x + 2\cos 2x + 1)\, dx$ · · · · · · Use $\cos^2 2x \equiv \dfrac{1}{2}(\cos 4x + 1)$.

$\displaystyle\int \cos^4 x \, dx = \int \dfrac{1}{4}\left(\dfrac{1}{2}\cos 4x + \dfrac{1}{2} + 2\cos 2x + 1\right) dx$ · · · · Simplify.

$\displaystyle\int \cos^4 x \, dx = \int \left(\dfrac{1}{8}\cos 4x + \dfrac{1}{2}\cos 2x + \dfrac{3}{8}\right) dx$

$\displaystyle\int \cos^4 x \, dx = \dfrac{3}{8}x + \dfrac{1}{4}\sin 2x + \dfrac{1}{32}\sin 4x + c$

67

EXERCISE 5D

1 Find:

a $\displaystyle\int 5\cos^2 x\,dx$ **b** $\displaystyle\int 3\cos^2\left(\frac{x}{2}\right)dx$ **c** $\displaystyle\int \sin^2 4x\,dx$

d $\displaystyle\int 2\tan^2 3x\,dx$ **e** $\displaystyle\int 5\tan^2(2x)\,dx$ **f** $\displaystyle\int 3\cos^4 x\,dx$

2 Find the value of:

a $\displaystyle\int_0^{\frac{1}{3}\pi} 2\sin^2 x\,dx$ **b** $\displaystyle\int_{\frac{1}{6}\pi}^{\frac{1}{3}\pi} 2\tan^2 x\,dx$ **c** $\displaystyle\int_0^{\frac{1}{6}\pi} 3\cos^2 x\,dx$

d $\displaystyle\int_0^{\frac{1}{3}\pi} \cos^2 3x\,dx$ **e** $\displaystyle\int_0^{\frac{1}{2}\pi} 3\sin^2 2x\,dx$ **f** $\displaystyle\int_0^{\frac{1}{12}\pi} 2\tan^2 3x\,dx$

3 Find the value of:

a $\displaystyle\int_0^{\frac{1}{3}\pi}\left(2\cos^2 x+\frac{1}{\cos^2 x}\right)dx$ **b** $\displaystyle\int_0^{\frac{1}{6}\pi}(\cos 2x+\sin 2x)\,dx$

c $\displaystyle\int_0^{\frac{1}{3}\pi}(3\sin x+\cos x)^2\,dx$ **d** $\displaystyle\int_{\frac{1}{3}\pi}^{\frac{1}{2}\pi}(\cos x-\sin x)\,dx$

e $\displaystyle\int_0^{\frac{1}{4}\pi}\frac{2+\cos^4 x}{\cos^2 x}\,dx$ **f** $\displaystyle\int_0^{\frac{1}{6}\pi}\frac{3}{1+\cos 2x}\,dx$

4 Find the exact value of $\displaystyle\int_0^{\pi}\cos^2(3x)\,dx$.

5 Find the exact value of $\displaystyle\int_0^{\frac{\pi}{12}}\frac{1}{\cos^2 4x}\,dx$.

6 a Find the value of the constants A, B and C such that
$\sin^4 x\equiv A+B\cos 2x+C\cos 4x$.

b Hence evaluate $\displaystyle\int_0^{\frac{\pi}{2}}\sin^4 x\,dx$.

7 Let R be the region under the graph of $y=\sin^2 x$ over the interval $0\leqslant x\leqslant\pi$. Find:

a the area of R

b the volume of revolution formed by rotating R about the x-axis.

> **TIP**
> Remember, for rotations about the x-axis:
> $$V=\int_a^b \pi y^2\,dx.$$

P 8 a Prove that $\dfrac{2}{1 + \cos x} \equiv \sec^2\left(\dfrac{1}{2}x\right)$.

b Hence show that $\displaystyle\int_{-\frac{1}{2}\pi}^{\frac{1}{2}\pi} \dfrac{2}{(1 + \cos x)}\, dx = 4$.

P 9 a Prove that $\dfrac{1 - \sin 2x}{\operatorname{cosec} x - 2\cos x} \equiv \sin x$.

b Hence find $\displaystyle\int_{-\frac{1}{2}\pi}^{\frac{3}{4}\pi} \dfrac{1 - \sin 2x}{\operatorname{cosec} x - 2\cos x}\, dx$, giving your answer as an exact value.

10 Find the value of k if $\cos\left(x + \dfrac{\pi}{3}\right) - \cos\left(x - \dfrac{\pi}{3}\right) \equiv k \sin x$.

P2 ## 5.5 The trapezium rule

WORKED EXAMPLE 5.5

The graph shows the curve $y = x^2 e^x$.

Use the trapezium rule with 5 strips to estimate the shaded area, giving your answer correct to 4 significant figures. State, with a reason, whether the trapezium rule gives an under-estimate or an over-estimate of the true value.

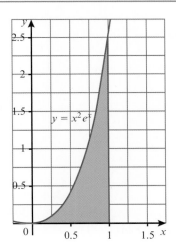

Answer

$a = 0$, $b = 1$ and $h = 0.2$

x	0	0.2	0.4	0.6	0.8	1
y	0	0.04886	0.23869	0.65596	1.42435	2.71828
	y_0	y_1	y_2	y_3	y_4	y_5

$$\text{Area} \approx \frac{h}{2}[y_0 + 2(y_1 + y_2 + y_3 + y_4) + y_5]$$

$$\approx \frac{0.2}{2}[0 + 2(0.04886 + 0.23869 + 0.65596 + 1.42435) + 2.71828]$$

$$\approx 0.74540 \ldots$$

$$\approx 0.7454 \text{ (4 significant figures)}$$

It can be seen from the graph that this is an over-estimate since the top edges of the strips all lie above the curve.

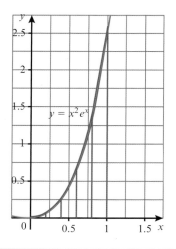

EXERCISE 5E

1 Use the trapezium rule, with the given number of intervals, to find the approximate value of each integral.

a i $\int_0^5 e^{-x^2} dx$, 5 intervals

ii $\int_0^2 \frac{1}{x^3 + 1} dx$, 4 intervals

b i $\int_0^2 \sin(\sqrt{x}) dx$, 5 intervals

ii $\int_3^4 \ln(x^3 - 2) dx$, 4 intervals

c i $\int_0^2 e^{\sqrt{x}} - 1 dx$, 6 intervals

ii $\int_0^1 \tan(x^2) dx$, 3 intervals

2 a Sketch the graph of $y = 3\ln(x - 1)$.

b Use the trapezium rule with five strips to estimate the value of $\int_2^4 3\ln(x-1) dx$. Give your answer to two decimal places.

c Explain whether your answer is an over-estimate or an under-estimate.

3 a Use the trapezium rule with four intervals to find an approximate value to 3 significant figures of $\int_4^5 e^{\sqrt{5-x}} dx$.

b Describe how you could obtain a more accurate approximation.

4 The diagram shows a part of the graph of $y = \cos(x^2)$.

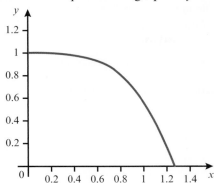

The graph crosses the x-axis at the point where $x = a$.

a Find the exact value of a.

b Use the trapezium rule with four intervals to find an approximation for $\displaystyle\int_0^a \cos(x^2)\,dx$. Give your answer to 3 significant figures.

c Is your approximation an over-estimate or an under-estimate? Explain your answer.

5 A particle moves in a straight line with velocity given by $v = e^{\sqrt{t}}$, where v is measured in $\mathrm{m\,s^{-1}}$ and t in seconds. Use the trapezium rule with 6 strips to find the approximate distance travelled by the particle in the first 3 seconds.

6 The velocity, $v\,\mathrm{m\,s^{-1}}$, of a particle moving in a straight line is given by $v = \sin(\sqrt{t})$. The diagram shows the velocity–time graph for the particle.

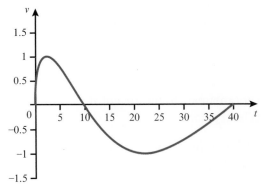

a The particle changes direction when $t = p$ and $t = q$ (with $p < q$). Find the exact values of p and q.

b Use the trapezium rule, with 8 equal intervals, to estimate to 3 significant figures the total distance travelled by the particle during the first q seconds.

71

7 The diagram shows a part of the graph with equation
$y = \ln(x)\sin(x)$. The coordinates of the maximum point are
(7.915, 2.065). Give your answers to 3 significant figures in this
question.

a Use the trapezium rule with four strips to find an approximate

value of $\displaystyle\int_{2\pi}^{3\pi} \ln x \sin x \, dx$. State whether your answer is an over-

estimate or an under-estimate.

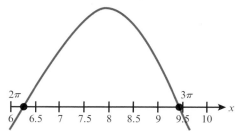

b Use four rectangles of equal width to find an upper bound for
$\displaystyle\int_{2\pi}^{3\pi} \ln x \sin x \, dx$.

c Write down values of L and U such that $L < \displaystyle\int_{2\pi}^{3\pi} \ln x \sin x \, dx < U$.
How can the difference between L and U be reduced?

8 a Use the trapezium rule, with three intervals each of width
$\dfrac{1}{18}\pi$, to estimate the value of $\displaystyle\int_{0}^{\frac{1}{6}\pi} \sec x \, dx$. Give your answer to
3 significant figures.

b State with a reason whether the trapezium rule gives an
over-estimate or an under-estimate of the rule of the integral
in this case.

9 A region R is bounded by part of the curve with equation
$y = \sqrt{64 - x^3}$, the positive x-axis and the positive y-axis. Use the
trapezium rule with 4 intervals to approximate to the area of R,
giving your answer correct to 1 decimal place.

10 a Use the trapezium rule with 6 ordinates to calculate an
approximation to $\displaystyle\int_{0}^{1} \sqrt{4 - x^2} \, dx$. Give your answer to 4 decimal
places.

b The graph of $y = \sqrt{4 - x^2}$ is a semicircle. Sketch the graph, and
hence calculate the area exactly.

c Find to 1 decimal place the percentage error of your answer to
part **a**.

END-OF-CHAPTER REVIEW EXERCISE 5

1 Show that $\displaystyle\int_{\frac{1}{6}\pi}^{\frac{1}{3}\pi}(3\tan^2 x - 2)\,dx = 2\sqrt{3} - \dfrac{5\pi}{6}$.

2 Find the exact value of $\displaystyle\int_{-3}^{-1}\left(\dfrac{1}{2 - 3x} - x\right)dx$, giving your answer in

the form $a + b\ln\left(\dfrac{c}{d}\right)$, where a, c and d are integers.

P2 **3** The diagram shows a part of the curve with equation
$y = \ln(x^2 + 1)$.

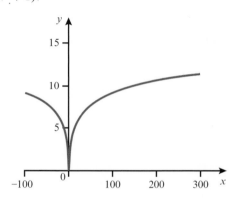

a Use the trapezium rule, with 5 strips of equal width, to estimate
the value of $\displaystyle\int_{0}^{200}\ln(x^2 + 1)\,dx$.

b State with a reason whether your answer is an under-estimate
or an over-estimate.

c Explain how you could find a more accurate estimate.

TIP

You should not
use a numerical
method with
definite integration
questions when an
algebraic method
is available to you,
unless you are
specifically asked
to do so.

4 Show that $\displaystyle\int_{0}^{\ln 2}(e^{-x} - 3)^2\,dx = 9\ln 2 - \dfrac{21}{8}$.

5 a Find $\displaystyle\int_{0}^{k}(2e^{-x} + 3e^{-2x})\,dx$, where k is a positive constant.

b Hence find the exact value of $\displaystyle\int_{0}^{\infty}(2e^{-x} + 3e^{-2x})\,dx$.

6 Show that $\displaystyle\int_{2}^{3}\dfrac{3}{1 - 5x}\,dx = -\dfrac{3}{5}\ln\dfrac{14}{9}$.

7 a Find the value of the constant A such that
$$\dfrac{6x^2 - 5x}{2x - 1} \equiv 3x - 1 - \dfrac{A}{2x - 1}.$$

b Hence show that $\displaystyle\int_{1}^{4}\dfrac{6x^2 - 5x}{2x - 1}\,dx = \dfrac{39}{2} - \dfrac{1}{2}\ln 7$.

8   a   Show that $2\cos^2 2x \equiv 1 + \cos 4x$.

    b   Hence show that $\displaystyle\int_{\frac{1}{4}\pi}^{\pi} 2\cos^2 2x \, dx = \frac{3\pi}{4}$.

9   a   Show that $\displaystyle\int \frac{1 + \sin^2 2x}{\cos^2 2x} \, dx$ can be written as $\tan 2x - x + c$.

    b   Hence find $\displaystyle\int_{-\frac{\pi}{8}}^{\frac{\pi}{8}} \frac{1 + \sin^2 2x}{\cos^2 2x} \, dx$ writing your answer as an exact value.

10 Find the volume of the solid of revolution formed by rotating about the x-axis the area between the curve $y = \sin x + \cos x$ and the x-axis from $x = 0$ to $x = \dfrac{\pi}{2}$.

- Locate approximately a root of an equation, by means of graphical considerations and/or searching for a sign change.
- Understand the idea of, and use the notation for, a sequence of approximations which converges to a root of an equation.
- Understand how a given simple iterative formula of the form $x_{n+1} = F(x_n)$ relates to the equation being solved, and use a given iteration, or an iteration based on a given rearrangement of an equation, to determine a root to a prescribed degree of accuracy.

6.1 Finding a starting point

WORKED EXAMPLE 6.1

a By sketching a suitable pair of graphs, show that the equation $\ln x = \dfrac{x}{4}$ has only one root for $0 \leqslant x \leqslant 2$.

b Verify by calculation that this root lies between $x = 1.4$ and $x = 1.5$.

Answer

a

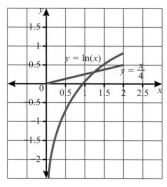

Draw the graphs of $y = \ln x$ and $y = \dfrac{x}{4}$ for $0 \leqslant x \leqslant 2$.

Both graphs are continuous in the given domain. The graphs intersect once only and so the equation $\ln x = \dfrac{x}{4}$ has only one root for $0 \leqslant x \leqslant 2$.

b $\ln x = \dfrac{x}{4}$ so $\ln x - \dfrac{x}{4} = 0$

Let $f(x) = \ln x - \dfrac{x}{4}$

$f(1.4) = \ln 1.4 - \dfrac{1.4}{4} = -0.0135\ldots$

$f(1.5) = \ln 1.5 - \dfrac{1.5}{4} = 0.0304\ldots\ldots$

Change of sign indicates the presence of a root.

TIP

Note that a change of sign between $x = a$ and $x = b$ implies that there is at least one root between those two values, but it does **not** tell us whether there is more than one.

EXERCISE 6A

1 For each of parts **a** to **f**, use the sign-change rule to determine the integer N such that the equation $f(x) = 0$ has a root in the interval $N < x < N + 1$.

a $f(x) = x^5 - 5x + 6$

b $f(x) = x + \sqrt{x^3 + 1} - 7$

c $f(x) = e^x - \dfrac{5}{x}$

d $f(x) = 1000 - e^x \ln x$

e $f(x) = \ln(x^2 + 1) - 12 - x$

f $f(x) = x^5 + x^3 - 1999$

TIP

Be careful! If the graph of the function has a vertical asymptote, or another break in its graph, there may be a change of sign even if the graph does not cross the x-axis.

2 Each of the following equations has a root between -3 and 3. In each case, find two integers between which the root lies.

a $x^3 - 4x - 4 = 0$

b $2\sin x - 4x + 1 = 0$

c $25 \ln x = 3x^2$

d $\cos(3 - x) + x^3 = -5$

3 For each of the following equations, show that there is a root in the given interval.

a i $x - 5 \ln x = 0$, between 1 and 2

  ii $3e^{2x} - 4x^2 = 0$, between -1 and 0

b i $\cos 2x = \sqrt{x}$, between 0 and 1

  ii $3\tan x = 5x^3$, between -0.5 and -1

4 For each equation, show that the given root is correct to the stated degree of accuracy.

a i $x^5 - 3x^2 + 1 = 0$, $x = 0.6$ (1 decimal place)

  ii $x^3 - 3x + 4 = 0$, $x = -2.2$ (1 decimal place)

b i $4\sin x - e^{-2x} = 0$, $x = 3.14$ (3 significant figures)

  ii $2\ln x - 3\cos x = 0$, $x = 1.36$ (3 significant figures)

c i $3\tan x = 5x^3$, $x = 1.31$ (2 decimal places)

  ii $2x = e^{-x}$, $x = 0.35$ (2 decimal places)

  d i $3e^x = x^4$, $x = 6.20$ (3 significant figures)

  ii $3 \cos x = \ln x$, $x = 5.30$ (3 significant figures)

5 a Show that the equation $x^3 - 3x - 1 = 0$ has a solution between 1 and 2.

  b Show that this solution equals 1.9 correct to one decimal place.

6 The equation $\ln\left(\dfrac{x}{3}\right) - \dfrac{x^2}{4} + 2 = 0$ has two solutions.

  a Show that one of the solutions equals 0.425 correct to 3 significant figures.

  b The other solution lies between positive integers k and $k + 1$. Find the value of k.

PS

7 a By sketching the graphs of $y = \ln x$ and $y = \dfrac{1}{x}$ on the same axes, show that there is one real root of the equation $\ln x - \dfrac{1}{x} = 0$.

  b The real root of $\ln x - \dfrac{1}{x} = 0$ is α. Find the integer n such that $n < \alpha < n + 1$.

PS

8 a By sketching the graphs of $y = e^x$ and $y = 5 - x^2$ on the same axes, show that the equation $x^2 - 5 + e^x = 0$ has one positive and one negative root.

  b Show that the negative root lies between -3 and -2.

  c The positive root α is such that $\dfrac{N}{10} < \alpha < \dfrac{N+1}{10}$, where N is an integer. Find the value of N.

9 A function is defined by $f(x) = \dfrac{x^2 + 2}{2x - 5}$.

  a Show that the equation $f(x) = 0$ has no solutions.

  b i Evaluate $f(2)$ and $f(3)$.

  ii Alicia says that the change of sign implies that the equation $f(x) = 0$ has a root between 2 and 3. Explain why she is wrong.

PS

10 Let $g(x) = \cos 8x$.

  a i Sketch the graph of $y = g(x)$ for $0 \leqslant x \leqslant \dfrac{\pi}{2}$.

  ii State the number of solutions of the equation $g(x) = 0$ between 0 and $\dfrac{\pi}{4}$.

b i State the values of g(0) and $g\left(\dfrac{\pi}{4}\right)$.

ii George says: 'These is no change of sign between 0 and $\dfrac{\pi}{4}$ so the equation g(x) = 0 has no roots in this interval.' Use your graph to explain why George's reasoning is incorrect.

iii Use the change of sign method (without referring to the graph) to show that the equation g(x) = 0 has two roots between 0 and $\dfrac{\pi}{4}$.

6.2 Improving your solution

WORKED EXAMPLE 6.2

The equation $x^3 - 3x - 5 = 0$ has one root, α.

a Show that this equation can be rearranged as $x = \dfrac{1}{3}(x^3 - 5)$.

b Alice uses the iterative formula $x_{n+1} = \dfrac{1}{3}(x_n^3 - 5)$ with a starting value of $x_0 = 2$ and correctly works out the first 6 iterations (to 5 decimal places where appropriate). Work out the results she should have obtained. Comment on their convergence.

c Otto rearranges the same equation correctly to give $x = \sqrt[3]{3x + 5}$. Using $x_{n+1} = \sqrt[3]{3x_n + 5}$ with a starting value of $x_0 = 2$, write down the results of the first 6 iterations he should have obtained (to 5 decimal places) and comment on their convergence.

d Using the results from parts **b** and **c**, calculate the root of the equation $x^3 - 3x - 5 = 0$ to 3 decimal places.

Answer

a $x^3 - 3x - 5 = 0$ · · · · · · · · · · Add 3x to both sides.

$x^3 - 5 = 3x$ · · · · · · · · · · Divide both sides by 3 and rearrange.

$x = \dfrac{1}{3}(x^3 - 5)$

b 2, 1, −1.33333, −2.45679, −6.60958, −97.91654, −312931.4537

The results of the iterations do not converge to a limit.

c $x_0 = 2$

$x_{n+1} = \sqrt[3]{3x_n + 5}$

$x_1 = \sqrt[3]{3(2) + 5} = 2.22398$

$x_2 = 2.26837$

$x_3 = 2.27697$

$x_4 = 2.27862$

$x_5 = 2.27894$

$x_6 = 2.27900$

The results suggest the terms converge to a limit, giving one root of the equation.

d   Using Otto's results, the terms get
steadily larger and the root (α) appears
to be 2.279 to 3 decimal places.

We can **prove** this, using a change of sign test.

When $\alpha = 2.279$ then
$2.2785 < \alpha < 2.2795$ and so

$f(2.2785) = 2.2785^3 - 3(2.2785) - 5$

$\qquad = -6.53 \times 10^{-3}$

$f(2.2795) = 2.2795^3 - 3(2.2795) - 5$

$\qquad = 6.06 \times 10^{-3}$

The change of sign test confirms the
root of the equation is 2.279 to
3 decimal places.

EXERCISE 6B

1   Use iteration with the given starting value to find the first five
approximations to the roots of the following equations. Give
your answers to three decimal places.

a   i $x = 2\ln(x + 2)$, $x_1 = 3$ ii $x = 3 - e^{-x}$, $x_1 = 4$

b   i $x = \dfrac{3}{x + 4} - 1$, $x_1 = -1$ ii $x = \cos(2x - 1)$, $x_1 = 1$

c   i $\ln x - x^2 + 2 = x$, $x_1 = 0.5$ ii $1.5\sin(x + 1) = x$, $x_1 = 1$

2   Use iteration with the given starting value to find an approximate
solution correct to 2 decimal places.

a   i $x = e^{-\frac{x}{2}}$, $x_1 = 0$ ii $x = \cos\left(\dfrac{x}{3}\right)$, $x_1 = 0$

b   i $x = \ln x + 3$, $x_1 = 4$ ii $x = \tan\left(\dfrac{x}{2}\right) + 0.2$, $x_1 = 1$

TIP

Using the **Ans** key
on your calculator
reduces the number
of key strokes
needed to use an
iterative process.

3   Each of the equations below is to be solved using iteration. Draw the graphs and use technology to investigate the following.

    i   Does the limit depend on the starting point?

    ii Does starting on different sides of the root give a different limit?

    iii If there is more than one root, which one does the sequence converge to?

    a $x = \sqrt[3]{x + 2}$ b $x = \ln(x + 2)$ c $x = e^{x-2}$

4   Use the iteration formula $x_{n+1} = \cos\left(\dfrac{x_n}{3}\right)$ with $x_1 = 0.5$ to find x_5. Give your answer correct to four decimal places.

This value of x_5 is an approximation to the equation $f(x) = 0$. Write down an expression for $f(x)$ and suggest the value of the root correct to two decimal places.

5   Show that the equation $x^5 + x - 19 = 0$ can be arranged into the form $x = \sqrt[3]{\dfrac{19 - x}{x^2}}$ and that the equation has a root α between $x = 1$ and $x = 2$. Use an iteration based on this arrangement, with initial approximation $x_0 = 2$, to find the values of $x_1, x_2, \ldots, x_6$. Investigate whether this sequence is converging to α.

6   a   Show that the equation $x^2 + 2x - e^x = 0$ has a root in the interval $2 < x < 3$.

    b   Use an iterative method based on the rearrangment $x = \sqrt{e^x - 2x}$, with initial approximation $x_0 = 2$, to find the value of x_{10} to 4 decimal places. Describe what is happening to the terms of this sequence of approximations.

7   Show that the equation $e^x = x^3 - 2$ can be arranged into the form $x = \ln(x^3 - 2)$. Show also that it has a root between 2 and 3. Use the iteration $x_{r+1} = \ln(x_r^3 - 2)$, commencing with $x_0 = 2$ as an initial approximation to the root, to show that this arrangement is not a suitable one for finding this root. Find an alternative arrangement of $e^x = x^3 - 2$ which can be used to find this root, and use it to calculate the root correct to 2 decimal places.

8   a   Show that the equation $x^3 - 3x^2 - 1 = 0$ has a root α between $x = 3$ and $x = 4$.

    b   The iterative formula $x_{r+1} = 3 + \dfrac{1}{x_r^2}$ is used to calculate a sequence of approximations to this root. Taking $x_0 = 3$ as an initial approximation to α, determine the values of x_1, x_2, x_3 and x_4 correct to 5 decimal places. State the values of α to 3 decimal places.

9 a Determine the value of the positive integer N such that the equation $12 - x - \ln x = 0$ has a root α such that $N < \alpha < N + 1$.

b Define the sequence $x_0, x_1, \ldots$ of approximations to α iteratively by $x_0 = N + \dfrac{1}{2}$, $x_{r+1} = 12 - \ln x_r$. Find the number of steps required before two consecutive terms of this sequence are the same when rounded to 4 significant figures. Show that this common value is equal to α to this degree of accuracy.

10 Find the missing constants to rearrange each of the following equations into the given equivalent form.

a i $2x^3 - 4x + 1 = 0 \Leftrightarrow x = \sqrt[3]{ax + b}$

ii $x - \dfrac{1}{2}x^4 - 3 = 0 \Leftrightarrow x = \sqrt[4]{ax + b}$

b i $x^3 + x^2 - 4 = 0 \Leftrightarrow x = \dfrac{a}{x} - bx^2$

ii $2x^3 - 2x^2 + 1 = 0 \Leftrightarrow x = \dfrac{ax^3 + b}{cx}$

c i $2x^3 - x + 5 = 0 \Leftrightarrow x = \sqrt{a + \dfrac{b}{x}}$

ii $x^2 - 3x^3 + 2 = 0 \Leftrightarrow x = \sqrt{cx + \dfrac{d}{x}}$

d i $x^3 - 3x^2 + 5x + 2 = 0 \Leftrightarrow x = \dfrac{ax^3 + b}{3x - 5}$

ii $2x^3 + x^2 - 3x + 1 = 0 \Leftrightarrow x = \dfrac{2x^3 + 1}{a - bx}$

6.3 Using iterative processes to solve problems involving other areas of mathematics

WORKED EXAMPLE 6.3

The diagram shows a sector ABC of a circle centre C and radius r. Angle ACB is θ radians. The ratio of the area of the shaded segment to the area of the triangle is $1 : 5$.

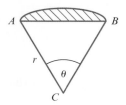

a Show that $5\theta - 6\sin\theta = 0$.

b Use the iterative formula $\theta_{n+1} = \dfrac{6}{5}\sin\theta_n$ with $\theta_0 = 1$ to find the value of θ correct to 2 decimal places. Write down the result of each iteration.

Answer

a   Area of segment $= \dfrac{1}{2}r^2\theta - \dfrac{1}{2}r^2\sin\theta$ .... Factorise.

$$= \dfrac{1}{2}r^2(\theta - \sin\theta)$$

$\therefore \dfrac{1}{2}r^2\sin\theta = 5 \times \dfrac{1}{2}r^2(\theta - \sin\theta)$ .... Shown.

$\sin\theta = 5\theta - 5\sin\theta$

$5\theta - 6\sin\theta = 0$

b

$\theta_1 = 1$	$\theta_{n+1} = \dfrac{6}{5}\sin\theta_n$	The same correct to 2 dp's.
	$\theta_2 = 1.009\,77$	No.
	$\theta_3 = 1.016\,05$	No.
	$\theta_4 = 1.020\,04$	No.
	$\theta_5 = 1.022\,55$	No.
	$\theta_6 = 1.024\,13$	No.
	$\theta_7 = 1.025\,12$	No.
	$\theta_8 = 1.025\,73$	Yes.

θ seems to be 1.03 correct to 2 decimal places.

When $\theta = 1.03$ then $1.025 < \theta < 1.035$ ..... To prove this, use the change of
sign test with $f(\theta) = 5\theta - 6\sin\theta$.

$f(1.025) = 5(1.025) - 6\sin 1.025$

$\qquad = -3.29 \times 10^{-3}$

$f(1.035) = 5(1.035) - 6\sin 1.035$

$\qquad = 1.58 \times 10^{-2}$

Change of sign indicates the presence of a root. Therefore $\theta = 1.03$.

EXERCISE 6C

 TIP

Remember to use radians when dealing with questions involving trigonometric functions.

1   The graph of $y = \sin\left(\dfrac{x}{2}\right) - x^2$ has a stationary point between 0 and 1.

   a   Show that the x-coordinate of the stationary point satisfies

   $$x = \dfrac{1}{4}\cos\left(\dfrac{x}{2}\right).$$

   b   Use iteration with a suitable starting point to find the x-coordinate of the stationary point correct to three decimal places.

2 A rectangle has two vertices on the x-axis, between $x = 0$ and $x = \pi$ and two vertices on the curve $y = \sin x$. Let the smaller of the x-coordinates of the vertices be a. It is required to find the rectangle with a maximum possible area.

   a Show that, for this rectangle, $2 \tan a = \pi - 2a$.

   b Use an iteration method with the starting value $a_0 = 0.7$ to find the value of a correct to four decimal places. Hence find the maximum possible area of the rectangle.

PS 3 **a** Show that the iteration given by $x_{n+1} = \dfrac{2 + kx_n}{x_n^2 + k}$ corresponds to the equation $x^3 = 2$, whatever the value of the constant k.

   b Taking $k = 3$, use the iteration, with $x_1 = 1$, to find the value of $\sqrt[3]{2}$ correct to 2 decimal places.

4 The diagram shows the graph of $y = e^{-x}$. The point P has coordinates (a, e^{-a}), and the lines PM and PN are parallel to the axes.

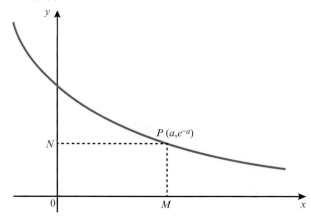

   a Find $\displaystyle\int_0^a e^{-x}\,dx$ in terms of a.

The area of the rectangle $OMPN$ is one quarter of the area under the curve $y = e^{-x}$ from $x = 0$ to $x = a$.

   b Show that $e^a = 4a + 1$.

   c Use the iteration $a_{n+1} = \ln(4a_n + 1)$, with $a_1 = 2$, to find the non-zero value of a satisfying the equation in part **b**. Give your answer correct to 1 decimal place.

5 The parametric equations of a curve are $x = t^2 - e^{-t}$, $y = t^2 - e^{-2t}$.

   a Find the equation of the tangent to the curve at the point where $t = 0$.

The curve cuts the y-axis at the point A.

b Show that the value of t at A lies between 0 and 1.

c Use the iteration $t_{n+1} = \sqrt{e^{-t_n}}$ to find this value of t correct to 2 significant figures, and hence determine the y-coordinate of A, correct to 1 significant figure.

6 The equation $\sin(x - 6) - \ln(x^2 + 1) = 0$, $x \in \mathbb{R}$ has a root in the interval $a < x < a + 1$, where a is a positive integer.

a Find the value of a.

b Using the iterative formula $x_{n+1} = \sqrt{e^{\sin(x_n - 6)} - 1}$ starting with $x_0 = a$ find three further approximations to this root giving your answers to 4 decimal places.

END-OF-CHAPTER REVIEW EXERCISE 6

1 The diagram shows a sector of a circle with radius 5 cm. The angle at the centre is θ. The shaded area equals 30 cm^2.

a Show that $\theta - \sin\theta = 2.4$.

b Show that the above equation has a root between 2 and 3.

c Use an iterative method with a suitable starting point to find the value of θ correct to two decimal places.

2 a Sketch the graphs of $y = e^{x-1}$ and $y = \ln(x + 2)$ on the same set of axes. State the number of solutions of the equation $e^{x-1} = \ln(x + 2)$.

b Show that the above equation has a solution between 1 and 2.

c Use an iteration of the form $x_{n+1} = A + \ln(\ln(x_n + B))$ to find this solution correct to two decimal places.

3 A curve is defined by $y = \dfrac{\sin x}{x^2}$ for $x > 0$.

a Show that the x-coordinate of any stationary point on the curve satisfies the equation $x = 2\tan x$.

One of the roots of this equation is between 4 and 5.

b By considering the derivative of $2\tan x$ prove that the iteration $x_{n+1} = 2\tan x_n$ does not converge to this root.

c Find an alternative rearrangement of the equation $x = 2\tan x$ and use it to find the x-coordinate of the stationary point on the curve $y = \dfrac{\sin x}{x^2}$ between $x = 4$ and $x = 5$. Give your answer correct to three decimal places.

4 a Show that the equation $x^3 - 3x - 10 = 0$ has a root between $x = 2$ and $x = 3$.

   b Find an approximation, correct to 2 decimal places, to this root using an iteration based on the equation in the form $x = (3x + 10)^{\frac{1}{3}}$ and starting with $x_1 = 3$.

5 Consider the equation $\ln(x - 2) = \frac{1}{2} \sin x$, where x is measured in radians.

   a By means of a sketch, show that this equation has only one solution.

   b Show that this solution lies between 3 and 4.

   c Show that the equation can be rearranged into the form $x = e^{a \sin x} + b$, where a and b are constants to be found.

   d Hence use a suitable iterative formula to find an approximate solution to the equation $\ln(x - 2) = \frac{1}{2} \sin x$, correct to 3 decimal places.

6 A rectangle is drawn inside the region bounded by the curve $y = \sin x$ and the x-axis, as shown in the diagram. The vertex A has coordinates $(x, 0)$.

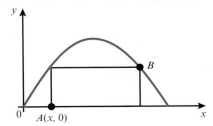

   a i Write down the coordinates of point B.

   ii Find an expression for the area of the rectangle in terms of x.

   b i Show that the stationary point of the area satisfies the equation $2 \sin x = (\pi - 2x) \cos x$.

   ii By sketching graphs, show that this equation has one root for $0 < x < \frac{\pi}{2}$.

   iii Use the second derivative to show that the stationary point is a maximum.

   c i The equation for the stationary point can be written as $x = \tan^{-1}\left(\frac{\pi}{2} - x\right)$. Use a suitable iterative formula, with $x_1 = 0.5$, to find the root of the equation $2 \tan x = \pi - 2x$ correct to three decimal places.

   ii Hence find the maximum possible area of the rectangle.

Chapter 7
Further algebra

P3 **This chapter is for Pure Mathematics 3 students only.**

- Recall an appropriate form for expressing rational functions in partial fractions, and carry out the decomposition, in cases where the denominator is no more complicated than:
  - $(ax + b)(cx + d)(ex + f)$
  - $(ax + b)(cx + d)^2$
  - $(ax + b)(cx^2 + d)$
- Use the expansion of $(1 + x)^n$, where n is a rational number and $|x| < 1$.

7.1 Improper algebraic fractions

WORKED EXAMPLE 7.1

Given $f(x) = \dfrac{x^3 - 2x^2 - 21x + 70}{x^2 + 2x - 15}$ and $x \neq 3$:

a Express $f(x)$ in the form $Ax + B + \dfrac{C}{g(x)}$ where $g(x)$ is linear.

b Hence solve the equation $f(x) = \dfrac{3x - 7}{x - 3}$

Answer

a
$$
\begin{array}{r}
x - 4 \\
x^2 + 2x - 15 \overline{)\, x^3 - 2x^2 - 21x + 70} \\
x^3 + 2x^2 - 15x \\
\hline
-4x^2 - 6x + 70 \\
-4x^2 - 8x + 60 \\
\hline
2x + 10
\end{array}
$$

$\therefore \dfrac{x^3 - 2x^2 - 21x + 70}{x^2 + 2x - 15} = x - 4 + \dfrac{2x + 10}{x^2 + 2x - 15}$

$\qquad\qquad = x - 4 + \dfrac{2(x + 5)}{(x + 5)(x - 3)}$

$\qquad\qquad = x - 4 + \dfrac{2}{x - 3}$

b $\dfrac{3x - 7}{x - 3}$

Divide the numerator by the denominator.

$\dfrac{3x - 7}{x - 3} = 3 + \dfrac{2}{x - 3}$

$\therefore 3 + \dfrac{2}{x - 3} = x - 4 + \dfrac{2}{x - 3}$

Subtract $\dfrac{2}{x - 3}$ from both sides.

$3 = x - 4$

$x = 7$

TIP

The resultant polynomial when one polynomial is divided by another is called the 'quotient'.

EXERCISE 7A

1 Express each of the following improper fractions as the sum of a polynomial and a proper fraction.

   a $\dfrac{6x}{2x+1}$ **b** $\dfrac{12x+1}{4x-2}$ **c** $\dfrac{3x^3-2}{2x-1}$

   d $\dfrac{x^3+2x^2-3x+1}{x^2+x+3}$ **e** $\dfrac{4x^3+3x^2-2x+1}{x^2+3}$ **f** $\dfrac{x^4+x^2-4}{x^2+2}$

2 Given that $\dfrac{x^3+2x^2-7}{x-1} \equiv Ax^2 + Bx + C + \dfrac{D}{x-1}$, find the values of A, B, C and D.

3 Given that $\dfrac{2x^4+3x^2-1}{x-1} \equiv Ax^3 + Bx^2 + Cx + D + \dfrac{E}{x-1}$, find the values of A, B, C, D and E.

4 Given that $\dfrac{3x^4+x^3-x^2+2x}{x^3+x} \equiv Ax + B + \dfrac{Cx+D}{x^2+1}$, find the values of A, B, C and D.

5 Find the quotient and remainder when $2x^2 - 3x + 4$ is divided by $2x - 1$.

6 Write $\dfrac{2x^2-x-28}{x^2-2x-8}$ in the form $A + \dfrac{B}{x+C}$.

7 The remainder when $x^2 + ax + 3$ is divided by $x - 2$ is 5. Find the value of a and then find the quotient.

P 8 When the polynomial f(x) is divided by $x - 2$, the quotient is the same as the remainder. Prove that f(x) is divisible by $x - 1$.

7.2 Partial fractions

WORKED EXAMPLE 7.2

Express $\dfrac{(x^2+3x-10)(x+1)}{x(x^2-4)}$ in partial fractions.

Answer

The degree of the denominator is the same as the degree of the numerator.   ••••••   The fraction is improper. Hence it must first be written as the sum of a polynomial and a proper fraction. However the fraction can be simplified first.

$\dfrac{(x^2+3x-10)(x+1)}{x(x^2-4)} \equiv \dfrac{(x+5)(x-2)(x+1)}{x(x+2)(x-2)}$ ••••••   Cancel.

$$\equiv \frac{(x+5)(x+1)}{x(x+2)}$$

$$\equiv \frac{x^2 + 6x + 5}{x^2 + 2x}$$

$$\begin{array}{r} 1 \\ x^2 + 2x \overline{)x^2 + 6x + 5} \\ \underline{x^2 + 2x} \\ 4x + 5 \end{array}$$

$$\frac{x^2 + 6x + 5}{x^2 + 2x} \equiv 1 + \frac{4x + 5}{x^2 + 2x}$$

Split the proper fraction $\dfrac{4x + 5}{x^2 + 2x}$ into partial fractions.

$$\frac{4x + 5}{x(x + 2)} \equiv \frac{A}{x} + \frac{B}{x + 2}$$

Multiply throughout by $x(x + 2)$.

$$4x + 5 \equiv A(x + 2) + Bx \text{------(1)}$$

Let $x = 0$ in equation (1).

$$5 = 2A$$

$$A = \frac{5}{2}$$

Let $x = -2$ in equation (1).

$$-3 = -2B$$

$$B = \frac{3}{2}$$

$$\frac{4x + 5}{x(x + 2)} \equiv \frac{5}{2x} + \frac{3}{2(x + 2)}$$

$$\therefore \frac{x^2 + 6x + 5}{x^2 + 2x} \equiv 1 + \frac{5}{2x} + \frac{3}{2(x + 2)}$$

EXERCISE 7B

1 Write the following expressions in terms of partial fractions.

a i $\dfrac{6 - 4x}{x(x - 3)(x - 2)}$ ii $\dfrac{3x + 4}{x(x + 1)(x + 2)}$

b i $\dfrac{13x + 17}{(x - 1)(x + 1)(x + 2)}$ ii $\dfrac{19x + 55}{(x - 3)(x + 4)(x + 1)}$

2 Express each of the following in partial fractions.

a $\dfrac{x^2 + x}{(x - 1)(x^2 + 1)}$ b $\dfrac{4 - x}{(x + 1)(x^2 + 4)}$ c $\dfrac{2x^2 + x - 2}{(x + 3)(x^2 + 4)}$

d $\dfrac{2x^2 + 11x - 8}{(2x - 3)(x^2 + 1)}$ e $\dfrac{x^2 - 3x + 14}{(3x + 2)(x^2 + 16)}$ f $\dfrac{3 + 17x^2}{(1 + 4x)(4 + x^2)}$

g $\dfrac{6 - 5x}{(1 + 2x)(4 + x^2)}$ h $\dfrac{x^2 + 18}{x(x^2 + 9)}$ i $\dfrac{17 - 25x}{(x + 4)(2x^2 + 7)}$

88

3 Express each of the following in partial fractions.

a $\dfrac{x^3 - 1}{x^2(x + 1)}$

b $\dfrac{x^3 + 2x + 1}{x(x^2 + 1)}$

c $\dfrac{x^3 + 3x^2 + x - 14}{(x + 4)(x^2 + 1)}$

d $\dfrac{2x^3 + 6x^2 - 3x - 2}{(x - 2)(x + 2)^2}$

e $\dfrac{6x^3 + x + 10}{(x - 2)(x + 2)(2x - 1)}$

f $\dfrac{-4x^3 + 16x^2 + 15x - 50}{x(4x^2 - 25)}$

g $\dfrac{x^3 + 2x + 1}{x(x + 1)(x - 1)}$

h $\dfrac{x^3 - 2x^2 + 3x + 6}{x^2(2 + x)}$

i $\dfrac{12x^3 - 20x^2 + 31x - 49}{(4x^2 + 9)(x - 1)}$

4 a Show that $\dfrac{x^2 - 3x + 5}{x - 1} = x - 2 + \dfrac{3}{x - 1}$.

   b Hence write $\dfrac{x^2 - 3x + 5}{(x - 1)(x - 2)}$ in terms of partial fractions.

5 Write in partial fractions $\dfrac{2x - 3a}{x^2 - 3ax + 2a^2}$ where a is a constant.

6 Express the following in terms of partial fractions.

a i $\dfrac{x}{(x + 1)^2}$

      ii $\dfrac{x}{(x - 2)^2}$

b i $\dfrac{16}{x^2(x + 4)}$

      ii $\dfrac{1}{x^2(x - 1)}$

c i $\dfrac{9x + 9}{(x - 1)(x + 2)^2}$

      ii $\dfrac{9x}{(x + 1)(x - 2)^2}$

P 7 a Prove that if a function can be written as $\dfrac{A}{x - p} + \dfrac{B}{(x - p)^2}$ it can also be written as $\dfrac{Cx + D}{(x - p)^2}$.

   b Write $\dfrac{1}{(x - 1)(x - 2)^2}$ in the form $\dfrac{A}{x - 1} + \dfrac{Bx + C}{(x - 2)^2}$.

8 Write $\dfrac{x(a + 1) - a^2}{x(x - a)^2}$ in terms of partial fractions.

9 a Simplify $f(x) = \dfrac{3x + 3}{6x^2 + 13x + 6} \times \dfrac{3x + 2}{x^2 + 3x + 2}$.

   b Hence write $f(x)$ in terms of partial fractions.

P 10 If two resistors with resistance R_1 and R_2 are connected in parallel, the combined system has resistance R_T. These are related by the equation $\dfrac{1}{R_T} = \dfrac{1}{R_1} + \dfrac{1}{R_2}$.

   a Find and simplify an expression for R_T in terms of R_1 and R_2.

   b Hence prove that $R_T < R_1$.

PS 11 Express the algebraic fraction $\dfrac{-2}{(n + 1)(n + 2)}$ in partial fractions, hence find the sum of the series $\dfrac{-2}{3 \times 4} + \dfrac{-2}{4 \times 5} + \ldots + \dfrac{-2}{(n + 1)(n + 2)} + \ldots$ between $n = 2$ and $n = \infty$.

7.3 Binomial expansion of $(1 + x)^n$ for values of n that are not positive integers

WORKED EXAMPLE 7.3

a Expand $(1 - 3x)^{\frac{1}{5}}$ in ascending powers of x up to and including the term in x^3, stating the validity of the expansion.

b Using your series with $x = \dfrac{1}{32}$, find an approximation for $29^{\frac{1}{5}}$ giving your answer to 5 decimal places.

Answer

a $(1 - 3x)^{\frac{1}{5}}$

$$= 1 + \frac{1}{5}(-3x) + \frac{\left(\frac{1}{5}\right)\left(\frac{1}{5} - 1\right)}{2!}(-3x)^2$$

$$+ \frac{\left(\frac{1}{5}\right)\left(\frac{1}{5} - 1\right)\left(\frac{1}{5} - 2\right)}{3!}(-3x)^3 + \dots$$

$$= 1 - \frac{3}{5}x - \frac{18}{25}x^2 - \frac{162}{125}x^3 - \dots$$

Valid for $|x| < \dfrac{1}{3}$

Use $n = \dfrac{1}{5}$ and replace x by $-3x$ in the binomial formula:

$$(1 + x)^n = 1 + nx + \frac{n(n-1)}{2!}x^2$$
$$+ \frac{n(n-1)(n-2)}{3!}x^3 + \dots$$

where n is rational and $|x| < 1$.

b $\left(1 - \dfrac{3}{32}\right)^{\frac{1}{5}} = \left(\dfrac{29}{32}\right)^{\frac{1}{5}} = \dfrac{1}{2}(29)^{\frac{1}{5}}$

Having substituted $x = \dfrac{1}{32}$ into $(1 - 3x)^{\frac{1}{5}}$ and also into the expanded form.

$$\frac{1}{2}(29)^{\frac{1}{5}} = 1 - \frac{3}{5}\left(\frac{1}{32}\right) - \frac{18}{25}\left(\frac{1}{32}\right)^2$$

$$- \frac{162}{125}\left(\frac{1}{32}\right)^3 - \dots$$

$$= 1 - 0.1875 - 0.000703125$$
$$- 0.000039550781 - \dots$$

$(29)^{\frac{1}{5}} = 1.96101$ to 5 decimal places

EXERCISE 7C

1 Expand the following in ascending powers of x up to and including the terms in x^2.

a $(1+x)^{-3}$ **b** $(1+x)^{-5}$

c $(1-x)^{-4}$ **d** $(1-x)^{-6}$

2 Find the coefficient of x^3 in the expansions of the following.

a $(1-x)^{-7}$ **b** $(1+2x)^{-1}$ **c** $(1+3x)^{-3}$

d $(1-4x)^{-2}$ **e** $\left(1-\dfrac{1}{3}x\right)^{-6}$ **f** $(1+ax)^{-4}$

g $(1-bx)^{-4}$ **h** $(1-cx)^{-n}$

3 Find the expansion of the following in ascending powers of x up to and including the terms in x^2.

a $(1+4x)^{\frac{1}{2}}$ **b** $(1+3x)^{-\frac{1}{3}}$

c $(1-6x)^{\frac{4}{3}}$ **d** $\left(1-\dfrac{1}{2}x\right)^{-\frac{1}{4}}$

4 Find the coefficient of x^3 in the expansions of the following.

a $(1+2x)^{\frac{3}{2}}$ **b** $(1-5x)^{-\frac{1}{2}}$ **c** $\left(1+\dfrac{3}{2}x\right)^{\frac{1}{3}}$

d $(1-4x)^{\frac{3}{4}}$ **e** $(1-7x)^{-\frac{1}{7}}$ **f** $(1+\sqrt{2}x)^{\frac{1}{2}}$

g $(1+ax)^{\frac{3}{2}}$ **h** $(1-bx)^{-\frac{1}{2}n}$

5 **a** Find the first three terms in the expansion of $\dfrac{1}{(4x^2+4x+1)}$.

b Find the values of x over which this expansion is valid.

6 **a** Use the binomial expansion to show that $\sqrt{1+\dfrac{x}{9}}=1+\dfrac{x}{18}-\dfrac{x^2}{648}$.

b State the range of values for which this expansion converges.

c Deduce the first three terms of the binomial expansion of:

i $\sqrt{1-\dfrac{x}{9}}$ **ii** $\sqrt{1+\left(\dfrac{x}{3}\right)^2}$ **iii** $\sqrt{9+x}$

d Use the first three terms of the expansions to find an approximation for $\sqrt{10}$ to four decimal places.

> **TIP**
>
> Saying 'an expansion is valid' is another way of saying that it **converges**.

91

7 a Find the first four terms of $\sqrt{1-4x}$ in ascending powers of x.

b State the range of values for which this expansion is valid.

c Hence approximate $\sqrt{96}$ to 5 decimal places.

d Hence approximate $\sqrt{0.006}$ to 4 decimal places.

8 The cubic term in the expansion of $(1+ax)^{-2}$ is $-256x^3$. Find the value of a.

9 Given that the expansion of $(1+ax)^n$ is $1-12x+90x^2+bx^3+\ldots$ find the value of b.

10 Given that the expansion of $(1+ax)^n$ is $1-x-\dfrac{x^2}{2}+bx^3+\ldots$ find the value of b.

7.4 Binomial expansion of $(a+x)^n$ for values of n that are not positive integers

WORKED EXAMPLE 7.4

Expand $(4-3x)^{-3}$ in ascending powers of x, up to and including the term in x^3 and state the range of values of x for which the expansion is valid.

TIP

$$(a+x)^n = a^n\left(1+\frac{x}{a}\right)^n$$

Answer

$$(4-3x)^{-3} = (4)^{-3}\left(1-\frac{3x}{4}\right)^{-3}$$

$$= (4)^{-3}\Bigg[1+(-3)\left(-\frac{3x}{4}\right)$$
$$+\frac{(-3)(-4)}{2!}\left(-\frac{3x}{4}\right)^2$$
$$+\frac{(-3)(-4)(-5)}{3!}\left(\frac{3x}{4}\right)^3-\ldots\Bigg]$$

$$= \frac{1}{64}\left[1+\frac{9}{4}x+\frac{27}{8}x^2+\frac{135}{32}x^3+\ldots\right]$$

$$= \frac{1}{64}+\frac{9}{256}x+\frac{27}{512}x^2+\frac{135}{2048}x^3+\ldots$$

Valid for $|x|<\dfrac{4}{3}$.

1 Expand each of the following up to and including the term in x^3. State the range of values for which each expansion is valid.

   a $(9 - 4x)^{-\frac{1}{2}}$

   b $(8 + 3x)^{\frac{2}{3}}$

   c $\dfrac{1}{(2 - x)^3}$

   d $\sqrt{4 - x}$

   e $\dfrac{1}{(3 - 2x)^2}$

   f $(2 + x)^{-1}$

2 Expand each of the following up to and including the term in x^2.

   a $(2 + 5x)(1 - 3x)^{-2}$

   b $\dfrac{7 - 3x}{(1 - x)^{\frac{1}{2}}}$

   c $\dfrac{(2 - x^2)^2}{(x + 4)^3}$

3 Find the first three non-zero terms, in ascending powers of x, in the expansion of $\dfrac{1}{\sqrt{4 + x}}$, stating the range of x for which this is valid.

4 a Find the first three terms of the binomial expansion of $\sqrt[3]{8 + x}$.

   b Hence find an approximation for $\sqrt[3]{8100}$ to two decimal places, showing your reasoning.

5 Find the first four terms in the expansion of each of the following in ascending powers of x. State the interval of values of x for which each expansion is valid.

   a $\sqrt[3]{8 - 16x}$

   b $\dfrac{2}{2 - x}$

   c $\dfrac{1}{(2 + x)^3}$

   d $\dfrac{4x}{\sqrt{4 + x^3}}$

   e $\sqrt[4]{1 + 8x}$

   f $\dfrac{12}{(\sqrt{3} - x)^4}$

6 Find the first three terms in the series expansion of $\dfrac{\sqrt{1 + 2x}}{(1 - x)^4}$ and state the range of values for which the series is valid.

7 Find the coefficient of x^2 in the expansion of $\dfrac{2 + x}{\sqrt{4 - 2x}}$, $|x| < 2$.

8 Show that for small values of x, the expansion of $(2 - 5x)(2x + 1)^{-\frac{1}{2}}$, $|x| < \dfrac{1}{2}$ is
   $2 - 7x + 8x^2 - \dfrac{25}{2}x^3$.

 9 Expand $\dfrac{5 + x}{2 - x + x^2}$ in ascending powers of x up to the term in x^3.

 10 Expand $(1 - x + x^2)^{\frac{1}{2}}$ as a series in ascending powers of x up to and including the terms in x^3.

7.5 Partial fractions and binomial expansions

WORKED EXAMPLE 7.5

Given that $f(x) = \dfrac{x}{(3 - 2x)(2 - x)}$, express f(x) in partial fractions and hence obtain the expansion of f(x) in ascending powers of x, up to and including the term in x^3. State the range of values of x for which the expansion is valid.

Answer

$$\frac{x}{(3 - 2x)(2 - x)} \equiv \frac{A}{3 - 2x} + \frac{B}{2 - x}$$

Multiply throughout by $(3 - 2x)(2 - x)$

$$x \equiv A(2 - x) + B(3 - 2x)\text{--------}(1)$$

Let $x = 2$ in equation (1).

$$2 = -B$$
$$B = -2$$

Let $x = \dfrac{3}{2}$ in equation (1).

$$\frac{3}{2} = \frac{1}{2}A$$
$$A = 3$$

$$\therefore \frac{x}{(3 - 2x)(2 - x)} \equiv \frac{3}{3 - 2x} - \frac{2}{2 - x} \equiv 3(3 - 2x)^{-1} - 2(2 - x)^{-1}$$

Simplify.

$$\equiv 3(3)^{-1}\left(1 - \frac{2}{3}x\right)^{-1} - 2(2)^{-1}\left(1 - \frac{1}{2}x\right)^{-1}$$

$$\equiv \left(1 - \frac{2}{3}x\right)^{-1} - \left(1 - \frac{1}{2}x\right)^{-1}$$

$$\left(1 - \frac{2}{3}x\right)^{-1}$$

$$= 1 + (-1)\left(-\frac{2}{3}x\right) + \frac{(-1)(-2)}{2!}\left(-\frac{2}{3}x\right)^2$$

$$+ \frac{(-1)(-2)(-3)}{3!}\left(-\frac{2}{3}x\right)^3 + \dots.$$

$$= 1 + \frac{2}{3}x + \frac{4}{9}x^2 + \frac{8}{27}x^3 + \dots$$

$$\left(1 - \frac{1}{2}x\right)^{-1}$$

$$= 1 + (-1)\left(-\frac{1}{2}x\right) + \frac{(-1)(-2)}{2!}\left(-\frac{1}{2}x\right)^2$$

$$+ \frac{(-1)(-2)(-3)}{3!}\left(-\frac{1}{2}x\right)^3 + \dots.$$

$$= 1 + \frac{1}{2}x + \frac{1}{4}x^2 + \frac{1}{8}x^3 + \dots$$

So:

$$f(x) = \left(1 + \frac{2}{3}x + \frac{4}{9}x^2 + \frac{8}{27}x^3 + \ldots\right) - \left(1 + \frac{1}{2}x + \frac{1}{4}x^2 + \frac{1}{8}x^3 + \ldots\right)$$

$$f(x) = \frac{1}{6}x + \frac{7}{36}x^2 + \frac{37}{216}x^3 + \ldots$$

$\left(1 - \frac{2}{3}x\right)^{-1}$ is valid for $\left|\frac{2}{3}x\right| < 1$ i.e. $-\frac{3}{2} < x < \frac{3}{2}$

$\left(1 - \frac{1}{2}x\right)^{-1}$ is valid for $\left|\frac{1}{2}x\right| < 1$ i.e. $-2 < x < 2$

The expansion is valid for the range of values of x satisfying both $-\frac{3}{2} < x < \frac{3}{2}$ and $-2 < x < 2$.

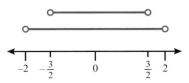

Hence the expansion is valid for $-\frac{3}{2} < x < \frac{3}{2}$.

EXERCISE 7E

1   a   Decompose $\dfrac{3x + 2}{(x + 1)(2x + 1)}$ into partial fractions.

   b   Hence find the first three terms in the binomial expansion of $\dfrac{3x + 2}{(x + 1)(2x + 1)}$.

   c   Write down the set of values for which this expansion is valid.

2   a   Express $\dfrac{5x + 8}{(2 - x)(x + 1)^2}$ in partial fractions.

   b   Find the first three terms, in ascending powers of x, in the binomial expansion of
       $\dfrac{5x + 8}{(2 - x)(x + 1)^2}$.

   c   Find the values of x for which this expansion converges.

3   Find the first three terms of the binomial expansion for $\dfrac{1}{(1 + 2x)(1 + x)}$.

4   Split $\dfrac{3}{8x^2 + 6x + 1}$ into partial fractions and hence find the binomial expansion of $\dfrac{3}{8x^2 + 6x + 1}$
   up to and including the term in x^3. State the values of x for which the expansion is valid.

5 **a** Write $\dfrac{3x + 16}{(3 - x)(x + 2)^2}$ in partial fractions.

   b Hence find the first three terms in the expansion of $\dfrac{3x + 16}{(3 - x)(x + 2)^2}$.

   c Write down the set of x values for which this expansion is valid.

6 It is given that $f(x) = \dfrac{4 + 3x}{(1 + 2x)(2 - x)}$.

   a Express $f(x)$ in the form $\dfrac{A}{2 - x} + \dfrac{B}{1 + 2x}$, where A and B are integers.

   b **i** Find the first three terms of the binomial expansion of $f(x)$ in the form $a + bx + cx^2$, where a, b and c are rational numbers.

   ii Explain why the binomial expansion cannot be expected to give a good approximation to $f(-0.5)$.

END-OF-CHAPTER REVIEW EXERCISE 7

1 Write $\dfrac{3x^2 - a^2}{x^2(x - a)}$ in terms of partial fractions.

P **2** Given that $\dfrac{A}{x + a} + \dfrac{B}{x + b} + \dfrac{C}{x + c} = \dfrac{f(x)}{(x + a)(x + b)(x + c)}$, prove that if $f(x)$ is linear then $A + B + C = 0$.

3 **a** Find the first two terms in ascending powers of x, in the expansion of $\sqrt{\dfrac{1 + 5x}{1 + 12x}}$.

   b Over what range of values is this expansion valid?

   c By substituting $x = 0.01$, find the approximation to $\sqrt{15}$ to two decimal places.

PS **4** Is it possible to find a binomial expansion for $\sqrt{x - 1}$?

5 Find the first four terms in the expansion of $\dfrac{1}{1 + 2x + x^2}$.

6 Find the first three non-zero terms in ascending order in the expansion of $\sqrt{1 - x}\sqrt{1 + x}$.

7 The first three terms in the binomial expansion of $\dfrac{1}{(1 + ax)^b} + \dfrac{1}{(1 + bx)^a}$ are $2 - 6x + 15x^2$.
   Find the values of a and b.

8 **a** Find the first three non-zero terms of the binomial expansion of $\sqrt[3]{\dfrac{1 + 2x}{1 - x}}$.

   b By setting $x = 0.4$, find an approximation for $\sqrt[3]{3}$ to five decimal places.

9 Given that the expansion of $(1 + ax)^n$ is $1 - 9x + 54x^2 + bx^3$ find the value of b.

10 Find the first three terms of the expansion of $\dfrac{1}{1 + x + x^2}$.

11 a $f(x) = \dfrac{x}{1+x}$ can be written in the form $Ax + Bx^2 + Cx^3 + \ldots$ Find the values of A, B and C and state the set of values of x for which this converges.

b Show that $f(x)$ can be written in the form $\dfrac{1}{1 + \dfrac{1}{x}}$.

c $f(x)$ can be written in the form $P + \dfrac{Q}{x} + \dfrac{R}{x^2} + \ldots$ Find the values of P, Q and R and state the set of values of x for which this converges.

d Use an appropriate expansion to approximate $\dfrac{100}{101}$ to four decimal places, showing your reasoning.

e Use an appropriate expansion to approximate $\dfrac{1}{51}$ to five significant figures, showing your reasoning.

PS

12 In special relativity the energy of an object with mass m and speed v is given by $E = \dfrac{mc^2}{\sqrt{1 - \dfrac{v^2}{c^2}}}$, where $c \approx 3 \times 10^8 \, \mathrm{m\,s^{-1}}$ (the speed of light).

a Find the first three non-zero terms of the binomial expansion in increasing powers of v, stating the range over which it is valid.

Let E_2 be the expansion containing two terms and E_3 be the expansion containing three terms.

b By what percentage is E_3 bigger then E_2 if v is:

    i 10% of the speed of light   **ii** 90% of the speed of light?

c Prove that $E > E_3 > E_2$.

Chapter 8
Further calculus

P3 **This chapter is for Pure Mathematics 3 students only.**

- Use the derivative of $\tan^{-1} x$.
- Extend the ideas of 'reverse differentiation' to include the integration of $\dfrac{1}{x^2 + a^2}$.
- Recognise an integrand of the form $\dfrac{k f'(x)}{f(x)}$, and integrate such functions.
- Use a given substitution to simplify and evaluate either a definite or an indefinite integral.
- Integrate rational functions by means of decomposition into partial fractions.
- Recognise when an integrand can usefully be regarded as a product, and use integration by parts.

8.1 Derivative of $\tan^{-1} x$

$$\frac{d}{dx}(\tan^{-1} x) = \frac{1}{x^2 + 1}$$

WORKED EXAMPLE 8.1

Differentiate with respect to x.

   a $y = x \tan^{-1} x^2$

   b $y = \tan^{-1}(e^{3x})$

   c $y = 4 \tan^{-1}(3x^4)$

Answer

   a $y = x \tan^{-1} x^2$ Use the product rule: $u = x$ $v = \tan^{-1} x^2$

$$\frac{dy}{dx} = \tan^{-1} x^2 \times 1 + x\left(\frac{d}{dx}(\tan^{-1}(x^2))\right)$$ Use the chain rule.

$$\frac{dy}{dx} = \tan^{-1} x^2 + 2x \times \frac{x}{x^4 + 1}$$

$$\frac{dy}{dx} = \tan^{-1} x^2 + \frac{2x^2}{x^4 + 1}$$

   b $y = \tan^{-1}(e^{3x})$ Use the chain rule: $u = e^{3x}$ $y = \tan^{-1} u$

$$\frac{dy}{dx} = \frac{dy}{du} \times \frac{du}{dx}$$

TIP

$$\frac{d}{dx}(\tan^{-1} x) = \frac{1}{x^2 + 1}$$

TIP

Product rule:

$$\frac{d}{dx} uv = v\frac{du}{dx} + u\frac{dv}{dx}$$

$$\frac{dy}{dx} = \frac{1}{e^{6x} + 1} \times 3e^{3x}$$

$$\frac{dy}{dx} = \frac{3e^{3x}}{e^{6x} + 1}$$

c $\quad y = 4\tan^{-1}(3x^4)$ .... Use the chain rule: $u = 3x^4$ $\quad y = 4\tan^{-1}u$

$$\frac{dy}{dx} = \frac{dy}{du} \times \frac{du}{dx}$$

$$\frac{dy}{dx} = 4 \times \frac{1}{9x^8 + 1} \times 12x^3$$

$$\frac{dy}{dx} = \frac{48x^3}{9x^8 + 1}$$

EXERCISE 8A

1 Differentiate with respect to x.

   a $\quad \tan^{-1} 6x$ b $\quad \tan^{-1}\frac{1}{2}x$ c $\quad \tan^{-1}\frac{2x}{3}$

   d $\quad \tan^{-1}(3x - 2)$ e $\quad \tan^{-1} x^3$ f $\quad \tan^{-1}\left(\frac{3x}{x-1}\right)$

2 Differentiate with respect to x.

   a $\quad 3x\tan^{-1} 2x$ b $\quad \frac{\tan^{-1} 4x}{x}$ c $\quad e^{-x}\tan^{-1} 2x$

   d $\quad e^{\tan^{-1} x}$ e $\quad \tan^{-1}(\ln x)$ f $\quad \frac{e^x}{\tan^{-1} x}$

3 Find the equation of the tangent to the curve $y = \tan^{-1}\left(\frac{x}{3}\right)$, at the point where $x = 3$.

4 Find the equation of the normal to the curve $y = \tan^{-1} 3x$, at the point where $x = \frac{1}{\sqrt{3}}$.

 5 Given that $y = x - \tan^{-1} x$, show that $\frac{d^2y}{dx^2} = 2x\left(1 - \frac{dy}{dx}\right)^2$.

8.2 Integration of $\dfrac{1}{x^2 + a^2}$

TIP

$$\int \frac{1}{x^2 + a^2}\,dx = \frac{1}{a}\tan^{-1}\frac{x}{a} + c$$

WORKED EXAMPLE 8.2

Find the exact value of $\int_0^{\sqrt{3}} \dfrac{1}{x^2 + 9}\, \mathrm{d}x$.

Answer

$$\int_0^{\sqrt{3}} \frac{1}{x^2 + 9}\, \mathrm{d}x = \left[\frac{1}{3} \tan^{-1} \frac{x}{3} \right]_0^{\sqrt{3}}$$

$$= \left(\frac{1}{3} \tan^{-1} \frac{\sqrt{3}}{3} \right) - \left(\frac{1}{3} \tan^{-1} 0 \right)$$

$$= \left(\frac{1}{3} \times \frac{\pi}{6} \right) - \left(\frac{1}{3} \times 0 \right)$$

$$= \frac{\pi}{18}$$

TIP

Do not confuse this type of question with $\int_0^{\sqrt{3}} \dfrac{1}{x^2 - 9}$ which would be worked out using partial fractions after writing:

$$\int_0^{\sqrt{3}} \frac{1}{(x-3)(x+3)}$$

EXERCISE 8B

1 Find the following integrals.

a $\displaystyle\int \frac{1}{4x^2 + 16}\, \mathrm{d}x$

b $\displaystyle\int \frac{1}{1 + 9x^2}\, \mathrm{d}x$

c $\displaystyle\int \frac{1}{x^2 + 36}\, \mathrm{d}x$

d $\displaystyle\int \frac{1}{4x^2 + 5}\, \mathrm{d}x$

e $\displaystyle\int \frac{1}{9x^2 + 3}\, \mathrm{d}x$

f $\displaystyle\int \frac{1}{9 + 2x^2}\, \mathrm{d}x$

2 Find the exact value of each of these integrals.

a $\displaystyle\int_{-3}^{0} \frac{1}{3x^2 + 9}\, \mathrm{d}x$

b $\displaystyle\int_{0}^{1} \frac{2}{x^2 + 1}\, \mathrm{d}x$

c $\displaystyle\int_{-\sqrt{3}}^{\sqrt{3}} \frac{3}{x^2 + 9}\, \mathrm{d}x$

3 The diagram shows part of the curve $y = \dfrac{4}{4x^2 + 1}$. Find the area of the shaded region giving your answer to 3 significant figures.

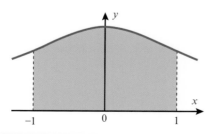

8.3 Integration of $\dfrac{k\mathrm{f}'(x)}{\mathrm{f}(x)}$

> **TIP**
>
> $$\int \frac{\mathrm{f}'(x)}{\mathrm{f}(x)}\,\mathrm{d}x = \ln|\mathrm{f}(x)| + c$$
>
> $$\int \frac{k\mathrm{f}'(x)}{\mathrm{f}(x)}\,\mathrm{d}x = k\ln|\mathrm{f}(x)| + c$$

WORKED EXAMPLE 8.3

Find $\displaystyle\int \tan x\,\mathrm{d}x$.

Answer

$$\int \tan x\,\mathrm{d}x \quad\cdots\cdots\cdots\cdots\cdots\cdots\quad \text{Write } \tan x = \frac{\sin x}{\cos x}.$$

If $\mathrm{f}(x) = \cos x$ then
$\mathrm{f}'(x) = -\sin x$

$$\int \tan x\,\mathrm{d}x = \int \frac{-\mathrm{f}'(x)}{\mathrm{f}(x)} = -\int \frac{\mathrm{f}'(x)}{\mathrm{f}(x)} = -\ln|\mathrm{f}(x)| + c$$

$$\int \tan x\,\mathrm{d}x = -\ln\cos x + c$$

> **TIP**
>
> $-\ln\cos x$ can be written as $\ln(\cos x)^{-1}$ or $\ln(\sec x)$. Do not confuse $\ln(\cos x)^{-1}$ with $\ln\cos^{-1} x$.

EXERCISE 8C

1 Work out the following integrals.

a $\displaystyle\int \frac{\cos x}{1 + \sin x}\,\mathrm{d}x$

b $\displaystyle\int \frac{x^2}{1 + x^3}\,\mathrm{d}x$

c $\displaystyle\int \cot x\,\mathrm{d}x$

d $\displaystyle\int \frac{e^x}{4 + e^x}\,\mathrm{d}x$

e $\displaystyle\int \frac{2e^{3x}}{5 - e^{3x}}\,\mathrm{d}x$

f $\displaystyle\int \tan 3x\,\mathrm{d}x$

2 Evaluate each of the following integrals, giving your answer in an exact form.

a $\displaystyle\int_{1}^{2} \frac{e^x}{e^x - 1}\,\mathrm{d}x$

b $\displaystyle\int_{4}^{5} \frac{x - 2}{x^2 - 4x + 5}\,\mathrm{d}x$

c $\displaystyle\int_{0}^{\frac{1}{6}\pi} \frac{\sin 2x}{1 + \cos 2x}\,\mathrm{d}x$

3 Show that $\displaystyle\int_{2}^{5}\frac{2x}{2x^2-1}\,dx = \ln k$ where k is an integer to be found.

PS **4** Calculate the area of the shaded region in the graph represented by $\displaystyle\int_{0}^{B}\frac{\cos x}{2+3\sin x}\,dx$, where B is the intersection of the graph $y = \dfrac{\cos x}{2+3\sin x}$ with the x-axis. Give your answer as an exact value in the form $a\ln b$.

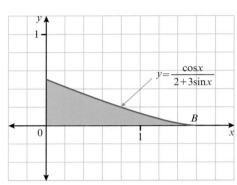

PS **5** Show that $\displaystyle\int_{1}^{3}\frac{(2x-3)\sqrt{x^2-3x+3}}{x^2-3x+3}\,dx = a\sqrt{b}+c$, where a, b and c are integers to be found.

6 a Find the area of the region enclosed by the curve with equation $y = \tan x$, the x-axis and the lines $x = 0$ and $x = \dfrac{1}{3}\pi$.

   b Find the volume generated when this area is rotated about the x-axis.

8.4 Integration by substitution

WORKED EXAMPLE 8.4

Use the substitution $u = 2x + 1$ to find $\displaystyle\int_{0}^{4}\frac{6x}{\sqrt{2x+1}}\,dx$.

Answer

$u = 2x + 1 \Rightarrow x = \dfrac{1}{2}(u-1)$

$u = 2x + 1 \Rightarrow \dfrac{du}{dx} = 2 \Rightarrow dx = \dfrac{1}{2}\,du$

$x = 4 \Rightarrow u = 2(4) + 1 = 9$ .... Find the new limits for u.

$x = 0 \Rightarrow u = 2(0) + 1 = 1$

TIP

Note that, given the choice, the same answer would be obtained by using $u^2 = 2x + 1$ throughout this question.

102

$$\int_{x=0}^{x=4} \frac{6x}{\sqrt{2x+1}}\,dx = \int_{u=1}^{u=9} \frac{3(u-1)}{2\sqrt{u}}\,du$$

Write the integral in terms of u and simplify.

$$= \int_{1}^{9} \frac{3}{2}(u^{\frac{1}{2}} - u^{-\frac{1}{2}})\,du$$

$$= \frac{3}{2}\int_{1}^{9} (u^{\frac{1}{2}} - u^{-\frac{1}{2}})\,du$$

Integrate with respect to u.

$$= \frac{3}{2}\left[\frac{2}{3}u^{\frac{3}{2}} - 2u^{\frac{1}{2}}\right]_{1}^{9}$$

Evaluate the function at the limits.

$$= \frac{3}{2}(18 - 6) - \frac{3}{2}\left(\frac{2}{3} - 2\right)$$

$$= 18 + 2$$

$$= 20$$

1 Use the given substitutions to find the following integrals.

a $\displaystyle\int \frac{1}{x - 2\sqrt{x}}\,dx, \ x = u^2$

b $\displaystyle\int \frac{1}{(3x+4)^2}\,dx, \ 3x+4 = u$

c $\displaystyle\int \sin\left(\frac{1}{3}\pi - \frac{1}{2}x\right)dx, \ \frac{1}{3}\pi - \frac{1}{2}x = u$

d $\displaystyle\int x(x-1)^5\,dx, \ x = 1 + u$

e $\displaystyle\int \frac{e^x}{1+e^x}\,dx, \ x = \ln u$

f $\displaystyle\int \frac{1}{3\sqrt{x}+4x}\,dx, \ x = u^2$

g $\displaystyle\int 3x\sqrt{x+2}\,dx, \ x = u^2 - 2$

h $\displaystyle\int \frac{x}{\sqrt{x-3}}\,dx, \ x = 3 + u^2$

i $\displaystyle\int \frac{1}{x \ln x}\,dx, \ x = e^u$

j $\displaystyle\int \frac{1}{\sqrt{4-x^2}}\,dx, \ x = 2\sin u$

2 a Use the substitution $x = \tan u$ to show that $\displaystyle\int \frac{1}{1+x^2}\,dx = \tan^{-1} x + k$.

b Use the substitution $x = \ln u$ to find $\displaystyle\int \frac{e^x}{1 + e^{2x}}\,dx$.

3 Use the given substitutions to find the following integrals.

a $\displaystyle\int_0^1 \frac{e^x}{1 + e^x}\,dx,\ x = \ln u$

b $\displaystyle\int_9^{16} \frac{1}{x - 2\sqrt{x}}\,dx,\ x = u^2$

c $\displaystyle\int_1^2 x(x - 1)^2\,dx,\ x = 1 + u$

d $\displaystyle\int_1^2 x\sqrt{x - 1}\,dx,\ x = 1 + u$

e $\displaystyle\int_0^1 \frac{1}{\sqrt{4 - x^2}}\,dx,\ x = 2\sin u$

f $\displaystyle\int_6^9 \frac{x^2}{\sqrt{x - 5}}\,dx,\ x = 5 + u$

g $\displaystyle\int_{-4}^4 \sqrt{16 - x^2}\,dx,\ x = 4\sin u$

h $\displaystyle\int_1^6 \frac{1}{4 + x^2}\,dx,\ x = 2\tan u$

i $\displaystyle\int_e^{e^2} \frac{1}{x(\ln x)^2}\,dx,\ x = e^u$

j $\displaystyle\int_0^{\frac{1}{2}} \frac{1}{(1 - x^2)^{\frac{3}{2}}}\,dx,\ x = \sin u$

k $\displaystyle\int_1^8 \frac{1}{x(1 + \sqrt[3]{x})}\,dx,\ x = u^3$

4 Use the substitution $x = \sin^2 u$ to calculate $\displaystyle\int_0^{\frac{1}{2}} \sqrt{\frac{x}{1 - x}}\,dx$.

5 Use the given substitutions to find the following integrals.

a $\displaystyle\int 2x(x^2 + 1)^3\,dx,\ u = x^2 + 1$

b $\displaystyle\int x\sqrt{4 + x^2}\,dx,\ u = 4 + x^2$

c $\displaystyle\int \sin^5 x \cos x\,dx,\ u = \sin x$

d $\displaystyle\int \tan^3 x \sec^2 x\,dx,\ u = \tan x$

e $\displaystyle\int \frac{2x^3}{\sqrt{1 - x^4}}\,dx,\ u = 1 - x^4$

f $\displaystyle\int \cos^3 2x \sin 2x\,dx,\ u = \cos 2x$

6 Use the given trigonometric substitutions to evaluate the following infinite and improper integrals. Give your answers as exact values.

a $\displaystyle\int_0^\infty \frac{1}{x^2 + 4}\,dx,\ x = 2\tan u$

b $\displaystyle\int_{-\infty}^\infty \frac{1}{9x^2 + 4}\,dx,\ x = \frac{2}{3}\tan u$

c $\displaystyle\int_0^1 \frac{1}{\sqrt{x(1 - x)}}\,dx,\ x = \sin^2 u$

d $\displaystyle\int_1^\infty \frac{1}{(1 + x^2)^{\frac{3}{2}}}\,dx,\ x = \tan u$

e $\displaystyle\int_1^\infty \frac{1}{x\sqrt{x^2 - 1}}\,dx,\ x = \sec u$

7 Use the given substitutions to evaluate the following definite integrals.

a **i** $\displaystyle\int_1^3 4x(2x + 1)^3\,dx,\ u = 2x + 1$

ii $\displaystyle\int_0^1 6x(3x - 2)^4\,dx,\ u = 3x - 2$

b **i** $\displaystyle\int_0^{\frac{\pi}{2}} \cos x \sin^5 x\,dx,\ u = \sin x$

ii $\displaystyle\int_0^{\frac{\pi}{4}} \sec^2 x \tan^2 x\,dx,\ u = \tan x$

c **i** $\displaystyle\int_2^3 \left(\frac{x}{4 - x}\right)^2\,dx,\ u = 4 - x$

ii $\displaystyle\int_1^3 \frac{x^3}{(x + 2)^2}\,dx,\ u = x + 2$

8   Use the substitution $x = e^u$ to find $\int \dfrac{\sec^2 (\ln (x^2))}{2x} dx$.

9   By using the substitution $u = e^x$, find the exact value of $\displaystyle\int_0^{\ln 3} \dfrac{1}{e^x + e^{-x}} dx$.

10 Find the equation of the curve which has gradient $\dfrac{dy}{dx} = 3 \tan x$ and passes through the point $(0, 4)$.

11 a   Given that $y = \dfrac{x + 1}{\sqrt{x + 2}}$, find $\dfrac{dy}{dx}$. Give your answer in the form $\dfrac{Ax + B}{2(x + 2)^{\frac{3}{2}}}$, where A and B are integers.

    The diagram shows part of the curve $y = \dfrac{x}{(x + 2)^{\frac{3}{2}}}$.

    b   Find the coordinates of the stationary point on the curve.

    c   Find the shaded area enclosed by the curve, the x-axis and the lines $x = 2$ and $x = 7$.

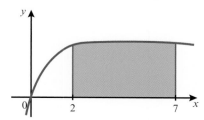

8.5 The use of partial fractions in integration

WORKED EXAMPLE 8.5

Find $\int \dfrac{x}{x^2 - 9} dx$.

Answer

$$\dfrac{x}{x^2 - 9} \equiv \dfrac{A}{x - 3} + \dfrac{B}{x + 3}$$

$$x \equiv A(x + 3) + B(x - 3)$$

First split into partial fractions. Multiply throughout by $(x + 3)(x - 3)$.

Let
$x = 3 \quad 3 = 6A \Rightarrow A = \dfrac{1}{2}$

Let
$x = -3 \quad -3 = -6B \Rightarrow B = \dfrac{1}{2}$

$$\therefore \int \frac{x}{x^2 - 9}\,dx = \int \left(\frac{1}{2(x-3)} + \frac{1}{2(x+3)}\right)dx$$

$$= \frac{1}{2}\int \left(\frac{1}{x-3} + \frac{1}{x+3}\right)dx$$

$$= \frac{1}{2}\ln|x-3| + \frac{1}{2}\ln|x+3| + c$$

$$= \frac{1}{2}\ln|(x-3)(x+3)| + c$$

$$= \frac{1}{2}\ln|x^2 - 9| + c$$

EXERCISE 8E

1 Find the following integrals by splitting them into partial fractions.

a i $\int \dfrac{5x-29}{(x-3)(x-10)}\,dx$ **ii** $\int \dfrac{x-7}{(x+1)(x-3)}\,dx$

b i $\int \dfrac{1}{x^2-1}\,dx$ **ii** $\int \dfrac{x}{x^2-1}\,dx$

c i $\int \dfrac{1-2x}{(x-2)(1-x)}\,dx$ **ii** $\int \dfrac{3x-1}{(1-x)(1+x)}\,dx$

d i $\int \dfrac{3(2x^2+2x+3)}{x^3+3x^2}\,dx$ **ii** $\int \dfrac{4x^2-5x+2}{x^3-2x^2}\,dx$

e i $\int \dfrac{6x+2}{(x-1)^2(x+3)}\,dx$ **ii** $\int \dfrac{-(2x+5)}{(x+1)^2(x-2)}\,dx$

2 **a** Write $\dfrac{5}{x^2+x-6}$ as a sum of partial fractions.

b Hence find $\int \dfrac{5}{x^2+x-6}\,dx$, giving your answer in the form $\ln|f(x)| + c$.

3 Find the exact value of $\displaystyle\int_0^1 \dfrac{4}{x^2-4}\,dx$.

4 **a** Split $\dfrac{5-x}{2+x-x^2}$ into partial fractions.

b Given that $\displaystyle\int_0^1 \dfrac{5-x}{2+x-x^2}\,dx = \ln k$, find the value of k.

PS 5 Find the exact value of $\displaystyle\int_3^4 \dfrac{8-3x}{3x^3-4x^2+4x}\,dx$. Give your answer in the form $\ln p + \dfrac{1}{q}$, where p and q are rational numbers.

6 a Write $\dfrac{x+5}{(x-1)(x+2)}$ in partial fractions.

   b Hence find, in the form $\ln k$, the exact value $\displaystyle\int_5^7 \dfrac{x+5}{(x-1)(x+2)}\,dx$.

7 Given that $\displaystyle\int_{-a}^{a} \dfrac{2}{1-x^2}\,dx = 2$, find the exact value of a.

8 The region bounded by the curve with equation $y = \sqrt{\dfrac{10x}{(x+4)(x^2+4)}}$, the x-axis and the
lines with equations $x=0$ and $x=2$ is rotated through 2π radians about the x-axis. Calculate
the volume of the solid of revolution formed.

9 a Express $\dfrac{2x+1}{(x-2)(x^2+1)}$ in partial fractions.

   b Hence show that $\displaystyle\int_0^1 \dfrac{2x+1}{(x-2)(x^2+1)}\,dx = -\dfrac{3}{2}\ln 2$.

8.6 Integration by parts

WORKED EXAMPLE 8.6

Find $\displaystyle\int_0^\infty x e^{-ax}\,dx$ where a is positive.

Answer

$\displaystyle\int_0^\infty x e^{-ax}\,dx$

$u = x \Rightarrow \dfrac{du}{dx} = 1$

Begin by finding the integrals from 0 to s and then consider their limits as $s \to \infty$.

$\dfrac{dv}{dx} = e^{-ax} \Rightarrow v = -\dfrac{1}{a}e^{-ax}$

Substitute into

$\displaystyle\int u \dfrac{dv}{dx}\,dx = uv - \int v \dfrac{du}{dx}\,dx$

$\displaystyle\int_0^s x e^{-ax}\,dx = \left[x\times\left(-\dfrac{1}{a}\right)e^{-ax}\right]_0^s - \int_0^s 1\times\left(-\dfrac{1}{a}\right)e^{-ax}\,dx$

$= \left(-\dfrac{1}{a}\right)se^{-as} - \left[\dfrac{1}{a^2}e^{-ax}\right]_0^s$

$= -\dfrac{1}{a}se^{-as} - \dfrac{1}{a^2}e^{-as} + \dfrac{1}{a^2}$

$s\to\infty \quad e^{-as}\to 0 \quad se^{(-as)}\to 0$

$\displaystyle\int_0^\infty x e^{-ax}\,dx = \dfrac{1}{a^2}$

107

1 Use integration by parts to integrate the following functions with respect to x.

   a $x \sin x$ **b** $3x\,e^x$ **c** $(x+4)e^x$

2 Use integration by parts to integrate the following functions with respect to x.

   a $x\,e^{2x}$ **b** $x \cos 4x$ **c** $x \ln 2x$

3 Find:

   a $\displaystyle\int x^5 \ln 3x\,dx$ **b** $\displaystyle\int x\,e^{2x+1}\,dx$ **c** $\displaystyle\int \ln 2x\,dx$

4 Find the exact values of:

   a $\displaystyle\int_1^e x \ln x\,dx$ **b** $\displaystyle\int_0^{\frac{1}{2}\pi} x \sin \tfrac{1}{2}x\,dx$ **c** $\displaystyle\int_1^e x^n \ln x\,dx \;\; (n>0)$

5 Find $\displaystyle\int x\tan^{-1}x\,dx$.

6 Find the area bounded by the curve $y = xe^{-x}$, the x-axis and the lines $x=0$ and $x=2$. Find also the volume of the solid of revolution obtained by rotating this region about the x-axis.

7 Find the area between the x-axis and the curve $y = x \sin 3x$ for $0 \leqslant x \leqslant \frac{1}{3}\pi$. Leave your answer in terms of π. Find also the volume of the solid of revolution obtained by rotating this region about the x-axis.

8 Find the exact value of $\displaystyle\int_1^e 3x^2 \ln(2x)\,dx$.

9 The region R in the diagram is enclosed between the graph of $y = \ln x$ and the x-axis between $x=2$ and $x=5$.

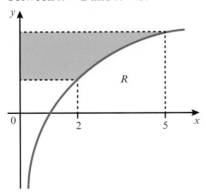

   a   Find the shaded area between the curve and the y-axis.

   b   Hence find the exact area of R.

END-OF-CHAPTER REVIEW EXERCISE 8

1 **a** Use the identity $\cos^2 x + \sin^2 x \equiv 1$ to show that $\cos(\sin^{-1} x) = \sqrt{1 - x^2}$.

   b The diagram shows part of the curve $y = \sin x$. Write down the x-coordinate of the point P.

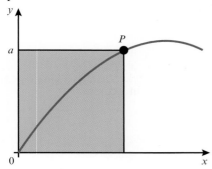

   c Find the red-shaded area in terms of a, writing your answer in a form without trigonometric functions.

   d By considering the blue-shaded area, find $\displaystyle\int_0^a \sin^{-1} x \, dx$ for $0 < a < 1$.

2 Find $\displaystyle\int_1^2 x^3 \ln x \, dx$, giving your answer in the form $\ln p - q$.

3 A curve is given by parametric equations $x = \cos t$, $y = \sin 2t$, for $0 \leqslant t \leqslant 2\pi$. The curve crosses the x-axis at point A, and B is a maximum point on the curve.

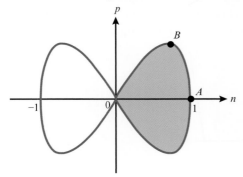

   a Find the exact coordinates of B.

   b i Find the values of t at the points O and A.

   ii Find the shaded area.

4 Use the given substitution and then use integration by parts to complete the integration.

   a $\displaystyle\int \cos^{-1} x \, dx, \quad x = \cos u$

   b $\displaystyle\int \tan^{-1} x \, dx, \quad x = \tan u$

   c $\displaystyle\int (\ln x)^2 \, dx, \quad x = e^u$

109

5　a　Show that the substitution $y = e^{-x}$ transforms the integral $\displaystyle\int_0^{\ln 2} \frac{1}{1 + e^{-x}} dx$ to $\displaystyle\int_{\frac{1}{2}}^1 \frac{1}{y(1 + y)} dy$.

　　b　Hence, or otherwise, evaluate $\displaystyle\int_0^{\ln 2} \frac{1}{1 + e^{-x}} dx$.

6　a　Find $\displaystyle\int x \ln x\, dx$.

　　b　Show that $\dfrac{1}{\sin x \cos x} \equiv \dfrac{\sec^2 x}{\tan x}$, and hence evaluate $\displaystyle\int_{\frac{1}{6}\pi}^{\frac{1}{3}\pi} \frac{1}{\sin x \cos x} dx$ using substitution
　　　with $u = \tan x$.

7　a　Differentiate $x\sqrt{2 - x}$ with respect to x.

　　b　Find $\displaystyle\int x\sqrt{2 - x}\, dx$:

　　　i　by using the substitution $2 - x = u$
　　　ii　by integration by parts.

8　Calculate the exact value of $\displaystyle\int_1^4 \frac{x^2}{x^3 + 1} dx$.

9　Use the substitution $u = \sin x$ to calculate the exact value of $\displaystyle\int_0^{\frac{1}{2}\pi} \sin^3 x \cos x\, dx$.

10　This sketch shows part of the graph of the function $y = x \sin x + \cos x$. The point labelled A is
　　the first stationary point with $x > 0$, and has coordinates (x_A, y_A).

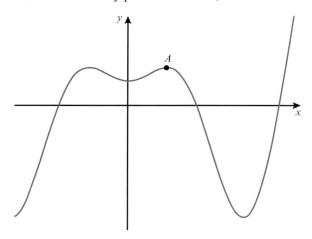

　　a　Find the coordinates of the point A.
　　b　Find the exact area enclosed by the graph of $y = x \sin x + \cos x$, the x-axis, the y-axis and
　　　the line $x = x_A$.

11　Calculate $\displaystyle\int_1^2 \frac{2x^3 + 3x^2 + 28}{(x + 2)(x^2 + 4)} dx$, giving your answer in exact form.

Vectors

P3 **This chapter is for Pure Mathematics 3 students only.**

- Use standard notations for vectors in 2-dimensions and 3-dimensions.
- Add and subtract vectors, multiply a vector by a scalar and interpret these operations geometrically.
- Calculate the magnitude of a vector and find and use unit vectors.
- Use displacement vectors and position vectors.
- Find the vector equation of a line.
- Find whether two lines are parallel, intersect or are skew.
- Find the common point of two intersecting lines.
- Find and use the scalar product of two vectors.

9.1 Displacement or translation vectors

WORKED EXAMPLE 9.1

Points A, B and C are such that $\overrightarrow{AB} = \begin{pmatrix} -2 \\ 3 \end{pmatrix}$ and $\overrightarrow{AC} = \begin{pmatrix} 4 \\ -1 \end{pmatrix}$. Find the unit displacement vector in the direction $\overrightarrow{CB}$.

Answer

$\overrightarrow{CB} = \overrightarrow{CA} + \overrightarrow{AB}$ Substitute column vectors and sum components.

$\overrightarrow{CB} = \begin{pmatrix} -4 \\ 1 \end{pmatrix} + \begin{pmatrix} -2 \\ 3 \end{pmatrix}$

$\overrightarrow{CB} = \begin{pmatrix} -6 \\ 4 \end{pmatrix}$ Now find the magnitude by applying Pythagoras' theorem.

$|\overrightarrow{CB}| = \sqrt{(-6)^2 + 4^2}$

$|\overrightarrow{CB}| = \sqrt{52}$ Divide each component by the magnitude of $\overrightarrow{CB}$.

Unit displacement vector is $\overrightarrow{CB} = \begin{pmatrix} \dfrac{-6}{\sqrt{52}} \\ \dfrac{4}{\sqrt{52}} \end{pmatrix}$ or

$\overrightarrow{CB} = \dfrac{1}{\sqrt{52}}\begin{pmatrix} -6 \\ 4 \end{pmatrix}$ or $\overrightarrow{CB} = \dfrac{1}{\sqrt{13}}\begin{pmatrix} -3 \\ 2 \end{pmatrix}$ etc.

1 a Find a unit vector parallel to $\begin{pmatrix} 2 \\ 2 \\ 1 \end{pmatrix}$.

b Find the unit vector in the same direction as $\begin{pmatrix} 4 \\ -1 \\ 2\sqrt{2} \end{pmatrix}$.

2 Given that $\mathbf{a} = \begin{pmatrix} 2 \\ 0 \\ 2 \end{pmatrix}$ and $\mathbf{b} = \begin{pmatrix} 3 \\ 1 \\ 3 \end{pmatrix}$, find the value of the scalar p

such that $\mathbf{a} + p\mathbf{b}$ is parallel to the vector $\begin{pmatrix} 3 \\ 2 \\ 3 \end{pmatrix}$.

> **TIP**
>
> You may need to review geometrical properties of special quadrilaterals when doing this exercise.

3 In the parallelogram $ABCD$, $\overrightarrow{AB} = \mathbf{a}$ and $\overrightarrow{AD} = \mathbf{b}$. M is the midpoint of BC, Q is the point on the extended line AB such that $BQ = \frac{1}{2}AB$ and P is the point on the extended line BC such that $BC : CP = 3 : 1$, as shown on the diagram. Express the following vectors in terms of $\mathbf{a}$ and $\mathbf{b}$.

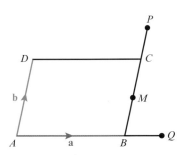

a i $\overrightarrow{AP}$ **ii** $\overrightarrow{AM}$

b i $\overrightarrow{QD}$ **ii** $\overrightarrow{MQ}$

c i $\overrightarrow{DQ}$ **ii** $\overrightarrow{PQ}$

> **TIP**
>
> Remember to use the correct notation when giving explanations. For example, $\overrightarrow{CB}$ is the translation vector from point C to point B. CB (or BC) is the (geometrical) line between point C and point B.

4 For the coordinate sets given, determine whether the three points A, B and C are collinear. If they are, find the ratio $AB : BC$.

a $A(2, 1)$, $B(-11, 14)$, $C(4, 3)$

b $A(4, 2a)$, $B(1, 3a + 2)$, $C(10, 4)$

c $A(a^2 + 2a, 3)$, $B(a^2 + a - 1, 1)$, $C(3a^2 + 2a - 2, 4a - 1)$

5 $\overrightarrow{AB} = \begin{pmatrix} 3 \\ -7 \end{pmatrix}$ and $\overrightarrow{CA} = \begin{pmatrix} -9 \\ 21 \end{pmatrix}$. Show that A, B and C are collinear and find the ratio $AB : BC$.

 6 Points A and B have coordinates $A(10, 1)$ and $B(2, 7)$. Point C lies on the line segment AB such that $AC : BC = x : 1 - x$, where $0 < x < 1$.

a Find the coordinates of C, in terms of x.

b Point D has coordinates $D(3, 2)$ and $CD = \sqrt{26}$. Find x.

P 7 The vertices of a quadrilateral $PQRS$ have coordinates $P(-2, 1)$, $Q(5, -3)$, $R(6, 0)$ and $S(-1, 5)$. The midpoints of the sides PQ, QR, RS and SP are A, B, C and D. Prove that $ABCD$ is a parallelogram.

8 $ABCD$ is a parallelogram with $\overrightarrow{AB} = \mathbf{p}$ and $\overrightarrow{BC} = \mathbf{q}$. Let M be the midpoint of the diagonal AC.

    a Express $\overrightarrow{AM}$ in terms of $\mathbf{p}$ and $\mathbf{q}$.

    b Show that M is also a midpoint of the diagonal BD.

P 9 Four points have coordinates $A(2, -1)$, $B(k, k + 1)$, $C(2k - 3, 3k + 2)$ and $D(k - 1, 2k)$.

    a Show that $ABCD$ is a parallelogram for all values of k.

    b Show that there is no value of k for which $ABCD$ is a rhombus.

P 10 OAB is a triangle with $\overrightarrow{OA} = \mathbf{a}$ and $\overrightarrow{OB} = \mathbf{b}$. M is the midpoint of AB and G is a point on OM such that $OG:GM = 2:1$. N is the midpoint of OA. Use vectors to prove that the points B, G and N are collinear.

11 Points M and N have coordinates $M(-6, 1)$ and $N(3, 5)$. Find a unit vector parallel to $\overrightarrow{MN}$.

12 Points P and Q have coordinates $(1, -8)$ and $(10, -2)$. N is a point on PQ such that $PN:NQ = 1:2$.

    a Find the coordinates of N.

    b Calculate the magnitudes of $\overrightarrow{OP}$, $\overrightarrow{ON}$ and $\overrightarrow{PN}$. Hence show that ONP is a right angle.

9.2 Position vectors

WORKED EXAMPLE 9.2

Points A and B have position vectors $\mathbf{a} = \begin{pmatrix} 2 \\ 2 \\ 1 \end{pmatrix}$ and $\mathbf{b} = \begin{pmatrix} 1 \\ -1 \\ 3 \end{pmatrix}$.

Point C lies on AB such that AC to BC is $2:3$.

Find the position vector of C giving your answer:

    a as a column vector

    b in terms of scalar multiples of the base vectors $\mathbf{i}$, $\mathbf{j}$ and $\mathbf{k}$.

Answer

To find $\overrightarrow{OC}$, first draw a diagram.

$\overrightarrow{OC} = \overrightarrow{OA} + \overrightarrow{AC}$

$\overrightarrow{OC} = \overrightarrow{OA} + \frac{2}{5}\overrightarrow{AB}$

$\overrightarrow{AB} = \overrightarrow{AO} + \overrightarrow{OB}$

$\overrightarrow{AB} = \begin{pmatrix} -2 \\ -2 \\ -1 \end{pmatrix} + \begin{pmatrix} 1 \\ -1 \\ 3 \end{pmatrix}$

$\overrightarrow{AB} = \begin{pmatrix} -1 \\ -3 \\ 2 \end{pmatrix}$

$\overrightarrow{OC} = \begin{pmatrix} 2 \\ 2 \\ 1 \end{pmatrix} + \frac{2}{5}\begin{pmatrix} -1 \\ -3 \\ 2 \end{pmatrix}$

a $\quad \overrightarrow{OC} = \begin{pmatrix} \frac{8}{5} \\ \frac{4}{5} \\ \frac{9}{5} \end{pmatrix}$ or $\frac{1}{5}\begin{pmatrix} 8 \\ 4 \\ 9 \end{pmatrix}$

as a column vector

b $\quad \overrightarrow{OC} = \frac{1}{5}(8\mathbf{i} + 4\mathbf{j} + 9\mathbf{k})$

EXERCISE 9B

1 Points A and B have position vectors $\mathbf{a} = \begin{pmatrix} 4 \\ 1 \\ 2 \end{pmatrix}$ and $\mathbf{b} = \begin{pmatrix} 2 \\ -1 \\ 3 \end{pmatrix}$. C is the midpoint of AB. Find the exact distance AC.

2 Points A, B and C have position vectors $\mathbf{a} = \mathbf{i} + 3\mathbf{j} - 4\mathbf{k}$, $\mathbf{b} = 3\mathbf{i} + 2\mathbf{j} + 2\mathbf{k}$ and $\mathbf{c} = -3\mathbf{i} + 3\mathbf{j} + 4\mathbf{k}$.

  a Find the position vector of the point D such that $ABCD$ is a parallelogram.

  b Prove that $ABCD$ is a rhombus.

3 Points A, B and C have position vectors $\mathbf{a} = -7\mathbf{i} + 11\mathbf{j} + 9\mathbf{k}$, $\mathbf{b} = 13\mathbf{i} - 4\mathbf{j} + 14\mathbf{k}$ and $\mathbf{c} = 3\mathbf{i} + \mathbf{j} + 4\mathbf{k}$.

  a Prove that the triangle ABC is isosceles.

  b Find the position vector of the point D such that the four points form a rhombus.

4 Points P and Q have position vectors $\mathbf{p} = 4\mathbf{i} - \mathbf{j} + 11\mathbf{k}$ and $\mathbf{q} = 3\mathbf{j} - \mathbf{k}$. S is the point on the line segment PQ such that $PS : SQ = 3 : 2$. Find the exact distance of S from the origin.

5 Points P and Q have position vectors $\mathbf{p} = 2\mathbf{i} - \mathbf{j} - 3\mathbf{k}$ and $\mathbf{q} = \mathbf{i} + 4\mathbf{j} - \mathbf{k}$.

   a Find the position vector of the midpoint M of PQ.

   b Point R lies on the line PQ such that $QR = QM$. Find the coordinates of R.

6 Given that $\mathbf{a} = \mathbf{i} - \mathbf{j} + 3\mathbf{k}$ and $\mathbf{b} = 2q\mathbf{i} + \mathbf{j} + q\mathbf{k}$, find the values of the scalars p and q such that $p\mathbf{a} + \mathbf{b}$ is parallel to the vector $\mathbf{i} + \mathbf{j} + 2\mathbf{k}$.

7 Points A and B have position vectors $\mathbf{a}$ and $\mathbf{b}$. Point M lies on AB and $AM : MB = p : q$. Express the position vector of M in terms of $\mathbf{a}$, $\mathbf{b}$, p and q.

P 8 In the diagram, O is the origin and points A and B have position vectors $\mathbf{a}$ and $\mathbf{b}$. P, Q and R are points on OA, OB and AB extended such that $OP : PA = 1 : 4$, $OQ : QB = 3 : 2$ and $AB : BR = 5 : 1$.

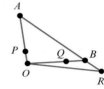

   Prove that:

   a PQR is a straight line

   b Q is the midpoint of PR.

9.3 The scalar product

TIP

$\mathbf{a}.\mathbf{b}$ is the same as $\mathbf{b}.\mathbf{a}$

WORKED EXAMPLE 9.3

If $\overrightarrow{BA} = 2\mathbf{i} + 3\mathbf{j} - \mathbf{k}$ and $\overrightarrow{AC} = -\mathbf{i} + 2\mathbf{k}$ find the angle BAC between the two vectors, to 3 significant figures.

Answer

$\overrightarrow{AB}.\overrightarrow{AC} = |\overrightarrow{AB}||\overrightarrow{AC}| \cos BAC$

$\overrightarrow{AB}.\overrightarrow{AC} = \sqrt{(-2)^2 + (-3)^2 + (1)^2} \sqrt{(-1)^2 + 0^2 + (2)^2} \cos BAC$

$(-2)(-1) + (-3)(0) + (1)(2) = \sqrt{14}\sqrt{5} \cos BAC$

$4 = \sqrt{14}\sqrt{5} \cos BAC$

$BAC = \cos^{-1} \dfrac{4}{\sqrt{14}\sqrt{5}}$

$BAC = 61.4°$

TIP

The scalar product of two vectors is $\mathbf{a}.\mathbf{b} = |\mathbf{a}| |\mathbf{b}| \cos \theta$.

TIP

The angle between two vectors is defined to be the angle made either when the direction of each vector is **away** from a point or when the direction of each vector is **towards** a point.

1 Which of the following vectors are perpendicular to each other?

    a $2\mathbf{i} - 3\mathbf{j} + 6\mathbf{k}$ **b** $2\mathbf{i} - 3\mathbf{j} - 6\mathbf{k}$

    c $-3\mathbf{i} - 6\mathbf{j} + 2\mathbf{k}$ **d** $6\mathbf{i} - 2\mathbf{j} - 3\mathbf{k}$

2 Use a vector method to calculate the angles between the following pairs of vectors, giving your answer in degrees to one decimal place, where appropriate.

    a $\begin{pmatrix} 2 \\ 1 \end{pmatrix}$ and $\begin{pmatrix} 1 \\ 3 \end{pmatrix}$ **b** $\begin{pmatrix} 4 \\ -5 \end{pmatrix}$ and $\begin{pmatrix} -5 \\ 4 \end{pmatrix}$ **c** $\begin{pmatrix} 4 \\ -6 \end{pmatrix}$ and $\begin{pmatrix} -6 \\ 9 \end{pmatrix}$

    d $\begin{pmatrix} -1 \\ 4 \\ 5 \end{pmatrix}$ and $\begin{pmatrix} 2 \\ 0 \\ -3 \end{pmatrix}$ **e** $\begin{pmatrix} 1 \\ 2 \\ -3 \end{pmatrix}$ and $\begin{pmatrix} 2 \\ 3 \\ -4 \end{pmatrix}$ **f** $\begin{pmatrix} 2 \\ -1 \\ 3 \end{pmatrix}$ and $\begin{pmatrix} 5 \\ -2 \\ -4 \end{pmatrix}$

3 Find the angle between the line joining $(1, 3, -2)$ to $(2, 5, -1)$ and the line joining $(-1, 4, 3)$ to $(3, 2, 1)$.

4 Find t if $\begin{pmatrix} -4 \\ t \\ 1-t \end{pmatrix}$ and $\begin{pmatrix} t \\ t \\ -6-t \end{pmatrix}$ are perpendicular vectors.

5 $ABCD$ is the base of a square pyramid of side 2 units, and V is the vertex. The pyramid is symmetrical, and of height 4 units. Calculate the acute angle between AV and BC, giving your answer in degrees correct to 1 decimal place.

6 Two aeroplanes are flying in directions given by the vectors $300\mathbf{i} + 400\mathbf{j} + 2\mathbf{k}$ and $-100\mathbf{i} + 500\mathbf{j} - \mathbf{k}$. A person from the flight control centre is plotting their paths on a map. Find the acute angle between their paths on the map.

7 Find the value of t such that the variable vector $\begin{pmatrix} 4 \\ 6 \\ 10 \end{pmatrix} + t\begin{pmatrix} -1 \\ 2 \\ 3 \end{pmatrix}$ is perpendicular

    to the vector $\begin{pmatrix} 4 \\ 2 \\ -7 \end{pmatrix}$. Find also the angle between the vectors $\begin{pmatrix} -1 \\ 2 \\ 3 \end{pmatrix}$ and $\begin{pmatrix} 4 \\ 2 \\ -7 \end{pmatrix}$.

    Give your answer in degrees correct to 1 decimal place.

8 The diagram shows the origin O, and points A and B whose position vectors are denoted by $\mathbf{a}$ and $\mathbf{b}$ respectively.

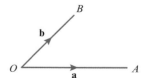

    a Copy the diagram, and show the positions of the points P and Q such that $\overrightarrow{OP} = 3\mathbf{a}$ and $\overrightarrow{OQ} = \mathbf{a} + \mathbf{b}$.

    b Given that $\mathbf{a} = \begin{pmatrix} 2 \\ 0 \end{pmatrix}$ and $\mathbf{b} = \begin{pmatrix} 1 \\ 1 \end{pmatrix}$, evaluate the scalar product $\overrightarrow{OQ}.\overrightarrow{BP}$.

    c Calculate the acute angle between the lines OQ and BP, giving your answer correct to the nearest degree.

9 The diagram shows a triangular pyramid $OABV$, whose base is the right-angled triangle OAB and whose vertical height is OV. The perpendicular unit vectors $\mathbf{i}$, $\mathbf{j}$ and $\mathbf{k}$ are directed along OA, OB and OV as shown, and the position vectors of A, B and V are given by $\overrightarrow{OA} = 10\mathbf{i}$, $\overrightarrow{OB} = 8\mathbf{j}$, $\overrightarrow{OV} = 6\mathbf{k}$.

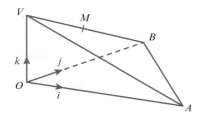

a The point M is the mid-point of VB. Find the position vector of M and the length of OM.

b The point P lies on OA, and has position vector $p\mathbf{i}$. Show that the value of the scalar product $\overrightarrow{VB}.\overrightarrow{MP}$ is -14.

c Explain briefly how you can deduce from part **b** that MP is never perpendicular to VB for any value of p.

d For the case where P is at the mid-point of OA, find angle $P\hat{M}B$, giving your answer correct to the nearest degree.

9.4 The vector equation of a line

WORKED EXAMPLE 9.4

a Find a vector equation for the line through $(2, -1)$ with gradient $\dfrac{3}{4}$.

b Hence find its Cartesian equation.

Answer

a The position vector of the point $(2, -1)$ is $\begin{pmatrix} 2 \\ -1 \end{pmatrix}$

$\mathbf{r} = \begin{pmatrix} 2 \\ -1 \end{pmatrix} + t\begin{pmatrix} 4 \\ 3 \end{pmatrix}$ .... This is the vector equation.

b $\mathbf{r} = \begin{pmatrix} 2 \\ -1 \end{pmatrix} + t\begin{pmatrix} 4 \\ 3 \end{pmatrix}$ .... Write $\mathbf{r}$ as a column vector and collect together the x, y components of the right hand side.

$\begin{pmatrix} x \\ y \end{pmatrix} = \begin{pmatrix} 2 + 4t \\ -1 + 3t \end{pmatrix}$ .... This can be written as two equations.

$x = 2 + 4t$ and $y = -1 + 3t$ ..... Now eliminate t to find the Cartesian equation.

$3x - 4y = 3(2 + 4t) - 4(-1 + 3t)$ .. Simplify.

$3x - 4y = 10$

> **TIP**
>
> The vector equation of the line is
> $r = \mathbf{a} + t\mathbf{b}$ where $\mathbf{a}$ is a point on the line, $\mathbf{b}$ is the direction vector of the line and t is a parameter.

> **TIP**
>
> Be careful! The direction vector is not $\begin{pmatrix} 3 \\ 4 \end{pmatrix}$ since 4 units across and 3 units up is $\begin{pmatrix} 4 \\ 3 \end{pmatrix}$.

1 Find a vector equation of the line which passes through $(1, 4, 2)$ and $(-2, 3, 3)$ and find the coordinates of its point of intersection with the line with vector equation $\mathbf{r} = \begin{pmatrix} 1 \\ 0 \\ 2 \end{pmatrix} + t\begin{pmatrix} 3 \\ -1 \\ -1 \end{pmatrix}$.

2 Write down vector equations for the lines through the given points in the specified directions. Then eliminate t to obtain the Cartesian equation.

   a $(2, -3)$, $\begin{pmatrix} 1 \\ 2 \end{pmatrix}$ b $(4, 1)$, $\begin{pmatrix} -3 \\ 2 \end{pmatrix}$

   c $(5, 7)$, parallel to the x-axis   d $(0, 0)$, $\begin{pmatrix} 2 \\ -1 \end{pmatrix}$

   e (a, b), $\begin{pmatrix} 0 \\ 1 \end{pmatrix}$ f $(\cos \alpha, \sin \alpha)$, $\begin{pmatrix} -\sin \alpha \\ \cos \alpha \end{pmatrix}$

3 Write down the vector equation of the straight line:

   a parallel to the vector $3\mathbf{i} - 2\mathbf{j}$ which passes through the point P with position vector $-\mathbf{i} + \mathbf{j}$

   b parallel to the line $r = 2\mathbf{i} + t(\mathbf{i} + 5\mathbf{j})$ which passes through point P with coordinates $(3, -1)$

   c which passes through the points with position vectors $\begin{pmatrix} -3 \\ 4 \end{pmatrix}$ and $\begin{pmatrix} -1 \\ 1 \end{pmatrix}$

   d parallel to the x-axis and through the point $(-2, 2, 1)$.

4 Find the value of the constant k if the two lines represented by the vector equations

$$\mathbf{r} = \begin{pmatrix} 3 \\ -1 \\ 0 \end{pmatrix} + t\begin{pmatrix} k \\ 2 \\ 0 \end{pmatrix} \text{ and } \mathbf{r} = -2\mathbf{i} + 4\mathbf{j} + s(6\mathbf{i} + 3\mathbf{j}) \text{ are parallel.}$$

5 B is at the foot of the perpendicular from a point $A(2, 4, 3)$ on the line which joins the points P and Q whose position vectors are $\overrightarrow{OP} = \begin{pmatrix} 1 \\ 2 \\ 4 \end{pmatrix}$ and $\overrightarrow{OQ} = \begin{pmatrix} 3 \\ 4 \\ 5 \end{pmatrix}$. Find the coordinates of B.

6 Relative to a fixed point O, points P and Q have position vectors $\begin{pmatrix} 9 \\ 5 \\ -3 \end{pmatrix}$ and $\begin{pmatrix} 11 \\ 7 \\ -3 \end{pmatrix}$ respectively.

   a Find, in vector form, an equation of the line L which passes through P and Q.

   The point R lies on the line L. OR is perpendicular to L.

   b Find:

      i the coordinates of R

      ii the exact area of triangle OPQ.

7 a Find (in $\mathbf{i}$, $\mathbf{j}$, $\mathbf{k}$ form), the vector equation $\mathbf{r}$ of a line whose parametric equations are

      $x = 3t + 2$ $y = 2t$ $z = -6t - 5$

   b Show that the point $(8, 4, -17)$ lies on this line.

8 The lines l_1 and l_2 have equations $\mathbf{r} = \begin{pmatrix} 3 \\ 5 \\ 1 \end{pmatrix} + s\begin{pmatrix} 1 \\ 2 \\ -4 \end{pmatrix}$ and $\mathbf{r} = \begin{pmatrix} 0 \\ 2 \\ 4 \end{pmatrix} + t\begin{pmatrix} 1 \\ -1 \\ 5 \end{pmatrix}$ respectively.

   a Show that l_1 and l_2 intersect, and find the position vector of the point of intersection.

   The plane p passes through the point with position vector $\begin{pmatrix} 3 \\ 5 \\ 1 \end{pmatrix}$ and is perpendicular to l_1.

   b Find the equation of p, giving your answer in the form $ax + by + cz = d$.

   c Find the position vector of the point of intersection of l_2 and p.

   d Find the acute angle between l_2 and p.

9 Find the distance of the point $(1,\ 1,\ 4)$ from the line $\mathbf{r} = \mathbf{i} - 2\mathbf{j} + \mathbf{k} + t(-2\mathbf{i} + \mathbf{j} + 2\mathbf{k})$.

9.5 Intersection of two lines

WORKED EXAMPLE 9.5

a Prove that the straight line L_1 with equation $\mathbf{r} = \begin{pmatrix} 1 \\ 2 \\ -3 \end{pmatrix} + t\begin{pmatrix} 2 \\ -1 \\ 4 \end{pmatrix}$ meets the line L_2

joining $(2, 4, 4)$ to $(3, 3, 5)$.

b Find the point of intersection.

c Find the cosine of the angle between the lines.

Answer

a $\mathbf{r} = \begin{pmatrix} 2 \\ 4 \\ 4 \end{pmatrix} + s\begin{pmatrix} 3-2 \\ 3-4 \\ 5-4 \end{pmatrix}$ Simplify to find L_2.

$\mathbf{r} = \begin{pmatrix} 2 \\ 4 \\ 4 \end{pmatrix} + s\begin{pmatrix} 1 \\ -1 \\ 1 \end{pmatrix}$ This is L_2.

$\begin{pmatrix} 1 \\ 2 \\ -3 \end{pmatrix} + t\begin{pmatrix} 2 \\ -1 \\ 4 \end{pmatrix} = \begin{pmatrix} 2 \\ 4 \\ 4 \end{pmatrix} + s\begin{pmatrix} 1 \\ -1 \\ 1 \end{pmatrix}$ Prove that L_2 intersects L_1.

$2t - s = 1$ ----------(1)   Now write as a set of three equations. Sets of three equations in two unknowns may or may not have a solution.

$-t + s = 2$ ----------(2)

$4t - s = 7$ ----------(3)

$2t - s = 1$ ----------(1)   Select any two equations.

$-t + s = 2$ ----------(2)

Solving gives $t = 3$ and $s = 5$ $\cdots\cdots$ Check by substituting into (3).

$4(3) - 5 = 7$ -------(3) $\cdots\cdots\cdots$ True, so all 3 equations are consistent with $t = 3$
$7 = 7$ and $s = 5$.

$\therefore$ The lines L_1 and L_2 intersect.

b $L_1: \mathbf{r} = \begin{pmatrix} 1 \\ 2 \\ -3 \end{pmatrix} + t\begin{pmatrix} 2 \\ -1 \\ 4 \end{pmatrix}$ $\cdots\cdots\cdots$ To find the intersection point, substitute
$t = 3$ into L_1.

The intersection point is
$(7, -1, \ 9)$.

c $\begin{pmatrix} 2 \\ -1 \\ 4 \end{pmatrix} \cdot \begin{pmatrix} 1 \\ -1 \\ 1 \end{pmatrix} = \left| \begin{pmatrix} 2 \\ -1 \\ 4 \end{pmatrix} \right| \left| \begin{pmatrix} 1 \\ -1 \\ 1 \end{pmatrix} \right| \cos \theta$

$2(1) - 1(-1) + 4(1) = \sqrt{2^2 + (-1)^2 + 4^2} \times \sqrt{1^2 + (-1)^2 + 1^2} \cos \theta$

$7 = \sqrt{21}\sqrt{3} \cos \theta$

$\cos \theta = \dfrac{\sqrt{7}}{3}$ $\cdots\cdots\cdots\cdots\cdots\cdots$ **Note:** You do not need to find θ in this question.

EXERCISE 9E

1 Find the point of intersection, if any, of each of the following pairs
of lines.

a $\mathbf{r} = \begin{pmatrix} 1 \\ 3 \\ 1 \end{pmatrix} + s\begin{pmatrix} -2 \\ -1 \\ 2 \end{pmatrix}, \mathbf{r} = \begin{pmatrix} 0 \\ -2 \\ 8 \end{pmatrix} + t\begin{pmatrix} 1 \\ -1 \\ 1 \end{pmatrix}$

b $\mathbf{r} = \begin{pmatrix} 1 \\ -1 \\ 2 \end{pmatrix} + s\begin{pmatrix} -1 \\ 2 \\ -1 \end{pmatrix}, \mathbf{r} = \begin{pmatrix} 1 \\ 3 \\ -1 \end{pmatrix} + t\begin{pmatrix} 2 \\ -8 \\ 5 \end{pmatrix}$

2 For each of the following sets of points A, B, C and D, determine
whether the lines AB and CD are parallel, intersect each other, or
are skew.

a $A(3, 2, 4)$, $B(-3, -7, -8)$, $C(0, 1, 3)$, $D(-2, 5, 9)$

b $A(3, 1, 0)$, $B(-3, 1, 3)$, $C(5, 0, -1)$, $D(1, 0, 1)$

c $A(-5, -4, -3)$, $B(5, 1, 2)$, $C(-1, -3, 0)$, $D(8, 0, 6)$

 TIP

Two lines in
3-dimensional space
could be:

- parallel

- not parallel but
  intersect

- not parallel and
  do not intersect
  (skew).

3 Two lines have equations $\mathbf{r} = \begin{pmatrix} 3 \\ 2 \\ -1 \end{pmatrix} + \lambda \begin{pmatrix} 1 \\ 2 \\ -1 \end{pmatrix}$ and

   $\mathbf{r} = \begin{pmatrix} 1 \\ 0 \\ -3 \end{pmatrix} + \mu \begin{pmatrix} 0 \\ -1 \\ 2 \end{pmatrix}$. Show that the lines intersect, and find the

   acute angle between the lines.

PS 4 Two lines are at an angle of 60° to each other. The first has

   equation $\mathbf{r} = \begin{pmatrix} 1 \\ 4 \\ 2 \end{pmatrix} + \lambda \begin{pmatrix} 1 \\ 0 \\ 1 \end{pmatrix}$ and the second has equation

   $\mathbf{r} = \begin{pmatrix} 1 \\ 4 \\ 2 \end{pmatrix} + \lambda \begin{pmatrix} 0 \\ 1 \\ k \end{pmatrix}$. Find k.

END-OF-CHAPTER REVIEW EXERCISE 9

1 **a** Find a vector equation for the line joining $(1, 1)$ and $(5, -1)$.

   b Another line has the vector equation $\mathbf{r} = \begin{pmatrix} 3 \\ 4 \end{pmatrix} + t \begin{pmatrix} 1 \\ 3 \end{pmatrix}$. Find the point of intersection of the two lines.

2 The line l_1 has equation $\mathbf{r} = 3\mathbf{i} + a\mathbf{j} - 2\mathbf{k} + s(\mathbf{i} + \mathbf{j} + \mathbf{k})$, and the line l_2 has equation $\mathbf{r} = \mathbf{i} + 4\mathbf{j} + b\mathbf{k} + t(\mathbf{i} - 2\mathbf{j} + 2\mathbf{k})$, where a and b are constants. Given that the lines intersect at the point A with coordinates $(4, p, q)$:

   a find, in any order, the values of a, b, p and q

   b find the acute angle between the lines.

PS 3 Find the intersection of the lines $\mathbf{r} = \begin{pmatrix} -1 \\ 0 \end{pmatrix} + s \begin{pmatrix} \cos \alpha \\ \sin \alpha \end{pmatrix}$ and $\mathbf{r} = \begin{pmatrix} 1 \\ 0 \end{pmatrix} + t \begin{pmatrix} -\sin \alpha \\ \cos \alpha \end{pmatrix}$, giving

   your answer in a simplified form. Interpret your answer geometrically.

PS 4 Four points A, B, C and D with position vectors $\mathbf{a}$, $\mathbf{b}$, $\mathbf{c}$ and $\mathbf{d}$ are vertices of a tetrahedron. The mid-points of BC, CA, AB, AD, BD, CD are denoted by P, Q, R, U, V, W. Find the position vectors of the mid-points of PU, QV and RW. What do you notice about the answers? State your conclusion as a geometrical theorem.

5 Find a vector equation of the line l containing the points $(1, 3, 1)$ and $(1, -3, -1)$.

   Find the perpendicular distance of the point with coordinates $(2, -1, 1)$ from l.

6 Determine whether the points with coordinates $P(5, 1, -6)$ and $Q(-7, 5, 9)$ lie on the line joining $A(1, 2, -1)$ to $B(-3, 3, 4)$.

7   Vectors $\mathbf{r}_1$ and $\mathbf{r}_2$ are given by $\mathbf{r}_1 = t\mathbf{i} + (2t - 1)\mathbf{j} - \mathbf{k}$ and $\mathbf{r}_2 = (1 - t)\mathbf{i} + 3t\mathbf{j} + (4t - 1)\mathbf{k}$, where t is a scalar.

   a Find the values of t for which $\mathbf{r}_1$ and $\mathbf{r}_2$ are perpendicular.

   When $t = 2$, $\mathbf{r}_1$ and $\mathbf{r}_2$ are the position vectors of the points P and Q respectively, with reference to an origin O.

   b Find $\overrightarrow{PQ}$.

   c Find the size of the acute angle QPO giving your answer to the nearest degree.

8   Find the exact distance of the point Q with coordinates $(1,\ 2,\ 3)$ from the straight line whose equation is $\mathbf{r} = 3\mathbf{i} + 4\mathbf{j} - 2\mathbf{k} + t(\mathbf{i} - 2\mathbf{j} + 2\mathbf{k})$.

9   The points P and Q have position vectors $\begin{pmatrix} 2 \\ -1 \\ -5 \end{pmatrix}$ and $\begin{pmatrix} 0 \\ 3 \\ -4 \end{pmatrix}$ respectively, relative to the origin.

   a Find in vector form the equation of line L_1 which passes through P and Q.

   The line L_2 has equation $r = \begin{pmatrix} 6 \\ -5 \\ 1 \end{pmatrix} + t\begin{pmatrix} x \\ -3 \\ 1 \end{pmatrix}$ where x is a constant. Given that L_1 and L_2 intersect:

   b find the value of x and the coordinates of the point where L_1 and L_2 intersect.

10 Find in degrees to the nearest degree, the obtuse angle between the lines with Cartesian equations $\dfrac{4 - x}{4} = \dfrac{y + 1}{7} = \dfrac{3 - z}{4}$ and $\dfrac{x - 2}{3} = \dfrac{y}{2} = \dfrac{z + 5}{-6}$.

- Formulate a simple statement involving a rate of change as a differential equation.
- Find, by integration, a general form of solution for a first order differential equation in which the variables are separable.
- Use an initial condition to find a particular solution.
- Interpret the solution of a differential equation in the context of a problem being modelled by the equation.

10.1 The technique of separating the variables

WORKED EXAMPLE 10.1

Find the general solution of each of the following.

a $\dfrac{dy}{dx} = xy \sin x$ **b** $\dfrac{dy}{dx} = y^2 \ln x$

Answer

a $\dfrac{dy}{dx} = xy \sin x$ $\cdots\cdots\cdots\cdots\cdots$ Separate the variables x and y.

$\dfrac{1}{y}\dfrac{dy}{dx} = x \sin x$ $\cdots\cdots\cdots\cdots\cdots$ Form integrals of both sides with respect to x.

$\displaystyle\int \dfrac{1}{y}\dfrac{dy}{dx}\, dx = \int x \sin x\, dx$ $\cdots\cdots$ Integrate each side. (Use integration by parts for the right hand side.)

 TIP

We studied integration by parts in Section 8.6.

$\ln |y| = -x\cos x + \displaystyle\int \cos x\, dx$

$\ln |y| = -x\cos x + \sin x + c$

$\ln |y| = \sin x - x\cos x + c$

$y = e^{\sin x - x\cos x + c}$

$y = e^{\sin x - x\cos x} \times e^c$ $\cdots\cdots\cdots\cdots$ Let $k = e^c$.

$y = ke^{\sin x - x\cos x}$

b $\dfrac{dy}{dx} = y^2 \ln x$ $\cdots\cdots\cdots\cdots\cdots$ Separate the variables x and y.

$\dfrac{1}{y^2}\dfrac{dy}{dx} = \ln x$ $\cdots\cdots\cdots\cdots\cdots$ Form integrals of both sides with respect to x.

$$\int \frac{1}{y^2} \frac{dy}{dx} dx = \int \ln x \, dx$$ ⋯⋯⋯ Use integration by parts for the right hand side.

$$-y^{-1} = x\ln x - x + c$$

$$\frac{1}{y} = -x\ln x + x - c$$ ⋯⋯⋯ Let $-c = k$.

$$\frac{1}{y} = -x\ln x + x + k$$

$$y = \frac{1}{x - x\ln x + k}$$

124

TIP

$$\int \ln x \, dx \to \int 1 \ln x \, dx$$

$$u = \ln x \quad \frac{du}{dx} = \frac{1}{x}$$

$$\frac{dv}{dx} = 1 \to v = x$$

$$\int u \frac{dv}{dx} dx = uv - \int v \frac{du}{dx} dx$$

$$\int \ln x \, dx = x\ln x - x + c$$

EXERCISE 10A

1 Find the general solution of the following differential equations.

a i $\dfrac{dy}{dx} = 3 \sin 2x$

ii $\dfrac{dy}{dx} = 4\cos\left(\dfrac{x}{3}\right)$

b i $3\dfrac{dy}{dx} - 2e^{2x} = 0$

ii $4e^{\frac{x}{2}} - \dfrac{dy}{dx} = 0$

c i $\cos^2 x \dfrac{dy}{dx} = 3$

ii $\cot^2 x \dfrac{dy}{dx} = 1$

d i $x^3 \dfrac{dy}{dx} = \ln x$

ii $\cos^2 x \dfrac{dy}{dx} = \sin x$

2 Find the particular solution of the following differential equations.

a i $\dfrac{dy}{dx} = \dfrac{2}{\sqrt{3x + 9}}$, $y = 2$ when $x = 0$

ii $\dfrac{dy}{dx} = \dfrac{1}{\sqrt{4 - x}}$, $y = 1$ when $x = 3$

b i $(x^2 + 1)\dfrac{dy}{dx} = 2x$, $y = 0$ when $x = 1$

ii $2x\dfrac{dy}{dx} = x^2 + 1$, $y = 1$ when $x = 1$

c **i** $\dfrac{1}{2} e^{3x} \dfrac{dy}{dx} = 3$, $y = 0$ when $x = 0$ **ii** $e^{2x-1} \dfrac{dy}{dx} = 4$, $y = 0$ when $x = \dfrac{1}{2}$

d **i** $\sec x \dfrac{dy}{dx} = \sin^3 x$, $y = \dfrac{13}{64}$ when $x = \dfrac{\pi}{3}$ **ii** $\cos^3 x \dfrac{dy}{dx} = \sin x$, $y = 5$ when $x = \dfrac{\pi}{4}$

3 Find the particular solutions of the following differential equations. You do not need to give the equation for y explicitly.

a **i** $\dfrac{dy}{dx} = \dfrac{\sin x}{\cos y}$, $y = 0$ when $x = \dfrac{\pi}{3}$ **ii** $\dfrac{dy}{dx} = \dfrac{\sec^2 x}{\sec^2 y}$, $y = 0$ when $x = \dfrac{\pi}{3}$

b **i** $\dfrac{dy}{dx} = x^2 y$, $y = 1$ when $x = 0$ **ii** $\dfrac{dy}{dx} = \dfrac{y^2}{x}$, $y = 1$ when $x = 1$

c **i** $\dfrac{dy}{dx} = 2e^{x+2y}$, $y = 0$ when $x = 0$ **ii** $\dfrac{dy}{dx} = e^{x-y}$, $y = 2$ when $x = 0$

4 Find the general solution of the following differential equations, giving your answer in the form $y = f(x)$, simplified as far as possible.

a **i** $2y \dfrac{dy}{dx} = 3x^2$ **ii** $\dfrac{1}{y^2} \dfrac{dy}{dx} = 2x$

b **i** $x \dfrac{dy}{dx} = \sec y$ **ii** $(x-2) \dfrac{dy}{dx} = \cos^2 y$

c **i** $(x-1) \dfrac{dy}{dx} = x(y+3)$ **ii** $\dfrac{(1-x^2)dy}{dx} = xy + y$

5 Find the general solution of the differential equation $x \dfrac{dy}{dx} + 4 = y^2$, giving your answer in the form $y = f(x)$.

6 Given that $\dfrac{dy}{dx} = \sqrt{\dfrac{1-y^2}{1-x^2}}$ and that $y = \dfrac{\sqrt{3}}{2}$ when $x = \dfrac{1}{2}$, show that $2y = x\sqrt{k} + \sqrt{1-x^2}$, where k is a constant to be found.

7 The population of fish in a lake, N thousand, can be modelled by the differential equation $\dfrac{dN}{dt} = (0.8 - 0.14t)N$, where t is the time, in years, since the fish were first introduced into the lake. Initially there are 2000 fish.

  a Show that the population initially increases and find when it starts to decrease.

  b Find the expression for N in terms of t.

  c Hence find the maximum population of fish in the lake.

  d What does this model predict about the size of the population in the long term?

8 Find the particular solution of the differential equation $\dfrac{dy}{dx} = \cos x \cos^2 y$ such that $y = \dfrac{\pi}{4}$ when $x = \dfrac{\pi}{6}$.

10.2 Forming a differential equation from a problem

WORKED EXAMPLE 10.2

In a simple model of a population of bacteria, the decay rate is assumed to be proportional to the number of bacteria.

a Let N be the number of bacteria after t minutes. Initially there are 3000 bacteria and this number decreases to 1800 after 12 minutes. Write and solve a differential equation to find the number of bacteria after t minutes.

b Comment on one limitation of this model.

Answer

a $\dfrac{\mathrm{d}N}{\mathrm{d}t} \propto N$ .... The rate of decay is proportional to N.

$\dfrac{\mathrm{d}N}{\mathrm{d}t} = -kN$ .... Separate the variables N and t.

$\dfrac{1}{N}\,\mathrm{d}N = -k\,\mathrm{d}t$ .... Form integrals of both sides.

$\displaystyle\int \dfrac{1}{N}\dfrac{\mathrm{d}N}{\mathrm{d}t}\,\mathrm{d}t = \int -k\,\mathrm{d}t$ .... Integrate each side.

$\ln|N| = -kt + c$ .... Since N cannot be negative, we do not need the modulus sign.

$\ln N = -kt + c$ .... When $t = 0$, $N = 3000$

$\ln 3000 = -k(0) + c$

$c = \ln 3000$

$\ln N = -kt + \ln 3000$

$kt = \ln\dfrac{3000}{N}$

$t = \dfrac{1}{k}\ln\dfrac{3000}{N}$ .... When $t = 12$, $N = 1800$

$12 = \dfrac{1}{k}\ln\dfrac{3000}{1800}$

$k = \dfrac{1}{12}\ln\dfrac{5}{3}$

$\ln N = -\dfrac{1}{12}\ln\dfrac{5}{3}t + \ln 3000$

$N = \mathrm{e}^{-\frac{1}{12}\ln\frac{5}{3}t + \ln 3000}$ or

$N = \dfrac{1}{\mathrm{e}^{\frac{1}{12}\ln\frac{5}{3}t + \ln 3000}}$

TIP

Initial conditions can be used to find the constant of integration.

b   Using this model, as t increases, N decreases and comes close to, but never actually reaches zero bacteria. This is **unlikely** to be the case in real life.

1   Write differential equations to describe the following situations. You do not need to solve the equations.

    a   **i**   A population increases at a rate equal to 5 times the size of the population (N).

        ii   The mass of a substance (M) decreases at a rate equal to three times the current mass.

    b   **i**   The rate of change of velocity is directly proportional to the velocity and inversely proportional to the square root of time.

        ii   The population size increases at a rate proportional to the square root of the population size (N) and to the cube root of time.

    c   **i**   The area of a circular stain increases at a rate proportional to the square root of the radius. Find an equation for the rate of change of radius with respect to time.

        ii   The volume of a sphere decreases at a constant rate of $0.8\,\text{m}^3\text{s}^{-1}$. Find an equation for the rate of decrease of the radius.

2   A tank contains 1000 litres of water, which contains 15 kg of a dissolved chemical. Water enters the tank from above at a rate of 10 litres/minute and the contents are thoroughly mixed. The resulting solution leaves the bottom of the tank at a rate of 10 litres/minute. Using A as the amount of chemical (in kg) present in the mixture after t minutes, form a differential equation and find how much of the chemical is in the tank at the end of t minutes.

3   A balloon is expanding and, at time t seconds, its surface area is $A\,\text{cm}^2$. The balloon's expansion is such that the rate of increase of A is proportional to $\dfrac{1}{\sqrt{A}}$. When the surface area is $1600\,\text{cm}^2$, it is increasing at $80\,\text{cm}^2\,\text{s}^{-1}$.

    a   Form a differential equation using this information.

       It is given that $A = 400\,\text{cm}^2$ when $t = 0$.

    b   Find to the nearest second, the time when $A = 1600\,\text{cm}^2$.

4 A tree is planted as a seedling of negligible height. The rate of increase in its height, in metres per year, is given by the formula $0.2\sqrt{25 - h}$, where h is the height of the tree, in metres, t years after it is planted.

    a Explain why the height of the tree can never exceed 25 metres.

    b Write down a differential equation connecting h and t, and solve it to find an expression for t as a function of h.

    c How long does it take for the tree to put on:

       i its first metre of growth   ii its last metre of growth?

    d Find an expression for the height of the tree after t years. Over what interval of values of t is this model valid?

5 A quantity has the value A at a time t seconds and is decreasing at a rate proportional to $\sqrt{A}$.

    a Write down a differential equation relating A and t.

    b By solving your differential equation, show that $A = (a - bt)^2$ where a and b are constants.

    c Given that when $t = 0$, $A = 400$, find the value of a.

    d Given also that when $t = 20$, $A = 100$, find the value of A when $t = 10$.

 TIP

Sometimes a problem has several variables and you need to use the geometric context and related rates of change to produce a single differential equation.

6 Alice is training for a race and, each day, she runs 15 km. On one particular day, after t hours she had run x km. During the run, she decided to vary her speed so that the rate of increase of x was directly proportional to x multiplied by the distance she had left to run.

    a Form a differential equation for x.

    b Given that after the first hour she had run 7.5 km, and that after $1\frac{1}{2}$ hours she had run 10 km, solve the differential equation and use it to find the **total** distance she had run after 2 hours.

7 A cylindrical tank with a cross sectional area $5\,\text{m}^2$ and height 4 m is initially filled with water. The water leaks out of the bottom of the tank at a rate of $0.08\sqrt{h}\,\text{m}^3\text{s}^{-1}$, where h is the height of water in the tank after t seconds.

    a Find an equation for $\dfrac{dh}{dt}$ in terms of h.

    b Hence find how long it takes for the tank to empty.

8   Newton's law of cooling states that the rate of change of
    temperature of a body is proportional to the difference in
    temperature between the body and its surroundings. A bottle of
    milk has a temperature of 5°C when it is initially taken out of the
    fridge, then it is placed on the table in the kitchen where the room
    temperature is 19°C. Initially, the milk is warming up at a rate of
    4.2°C per minute.

   a   Show that $\dfrac{d\theta}{dt} = 0.3(19 - \theta)$, where θ°C is the temperature of the
       milk and t is the time in minutes since the milk was taken out of
       the fridge.

   b   Solve the differential equation and hence find how long it takes,
       to the nearest minute, for the temperature of the milk to reach
       the kitchen temperature, correct to the nearest degree.

9   Consider the following model of population growth of an ants'
    nest: $\dfrac{dN}{dt} = 1.2N - 0.4N^2$, where N thousand is the population size
    at time t months.

   a   Suggest what the term $-0.4N^2$ could represent.

   b   Given that initially $N = 1.5$, solve the differential equation.

   c   Show that the solution may be written as $N = \dfrac{3}{1 + e^{-1.2t}}$.

       Hence describe what happens to the population in the long
       term.

END-OF-CHAPTER REVIEW EXERCISE 10

1 Find the general solution of the equations:

   a $\dfrac{dy}{dx} = \dfrac{2x(y^2 + 1)}{(x^2 + 1)}$

   b $\dfrac{dy}{dx} = \tan x \cot y$

2 Find the equations of the curves which satisfy the following differential equations and pass through the given points.

   a $\dfrac{dy}{dx} = \dfrac{y(x + 4)}{(1 + x)(2 - x)}$ $(3, 2)$

   b $\dfrac{dy}{dx} = \cot x \cot y$ $\left(\dfrac{1}{6}\pi, 0\right)$

   c $\dfrac{dy}{dx} = \dfrac{1 + y^2}{y(1 - x^2)}$ $\left(\dfrac{3}{2}, 2\right)$

   d $\dfrac{dy}{dx} = y \tan x$ $(0, 2)$

3 Find the general solution of the differential equations:

   a $4 + x\dfrac{dy}{dx} = y^2$

   b $e^y \dfrac{dy}{dx} - 1 = \ln x$

   c $y \cos x \dfrac{dy}{dx} = 2 - y\dfrac{dy}{dx}$

4 The size of an insect population n, which fluctuates during the year, is modelled by the equation $\dfrac{dn}{dt} = 0.01n(0.05 - \cos 0.02t)$, where t is the number of days from the start of observations. The initial number of insects is 5000.

   a Solve the differential equation to find n in terms of t.

   b Show that the model predicts that the number of insects will fall to a minimum after about 76 days, and find this minimum value.

5 One model for the growth of bacteria in a petri dish is given by the differential equation $\dfrac{dN}{dt} = \dfrac{N(1000 - N)}{200}$, where N is the number of bacteria (measured in thousands) present t hours after the start of the experiment. Initially, $N = 2$.

   a Determine a formula for N in terms of t.

   b Determine the number of bacteria present after 1 hours, according to this model, to 2 significant figures.

   c Describe the long-term behaviour of the number of bacteria predicted by this model.

6 The volume of a spherical balloon of radius r cm is V cm³, where $V = \dfrac{4}{3}\pi r^3$.

   a Find $\dfrac{dV}{dr}$.

   The balloon is filled in such a way that the volume, at time t seconds, increases according to the rule $\dfrac{dV}{dt} = \dfrac{1600}{(1 + t)^2}$. Initially, the volume of the balloon is zero.

   b Find $\dfrac{dr}{dt}$ in terms of r and t.

   c Solve the differential equation $\dfrac{dV}{dt} = \dfrac{1600}{(1 + t)^2}$ to obtain a formula for V in terms of t.

   d   Hence find, giving your answers to 2 significant figures:

      i   the radius of the balloon

      ii   the rate of increase of the radius of the balloon after 10 seconds.

M 7   A population of fish initially contains 250 fish, and increases at the rate of 10 fish per month. Let N be the number of fish after t months. In a simple model of population growth, the rate of increase is directly proportional to the population size.

   a   Show that $\dfrac{dN}{dt} = 0.04\,N$.

   b   Solve the differential equation and find how long it takes for the population of fish to reach 1000.

   c   Comment on the long-term suitability of this model.

   An improved model takes into account seasonal variation: $\dfrac{dN}{dt} = 0.04\,N\left(1 + 2.5\cos\left(\dfrac{\pi t}{6}\right)\right)$

   d   Given that initially there are 250 fish, find an expression for the size of the population after t months.

8   A particle moves in a straight line. Its acceleration depends on the displacement as follows: $\dfrac{dv}{dt} = -8e^{-4x}$.

   a   Find an expression for $\dfrac{dv}{dx}$ in terms of x and v.

   Initially the particle is at the origin and its speed is $2\,\mathrm{m\,s^{-1}}$. The velocity of the particle remains positive for $t > 0$.

   b   Show that $v = 2e^{-2x}$.

   c   Find expressions for the displacement and velocity in terms of time.

9   Water is flowing out of a small hole at the bottom of a conical container, which has a vertical axis. At time t, the depth of the water in the container is x and the volume of the water in the container is V (see diagram). You are given that V is proportional to x^3, and that the rate at which V decreases is proportional to $\sqrt{x}$.

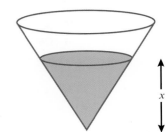

   a   Express $\dfrac{dV}{dt}$ in terms of x, $\dfrac{dx}{dt}$ and a constant.

   b   Show that x satisfies a differential equation of the form $\dfrac{dx}{dt} = -\dfrac{A}{x^{\frac{3}{2}}}$, where A is a positive constant.

   c   Find the general solution of the differential equation in part **b**.

   d   Given that $x = 4$ when $t = 0$ and that $x = 1$ when $t = 1$, find the value of t when $x = 0$.

10 The population of a community with finite resources is modelled by the differential equation $\dfrac{dn}{dt} = 0.01\,n\mathrm{e}^{-0.01t}$, where n is the population at time t. At time $t = 0$ the population is 5000.

    a Solve the differential equation, expressing $\ln n$ in terms of t.

    b What happens to the population as t becomes large?

11 An inverted cone has base radius 4cm and height 10cm. The cone is filled with water at a constant rate of $80\,\mathrm{cm}^3\,\mathrm{s}^{-1}$.

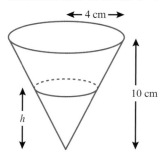

    a Show that the height of water (h) satisfies the differential equation $\pi h^2 \dfrac{dh}{dt} = 500$.

    b Given that the cone is initially empty, find how long it takes to fill it.

Chapter 11
Complex numbers

P3 **This chapter is for Pure Mathematics 3 students only.**

- Understand the idea of a complex number, recall the meaning of the terms real part, imaginary part, modulus, argument, conjugate and use the fact that two complex numbers are equal if and only if both their real and their imaginary parts are equal.
- Carry out operations of addition, subtraction, multiplication and division of two complex numbers expressed in Cartesian form $x + iy$.
- Use the result that, for a polynomial equation with real coefficients, any non-real roots occur in conjugate pairs.
- Represent complex numbers geometrically by means of an Argand diagram.
- Carry out operations of multiplication and division of two complex numbers expressed in polar form $r(\cos \theta + i \sin \theta) = re^{i\theta}$.
- Find the two square roots of a complex number.
- Understand in simple terms the geometrical effects of conjugating a complex number and of adding, subtracting, multiplying and dividing two complex numbers.
- Illustrate simple equations and inequalities involving complex numbers by means of loci in an Argand diagram.

11.1 Imaginary numbers

> **WORKED EXAMPLE 11.1**
>
> Without using a calculator (and writing your answers in their simplest form) find:
>
>   **a** $\sqrt{-36}$ **b** $\sqrt{-7}$ **c** $\sqrt{-72}$ **d** $6i^2 + (6i)^2$
>
>   **e** $-3i + (-2i)^5$ **f** $\sqrt{\dfrac{12i + 24i}{2i}}$ **g** $(2i^6)^{-3}$
>
> **Answer**
>
>   **a** $\sqrt{-36} = \sqrt{36 \times -1} = \sqrt{36} \times \sqrt{-1} = 6i$
>
>   **b** $\sqrt{-7} = \sqrt{7 \times -1} = \sqrt{7} \times \sqrt{-1} = i\sqrt{7}$
>
>   **c** $\sqrt{-72} = \sqrt{36 \times 2 - 1} = \sqrt{36} \times \sqrt{2} \times \sqrt{-1} = 6i\sqrt{2}$
>
>   **d** $6i^2 + (6i)^2 = 6i^2 + 36i^2 = 42i^2 = -42$
>
>   **e** $-3i + (-2i)^5 = -3i - 32i^5 = -3i - 32i = -35i$
>
>   **f** $\sqrt{\dfrac{12i + 24i}{2i}} = \sqrt{\dfrac{36i}{2i}} = 3\sqrt{2}$
>
>   **g** $(2i^6)^{-3} = 2^{-3}i^{-18} = \dfrac{1}{8i^{18}} = \dfrac{1}{-8} = -\dfrac{1}{8}$

EXERCISE 11A

Do **not** use a calculator in this exercise.

1 Write the following numbers in their simplest form.

a $\sqrt{-169}$

b $\sqrt{-\dfrac{64}{169}}$

c $\sqrt{-90}$

d $\sqrt{-64} + \sqrt{-16}$

2 Simplify:

a $(-5i)^2 + 5i^2$

b $3i - (i\sqrt{3})^4$

c $\dfrac{16i^2 - 64i^4}{4}$

d $\dfrac{-10}{12i^2}$

3 Solve:

a $x^2 + \dfrac{4}{9} = 0$

b $3x^2 + 4 = 0$

c $16x^2 + 25 = 0$

11.2 Complex numbers

WORKED EXAMPLE 11.2

One root of the quadratic equation $x^2 + px + q = 0$ is $2 - 3i$. Find the values of p and q.

Answer

If one root is $2 - 3i$, the other must be $2 + 3i$.

⋯⋯ Use this to find the roots α and β.

$\alpha + \beta = 4$ and
$\alpha\beta = (2 + 3i)(2 - 3i) = 13$

So the equation can be written
$x^2 - 4x + 13 = 0$

⋯⋯ Any quadratic equation can be written in the form $x^2 - (\text{sum of roots})x + (\text{product of roots}) = 0$

$\therefore p = -4, \ q = 13$

TIP

For any quadratic relationship $ax^2 + bx + c = 0$, the roots α and β satisfy the relationships
$\alpha + \beta = -\dfrac{b}{a}$ and
$\alpha\beta = \dfrac{c}{a}$.

EXERCISE 11B

Do **not** use a calculator in this exercise.

1 If $p = 2 + 3i$ and $q = 2 - 3i$, express the following in the form $a + bi$, where a and b are real numbers.

a $p + q$

b $p - q$

c pq

d $(p + q)(p - q)$

e $p^2 - q^2$

f $p^2 + q^2$

g $(p + q)^2$

h $(p - q)^2$

2 If $r = 3 + i$ and $s = 1 - 2i$, express the following in the form $a + bi$, where a and b are real numbers.

    a $r + s$ **b** $r - s$ **c** $2r + s$ **d** $r + si$

    e rs **f** r^2 **g** $\dfrac{r}{s}$ **h** $\dfrac{s}{r}$

    i $\dfrac{r}{i}$ **j** $(1 + i)r$ **k** $\dfrac{s}{1 + i}$ **l** $\dfrac{1 - i}{s}$

3 If $(2 + i)(x + yi) = 1 + 3i$, where x and y are real numbers, write two equations connecting x and y, and solve them.

4 If $p = 3 + 4i$, $q = 1 - i$ and $r = -2 + 3i$, solve the following equations for the complex number z.

    a $p + z = q$ **b** $2r + 3z = p$

    c $qz = r$ **d** $pz + q = r$

5 Solve these pairs of simultaneous equations for the complex numbers z and w.

    a $(1 + i)z + (2 - i)w = 3 + 4i$ **b** $5z - (3 + i)w = 7 - i$

        $iz + (3 + i)w = -1 + 5i$ $(2 - i)z + 2iw = -1 + i$

6 Solve the following quadratic equations, giving answers in the form $a + bi$, where a and b are real numbers.

    a $z^2 + 9 = 0$ **b** $z^2 + 4z + 5 = 0$

    c $z^2 - 6z + 25 = 0$ **d** $2z^2 + 2z + 13 = 0$

7 Write down the conjugates of:

    a $1 + 7i$ **b** $-2 + i$ **c** 5 **d** $3i$

8 Find in the form $a + bi$ (with $b > 0$) the complex number which satisfies the simultaneous equations $zz^* = 25$ and $z + z^* = 6$.

9 Find the quadratic equations which have the following roots:

    a $1 + 2i,\ 1 - 2i$ **b** $3 + 4i,\ 3 - 4i$ **c** $-1 + i\sqrt{5},\ -1 - i\sqrt{5}$

10 Find the real values of x and y, given that:
$$x(1 + 2i) + y(2 - i) = 4 + 3i$$

11 Find the complex numbers which satisfy the following equations.

    a $(1 + i)z = 1 + 3i$ **b** $z^2 + 4z + 13 = 0$

    c $(1 - i)z^2 - 4z + (1 + 3i) = 0$ **d** $\begin{cases} (1 - i)z + (1 + i)w = 2 \\ (1 + 3i)z - (4 + i)w = 3i \end{cases}$

 TIP

Use the quadratic formula.

135

11.3 The complex plane

Express:

a $5 + 12i$ in the form:

    i $r(\cos\theta + i\sin\theta)$

    ii $re^{i\theta}$

b $e^{-\frac{i\pi}{4}}$ in the form:

    i $\cos\theta + i\sin\theta \ (-\pi < \theta \leqslant \pi)$

    ii $a + ib \ (a, b \in \mathbb{R})$

Answer

a **i** $z = 5 + 12i$

        $r = |z| = \sqrt{5^2 + 12^2} = 13$

        $\tan\theta = \dfrac{12}{5}$

        $\theta = 1.18$ radians (3 significant figures)

        $z = 13\,(\cos 1.18 + i\sin 1.18)$

  ii $z = 13e^{1.18i}$

b **i** $e^{-\frac{i\pi}{4}} = \cos\left(-\dfrac{\pi}{4}\right) + i\sin\left(-\dfrac{\pi}{4}\right)$ Since $\cos(-\theta) = \cos\theta$ and $\sin(-\theta) = -\sin\theta$.

        $e^{-\frac{i\pi}{4}} = \cos\dfrac{\pi}{4} - i\sin\dfrac{\pi}{4}$

  ii $e^{-\frac{i\pi}{4}} = \cos\dfrac{\pi}{4} - i\sin\dfrac{\pi}{4}$

        $e^{-\frac{i\pi}{4}} = \dfrac{1}{\sqrt{2}} - i\dfrac{1}{\sqrt{2}}$

        $= \dfrac{1}{\sqrt{2}}(1 - i)$

        $= \dfrac{\sqrt{2}}{2} - \dfrac{\sqrt{2}}{2}i$

1 Points A, B and C represent i, $3 - i$ and $4 + 2i$ in an Argand diagram. D is the reflection of C in the line AB. Find the complex number which is represented by D.

2 If $s = 2\left(\cos\frac{1}{3}\pi + i\sin\frac{1}{3}\pi\right)$, $t = \cos\frac{1}{4}\pi + i\sin\frac{1}{4}\pi$ and $u = 4\left(\cos\left(-\frac{5}{6}\pi\right) + i\sin\left(-\frac{5}{6}\pi\right)\right)$,
write the following in modulus-argument form.

    a st **b** $\dfrac{s}{t}$ **c** $\dfrac{u}{s}$ **d** st^*

3 Give the answers to the following questions in modulus-argument form.

    a If $s = \cos\theta + i\sin\theta$, express s^* in terms of θ.

    b If $s = \cos\theta + i\sin\theta$, express $\dfrac{1}{s}$ in terms of θ.

    c If $t = r(\cos\theta + i\sin\theta)$, express t^* in terms of r and θ.

    d If $t = r(\cos\theta + i\sin\theta)$, express $\dfrac{1}{t}$ in terms of r and θ.

4 Write $1 + \sqrt{3}i$ and $1 - i$ in modulus-argument form. Hence express $\dfrac{(1 + \sqrt{3}i)^4}{(1 - i)^6}$ in the form $a + bi$.

5 Show in an Argand diagram the points representing the complex numbers i, $-i$ and $\sqrt{3}$. Hence write down the values of:

    a $\arg(\sqrt{3} - i)$ **b** $\arg(\sqrt{3} + i)$ **c** $\arg\dfrac{\sqrt{3} + i}{\sqrt{3} - i}$ **d** $\dfrac{2i}{\sqrt{3} + i}$

6 In an Argand diagram, plot the complex numbers:

    a $e^{\pi i}$ **b** $e^{\frac{1}{2}\pi i}$ **c** $2e^{-i}$ **d** e^{4i}

    e e^{1+i} **f** e^{-1+i} **g** e^{1-i}

7 If $z = \cos\theta + i\sin\theta$, find the modulus and argument of e^z in terms of θ.

8 Show these numbers on an Argand diagram, and write them in the form $a + bi$. Where appropriate, leave surds in your answers, or give answers correct to 2 decimal places.

    a $2\left(\cos\frac{1}{3}\pi + i\sin\frac{1}{3}\pi\right)$ **b** $10\left(\cos\frac{3}{4}\pi + i\sin\frac{3}{4}\pi\right)$

    c $5\left(\cos\left(-\frac{1}{2}\pi\right) + i\sin\left(-\frac{1}{2}\pi\right)\right)$ **d** $3(\cos\pi + i\sin\pi)$

    e $10(\cos 2 + i\sin 2)$ **f** $\cos(-3) + i\sin(-3)$

9 Write these complex numbers in modulus-argument form. Where appropriate, express the argument as a rational multiple of π. Otherwise, give the modulus and argument correct to 2 decimal places.

    a $1 + 2i$ **b** $3 - 4i$ **c** $-5 + 6i$ **d** $-7 - 8i$ **e** 1

    f $2i$ **g** -3 **h** $-4i$ **i** $\sqrt{2} - \sqrt{2}i$ **j** $-1 + \sqrt{3}i$

10 Use an Argand diagram to find, in the form $a + bi$, the complex number(s) satisfying the following pairs of equations.

    a $\arg z = \dfrac{1}{6}\pi$, $|z| = 2$ **b** $\arg (z - 3) = \dfrac{1}{2}\pi$, $|z| = 5$

    c $\arg (z - 4i) = \pi$, $|z + 6| = 5$ **d** $\arg (z - 2) = \dfrac{3}{4}\pi$, $|z + 2| = 3$

11.4 Solving equations

WORKED EXAMPLE 11.4

Without using a calculator:

    a find $\sqrt{16 - 30i}$

    b solve the quadratic equation $(2 - i)z^2 + (4 + 3i)z + (-1 + 3i) = 0$

Answer

    a $(a + bi)^2 = 16 - 30i$ Expand the left hand side.

        $a^2 + 2abi + b^2i^2 = 16 - 30i$

        $a^2 + 2abi - b^2 = 16 - 30i$ Equate imaginary parts.

        $2ab = -30$

        $b = -\dfrac{15}{a}$ Equate real parts.

        $a^2 - b^2 = 16$ Substitute for b.

        $a^2 - \dfrac{225}{a^2} = 16$ Multiply through by a^2.

        $a^4 - 225 = 16a^2$

        $a^4 - 16a^2 - 225 = 0$ Factorise.

        $(a^2 - 25)(a^2 + 9) = 0$ Since a is real, $a^2 + 9 \neq 0$.

        $a^2 - 25 = 0$

        $a = \pm 5$

        If $a = 5$ then $b = -\dfrac{15}{5} = -3$,

        If $a = -5$ then $b = -\dfrac{15}{-5} = 3$

        The square roots of $16 - 30i$ are $5 - 3i$ and $-5 + 3i$

b   Method 1

$$(2 - i)z^2 + (4 + 3i)z + (-1 + 3i) = 0$$

$$z = \frac{-(4 + 3i) \pm \sqrt{(4 + 3i)^2 - 4(2 - i)(-1 + 3i)}}{2(2 - i)}$$

Use the quadratic formula with $a = 2 - i$, $b = 4 + 3i$, $c = -1 + 3i$

$$z = \frac{-(4 + 3i) \pm \sqrt{7 + 24i - 4(2 - i)(-1 + 3i)}}{2(2 - i)}$$

$$z = \frac{-(4 + 3i) \pm \sqrt{3 - 4i}}{2(2 - i)}$$

Use the method of finding the square root in part **a**.

$$z = \frac{-(4 + 3i) \pm (2 - i)}{2(2 - i)}$$

$$z = \frac{-2 - 4i}{2(2 - i)} \text{ or } \frac{-6 - 2i}{2(2 - i)}$$

$$z = \frac{-1 - 2i}{2 - i} \text{ or } \frac{-3 - i}{2 - i}$$

$$z = \frac{(-1 - 2i)(2 + i)}{(2 - i)(2 + i)} \text{ or } \frac{(-3 - i)(2 + i)}{(2 - i)(2 + i)}$$

$$z = \frac{-5i}{5} \text{ or } \frac{-5 - 5i}{5}$$

$$z = -i \text{ or } -1 - i$$

Method 2

$$(2 - i)z^2 + (4 + 3i)z + (-1 + 3i) = 0$$
$$(2 + i)(2 - i)z^2 + (2 + i)(4 + 3i)z + (2 + i)(-1 + 3i) = 0$$
$$5z^2 + (5 + 10i)z + (-5 + 5i) = 0$$

Multiply through by $(2 - i)^* = 2 + i$

$$z^2 + (1 + 2i)z + (-1 + i) = 0$$

$$z = \frac{-(1 + 2i) \pm \sqrt{(1 + 2i)^2 - 4(1)(-1 + i)}}{2}$$

Use the quadratic formula with $a = 1$, $b = 1 + 2i$, $c = -1 + i$

$$z = \frac{-(1 + 2i) \pm \sqrt{-3 + 4i - 4(-1 + i)}}{2}$$

$$z = \frac{-(1 + 2i) \pm \sqrt{1}}{2}$$

$$z = \frac{-2i}{2} \text{ or } \frac{-2 - 2i}{2}$$

$$z = -i \text{ or } -1 - i$$

Given that $-2 + i$ is a root of the quartic equation
$z^4 + 2z^3 + 2z^2 + 10z + 25 = 0$, find the other roots.

Answer

$z^4 + 2z^3 + 2z^2 + 10z + 25 = 0$ .... If $-2 + i$ is a root of the equation, then the complex conjugate $-2 - i$ must also be a root.

$(z - (-2 + i))$ and $(z - (-2 - i))$ ..... These are the factors of the equation.

$(z - (-2 + i))(z - (-2 - i))$ .... This is the product of the quadratic factors.

$(z + 2 - i)(z + 2 + i)$ .... Expand the brackets using
$(z + 2)^2 + 1$ the difference of two squares.

$z^2 + 4z + 5$ is a quadratic factor ..... To find the other quadratic
of $z^4 + 2z^3 + 2z^2 + 10z + 25$. factor, do polynomial division.

$$
\begin{array}{r}
z^2 - 2z + 5 \\
z^2 + 4z + 5 \overline{)z^4 + 2z^3 + 2z^2 + 10z + 25} \\
z^4 + 4z^3 + 5z^2 \\
-2z^3 - 3z^2 + 10z \\
-2z^3 - 8z^2 - 10z \\
5z^2 + 20z + 25 \\
5z^2 + 20z + 25 \\
\hline
0
\end{array}
$$

$z^4 + 2z^3 + 2z^2 + 10z + 25 = 0$ .... Factorise.

$(z^2 + 4z + 5)(z^2 - 2z + 5) = 0$ ..... Use the quadratic formula to find the factors of $z^2 - 2z + 5$.

$z = \dfrac{2 \pm \sqrt{4 - 4(1)(5)}}{2}$

$z = \dfrac{2 \pm \sqrt{-16}}{2}$

$z = 1 \pm 2i$

The roots are
$-2 - i, -2 + i, 1 + 2i, 1 - 2i$

TIP

For a quartic equation there could be:
- 4 real roots or
- 2 real roots and a pair of complex conjugate roots or
- 2 pairs of complex conjugate roots.

EXERCISE 11D

1   Find the roots z_1 and z_2 of the equation $z^2 - 5 + 12i = 0$ in the form $a + bi$ where a and b are real.

2   Write the following polynomials as products of linear factors.

   a $z^2 + 25$ b $9z^2 - 6z + 5$

   c $4z^2 + 12z + 13$ d $z^4 - 16$

   e $z^4 - 8z^2 - 9$ f $z^3 + z - 10$

   g $z^3 - 3z^2 + z + 5$ h $z^4 - z^2 - 2z + 2$

P   3   Prove that $1 + i$ is a root of the equation $z^4 + 3z^2 - 6z + 10 = 0$. Find all the other roots.

P   4   Prove that $-2 + i$ is a root of the equation $z^4 + 24z + 55 = 0$. Find all the other roots.

P   5   Let $z = a + bi$, where a and b are real numbers. If $\dfrac{z}{z^*} = c + di$, where c and d are real, prove that $c^2 + d^2 = 1$.

6   Find:

   a   the square roots of $8\sqrt{3}i - 8$

   b   the fourth roots of $8\sqrt{3}i - 8$

   c   the value of $(1 + i)^{20}$

   d   the value of $(\sqrt{3} + i)^{60}$

7   Use the modulus-argument method to find the square roots of the following complex numbers.

   a $4\left(\cos\dfrac{2}{5}\pi + i\sin\dfrac{2}{5}\pi\right)$ b $9\left(\cos\dfrac{4}{7}\pi - i\sin\dfrac{4}{7}\pi\right)$

   c $-2i$ d $20i - 21$

   e $1 + i$ f $5 - 12i$

8   Find the square roots of:

   a $e^{\frac{2}{3}\pi i}$ b e^{1+2i}

11.5 Loci

WORKED EXAMPLE 11.6

A point P in the complex plane is represented by the complex number z. Sketch the locus of z in the following situations

a $\quad |z| = 6$ b $\quad |z - 2| = |z + 3i|$ c $\quad \arg(z + 1) = \dfrac{2\pi}{3}$

d $\quad |z - 2 + 5i| = 4$ e $\quad |z - 4| < 3$

Answer

a $\quad |z| = 6$ describes all points which are 6 units   ·····Geometrically.
from the origin.

    If $z = x + iy$ ·················Algebraically.

    $|z| = |x + iy| = 6$

    $x^2 + y^2 = 6^2$

    The locus of all points P lies on a circle centre ····Solution.
$(0, 0)$ radius 6.

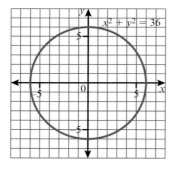

b $\quad |z - 2| = |z + 3i|$

    If $z = x + iy$, $|z - (-3i)|$ gives the distance   ······Geometrically.
from P to the point $(0, -3)$.

    $|z - 2|$ gives the distance from P to the
point $(2, 0)$.

    $|z - 2| = |z + 3i|$ is the set of all points which ······This is the perpendicular bisector
are equidistant from $(0, -3)$ and $(2, 0)$.   of the line joining these points.

    If $z = x + iy$, $|z + 3i| = |z - 2|$ ·············Algebraically.

    $|x + iy + 3i| = |x + iy - 2|$

    $x^2 + (y + 3)^2 = (x - 2)^2 + y^2$

    $x^2 + y^2 + 6y + 9 = x^2 - 4x + 4 + y^2$

$6y + 9 = -4x + 4$

$6y + 4x + 5 = 0$

The locus is all points P which lie on the line $6y + 4x + 5 = 0$ (the perpendicular bisector of $(0, -3)$ and $(2, 0)$).

············ Solution.

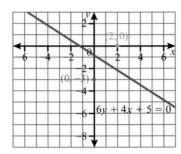

c $\arg(z + 1) = \dfrac{2\pi}{3}$ ······················ Geometrically.

This is the set of all points P on the line which passes through the point $(-1, 0)$ making an angle of $\dfrac{2\pi}{3}$ with the real x-axis.

$z = x + iy$ ···································· Algebraically.

$\arg(z + 1) = \dfrac{2\pi}{3}$

$\arg(x + 1 + iy) = \dfrac{2\pi}{3}$

$\dfrac{y}{x + 1} = \tan\dfrac{2\pi}{3} = -\sqrt{3}$

Giving the line $y = -\sqrt{3}(x + 1)$ ············ We need to restrict the line so $y \geqslant 0$.

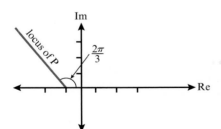

············ Solution: the locus is all points P (see diagram).

143

d $|z - 2 + 5i| = 4$

$z = x + iy$

$|z - (2 - 5i)| = 4$ represents a circle centre $(2, -5)$ radius 4

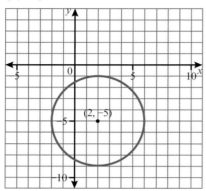

Solution: The locus of all points P is represented by a circle centre $(2, -5)$ radius 4.

e $|z - 4| < 3$

Since $|z - (4 + 0i)| = 3$ represents all points **on** the circumference of a circle centre $(4, 0)$ radius 3.

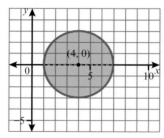

Solution: the locus is all points P **within** a circle (but not on the circumference) whose centre is $(4, 0)$ and radius 3.

EXERCISE 11E

1 Describe in words the locus represented by each of the following.

    a $|z - 2i| = 7$ **b** $|z + 1 - 3i| = 4$ **c** $|z - 2i| = |z - 2|$

2 Find the Cartesian equation for each locus.

    a $|z - 4i| = 3$ **b** $|z - 1 - 4i| = 5$

    c $|z| = |z - 4i|$ **d** $|z - 1 - 2i| = |z - 4 + i|$

3 On different diagrams, sketch the following loci. Shade any regions where needed.

    a $\arg z = \dfrac{\pi}{3}$ **b** $\arg (z + 2) = \dfrac{\pi}{4}$ **c** $\arg (z + 3) = -\dfrac{\pi}{6}$

4 Find the Cartesian equation for the locus given by:

a $|z| = \sqrt{26}$ 　　　　　　　　　b $|z| = |z - 2|$

Hence find the coordinates in the complex plane of where these two loci intersect. Sketch the two loci and show the points of intersection.

5 Given that z is a complex number, show by shading on an Argand diagram, the region for which $2 \leqslant |z - i| \leqslant 3$.

6 Shade on separate Argand diagrams the regions represented by:

a $|z - 2| \leqslant 3$ 　　　　　　　　　b $|z - 3| = |z - 2|$

END-OF-CHAPTER REVIEW EXERCISE 11

 Do **not** use a calculator in this exercise, **except** in Question 1.

1 Show that $1 + i$ is a root of the equation $z^3 + 4z^2 - 10z + 12 = 0$ and find the other roots.

2 If z is a real number and $z = \dfrac{k + 4i}{1 + ki}$ $k \in \mathbb{R}$, find the possible values of k.

3 a Find the modulus and argument of the complex number $2 + 2\sqrt{3}\,i$.

　　b Hence, or otherwise, find the two square roots of $2 + 2\sqrt{3}\,i$, giving your answers in the form $a + ib$.

　　c Find the exact solutions of the equation $iz^2 - 2\sqrt{2}z - 2\sqrt{3} = 0$, giving your answers in the form $a + ib$.

4 If $z = \cos\theta + i\sin\theta$, where $-\pi < \theta \leqslant \pi$, find the modulus and argument of:

a z^2

b $1 + z^2$
distinguishing the cases:

　　i $\theta = 0$ 　　　　　　ii $\theta = \dfrac{1}{2}\pi$ 　　　　　　iii $\theta = \pi$

　　iv $\theta = \dfrac{1}{2}\pi$ 　　　　v $0 < \theta < \dfrac{1}{2}\pi$ 　　　　vi $\dfrac{1}{2}\pi < \theta < \pi$

　　vii $-\dfrac{1}{2}\pi < \theta < 0$ 　　viii $-\pi < \theta < -\dfrac{1}{2}\pi$

5 $z = -3 + 4i$ and $zc = -14 + 2i$. Find:

a c in the form $a + bi$ $(a, b \in \mathbb{R})$

b the modulus and argument of c.

6 The cubic $2z^3 - 5z^2 + wz - 5 = 0$ has a solution $z = 1 - 2i$. Find:

a the other two solutions of the equation

b the value of w.

145

7 Solve:

a $z^3 - 27 = 0$ **b** $w^2 - i(w - 2) = w - 2$

PS

8 A snail starts at the origin of an Argand diagram and moves along the real axis for an hour, covering a distance of 8 metres. At the end of each hour it changes its direction by $\frac{1}{2}\pi$ anticlockwise; and in each hour it walks half as far as it did in the previous hour. Find where it is:

    a after 4 hours   **b** after 8 hours   **c** eventually.

9 a Convert $e^{-\frac{\pi i}{6}}$ to Cartesian form.

   b Write $z = 1 - i\sqrt{3}$ in the form $r(\cos\theta + i\sin\theta)$.

   c Express $8\left(\cos\frac{\pi}{6} - i\sin\frac{\pi}{6}\right)$ in the form $re^{i\theta}$.

   d Find the modulus and argument of $\dfrac{(1+i)^5}{(1-i)^7}$.

10 Sketch on separate Argand diagrams, the locus of points which satisfy:

    a $1 \leqslant |z + 1 - i| \leqslant 3$ **b** $|z - 2 + i| < 2$

11 Describe the points which satisfy:

    a $\arg\dfrac{z - 3}{z - 4i} = \dfrac{\pi}{2}$ **b** $\arg\dfrac{z - i}{z + i} = \dfrac{\pi}{4}$

12 The point A represents a complex number z where $|z + 1 - i| = 1$.

    a Find the Cartesian equation for the locus of A.

    b Sketch the locus of A on an Argand diagram.

    c Find the greatest and least values of:

      i $|z|$ **ii** $|z - 1|$

PS

13 One root of the cubic equation $z^3 + az + 10 = 0$ is $1 + 2i$.

    a Find the value of the real constant a.

    b Show all three roots of the equation on an Argand diagram.

    c Show that all three roots satisfy the equation $|6z - 1| = 13$.

Answers

Answers to proof-style questions are not included.

1 Algebra

Exercise 1A

1
a $3, -7$ **b** $8, -6$

c $0, 3$ **d** $3, -3\frac{2}{3}$

e $4, \frac{2}{3}$ **f** $-2, \frac{1}{2}$

g $-2, -8$ **h** $-4, \frac{10}{7}$

2 **a** $-1 \leqslant x \leqslant 1$ **b** $x \geqslant 1$ **c** $x \leqslant -1$

3 **a** $x \geqslant 1$ **b** $x \leqslant 0$ **c** $0 \leqslant x \leqslant 1$

4 **a** $-2, \frac{4}{3}$ **b** No solution

5 **a** ± 4 **b** $2, 3$

c $\sqrt{2} - 1, \sqrt{3} - 2$ **d** $\sqrt{7} - 2, 5$

e $\frac{1}{6}\left(1 - \sqrt{13}\right), \frac{1}{6}\left(1 + \sqrt{13}\right)$

f $\frac{1}{2}\left(5 - \sqrt{17}\right), \frac{1}{2}\left(5 + \sqrt{17}\right)$

6 **a** $x = 2, y = 1$ or $x = -\frac{10}{3}, y = \frac{11}{3}$

b $x = 0, y = 0$ or $x = -1, y = 3$

7 $x = \frac{1}{2}$ or $x = \frac{3}{2}$

8 **a** $x = \pm 2, x = \pm 3$

b

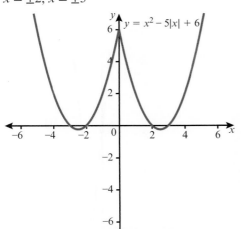

c $x = 0$

9 $x = \pm\dfrac{3}{4}$

10 $x = -\dfrac{16}{3}, y = -3$

Exercise 1B

1 **a** ∨ shaped graph, vertex $= (4, 0)$, y-intercept $= 4$

b ∨ shaped graph, vertex $= \left(\dfrac{5}{2}, 0\right)$, y-intercept $= 5$

c ∨ shaped graph, vertex $= (12, 0)$, y-intercept $= 3$

2 **a**

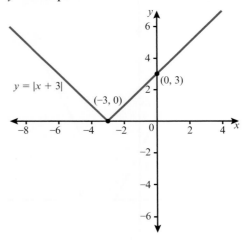

b

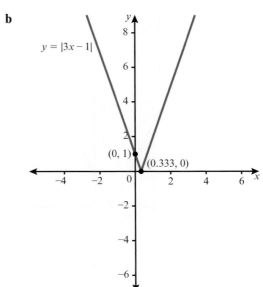

c

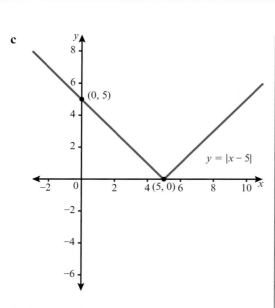

(0, 5)

$y = |x - 5|$

4 (5, 0) 6

d

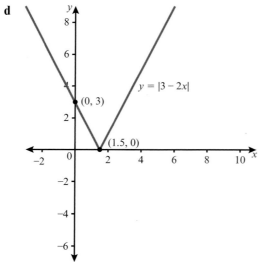

(0, 3)

$y = |3 - 2x|$

(1.5, 0)

e

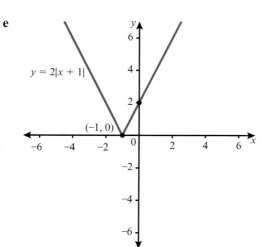

$y = 2|x + 1|$

(−1, 0)

f

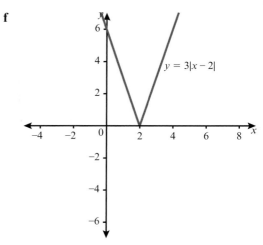

$y = 3|x - 2|$

g

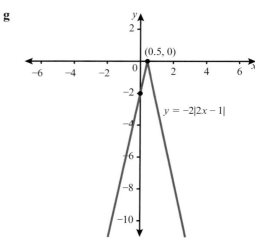

(0.5, 0)

$y = -2|2x - 1|$

h

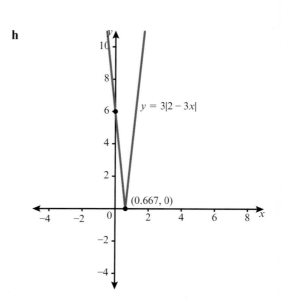

$y = 3|2 - 3x|$

(0.667, 0)

i

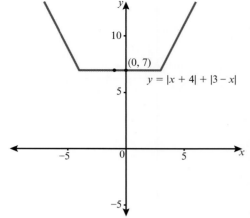

$(0, 7)$

$y = |x + 4| + |3 - x|$

j

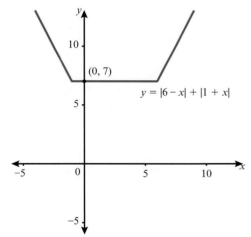

$(0, 7)$

$y = |6 - x| + |1 + x|$

k

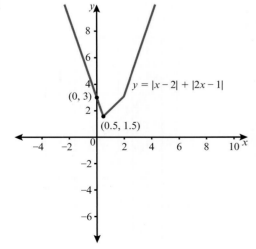

$(0, 3)$

$y = |x - 2| + |2x - 1|$

$(0.5, 1.5)$

l

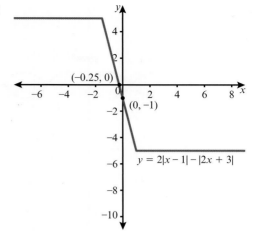

$(-0.25, 0)$

$(0, -1)$

$y = 2|x - 1| - |2x + 3|$

3

a Translation $\begin{pmatrix} 2 \\ 3 \end{pmatrix}$

b Translation $\begin{pmatrix} -3 \\ -2 \end{pmatrix}$

c Reflection in x-axis, translation $\begin{pmatrix} 0 \\ 1 \end{pmatrix}$

d Stretch, stretch factor $\frac{1}{3}$, in the x direction, translation $\begin{pmatrix} 0 \\ 1 \end{pmatrix}$

e Reflection in x-axis, translation $\begin{pmatrix} -2 \\ 2 \end{pmatrix}$

f Stretch, stretch factor 3, in the y direction, reflection in x-axis, translation $\begin{pmatrix} 0 \\ 1 \end{pmatrix}$

4

a

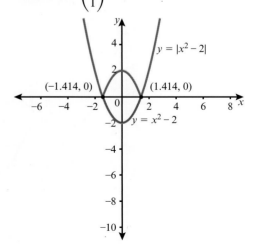

$y = |x^2 - 2|$

$(-1.414, 0)$

$(1.414, 0)$

$y = x^2 - 2$

149

b

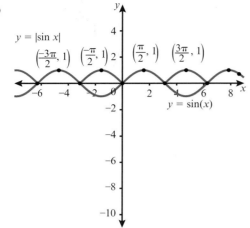

c

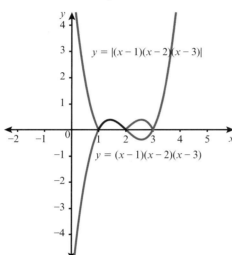

d

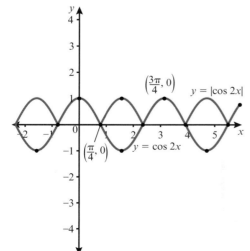

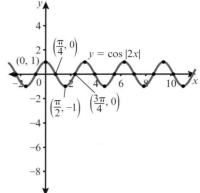

e

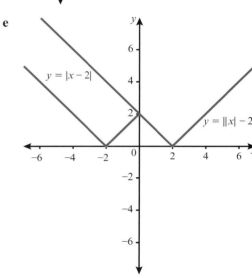

5 $-6 \leqslant f(x) \leqslant 3$

6   **a, b**

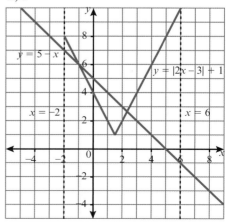

Vertex $\left(\dfrac{3}{2}, 1\right)$, y-intercept $(0, 4)$

c $x = -1$ or $x = \dfrac{7}{3}$

7 **a, b**

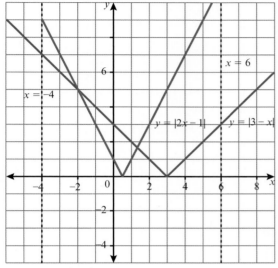

Vertex $\left(\dfrac{1}{2}, 0\right)$, y-intercept $(0, 1)$

c $x = -2$, $x = \dfrac{4}{3}$

8 **a**

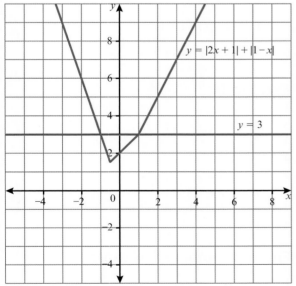

b $x = \pm 1$

9 **a** **i** $y = |x - 4|$ **ii** $y = |x + 2|$
    b **i** $y = |2x + 4|$ **ii** $y = |3x + 6|$
    c **i** $y = |3x - 3|$ **ii** $y = |2x - 5|$

10

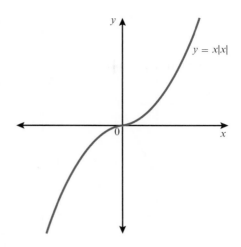

Exercise 1C

1 **a** $-3 < x < -1$
    b $x < -2$ or $x > 8$
    c $-5 \leqslant x \leqslant -2$
    d $x \leqslant -3\dfrac{1}{3}$ or $x \geqslant 2$
    e $x < -\dfrac{3}{4}$ or $x > \dfrac{1}{2}$
    f $x < -3$ or $x > -2\dfrac{1}{3}$
    g $1 < x < 3$
    h $x \leqslant 0$

2 **a**

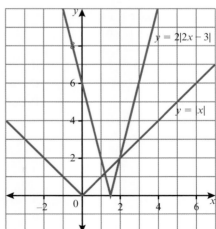

b $\dfrac{6}{5} < x < 2$

151

3 a

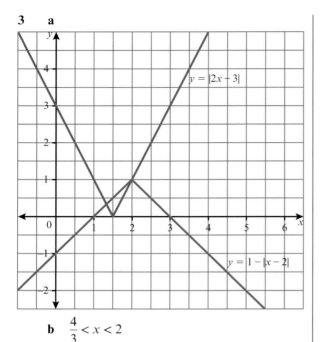

$y = |2x - 3|$

$y = 1 - |x - 2|$

b $\dfrac{4}{3} < x < 2$

4 **a** $2x - 1$ **b** 7 **c** $1 - 2x$

Exercise 1D

1 **a** $x^2 - 3, 7$
   b $x^2 + 2x + 15, 71$
   c $2x^2 - 6x + 22, -71$
   d $5x^2 + 20x + 77, 315$
   e $x^2 - x - 1, -6$
   f $2x^2 + 7x - 1, 3$

2 **a** **i** $x - 6$ **ii** $x + 7$
   b **i** $x^2 + 4x + 2$ **ii** $x^2 + 7x - 1$

3 **a** Proof   **b** Proof
4 Proof
5 Remainder $= 1$

Exercise 1E

1 **a** **i** No   **ii** Yes
   b **i** Yes   **ii** No
   c **i** Yes   **ii** No
   d **i** Yes   **ii** No
   e **i** No   **ii** No
2 **a** **i** $(x + 1)(x - 1)(x + 2)$
      ii $(x + 1)(x - 2)(x + 2)$

b **i** $(x - 2)^2(x - 3)$
   ii $(x + 2)^3$
c **i** $(x - 1)(x^2 - 2x + 10)$
   ii $(x - 3)(x^2 + x + 5)$
d **i** $(x - 1)(2x - 1)(3x - 1)$
   ii $(x + 2)(4x + 3)(3x - 5)$
3 **a** **i** $x = -3, 1, 4$ **ii** $x = -1, -3, 5$
   b **i** $x = 2, \dfrac{3 \pm \sqrt{5}}{2}$ **ii** $x = 1, \dfrac{5 \pm \sqrt{17}}{2}$
4 **a** **i** $x = 1, 2, 3$ **ii** $x = -2, 1, 3$
   b **i** $x = 1, -1$ **ii** $x = -3, 2, 4$
5 **a** Proof
   b $(x - 2)(x - 4)(x + 3) = -3, 2, 4$
6 **a** Proof
   b Proof
7 $c = 14, d = 8$
8 **a** $a = 2, b = 59$ **b** $(x + 8)$
9 $k = 0, 4$
10 $k = -\dfrac{1}{2}$
11 $a = 37, b = -30$
12 **a** $(x - 3)(x - 1)(x + 1)(x + 2), -2, -1, 1, 3$
   b $(x - 2)(x + 1)(x + 2)(x + 3), -3, -2, -1, 2$
   c $(x - 3)(x - 1)(x + 2)(2x + 1), -2, -\dfrac{1}{2}, 1, 3$
   d $(x + 1)(x - 2)(2x + 1)(3x + 2), -1, -\dfrac{2}{3}, -\dfrac{1}{2}, 2$
   e $(x - 1)^3(x + 1), -1, 1$
   f $(x - 2)^2(2x + 1)^2, -\dfrac{1}{2}, 2$

Exercise 1F

1 $5, -3$
2 $4, -3$
3 $2, 1$
4 $5, 3$
5 $a = 3, b = 2$
6 $p = 1, q = -3$
7 $a = 3, b = -1, c = -2$
8 Proof

End-of-chapter review exercise 1

1 $x \leqslant 0$ or $x \geqslant \dfrac{2k}{3}$

2 $x \geqslant 0$

3 a Vertical stretch with scale factor 3; reflection in the x-axis; translation 5 units up.

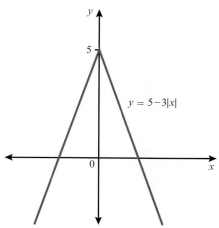

$y = 5 - 3|x|$

b 1.2, −0.8

c −0.8 ⩽ x ⩽ 1.2

4 $x \geqslant 0$

5

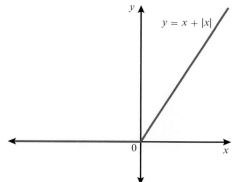

$y = x + |x|$

6 $b = 0, c = -3$

7 $a = -10, b = -18$

8 Proof

9 $a = 1, b = 2, c = -12, d = -18, e = 27$

10 $a = \pm 7$

2 Logarithmic and exponential functions

Exercise 2A

1 a $3 = \log_{10} 1000$

b $x = \log_{10} 500$

c $x = \log_{10} 0.02$

2 a 1.08   **b** 0.627   **c** −0.161

3 a $100\,000 = 10^5$

b $x = 10^{1.03}$

c $x = 10^{-0.2}$

4 a 21.4   **b** 5750   **c** 0.0251

5 a 4   **b** −5   **c** 2.5

d $\dfrac{1}{4}$ **e** $2\dfrac{1}{4}$ **f** 2.5

6 $x = 33$

7 $f^{-1}(x) = \dfrac{1}{2} \log_{10}(x - 5)$

8 $x = 562, y = 17.8$

Exercise 2B

1 a $3 = \log_5 125$ **b** $6 = \log_2 64$

c $-3 = \log_3 \dfrac{1}{27}$ **d** $-7 = \log_2 \dfrac{1}{128}$

e $x = \log_3 17$ **f** $y = \log_x 5$

g $2b = \log_a c$ **h** $3y = \log_x 0.5$

2 a $2^5 = 32$ **b** $3^5 = 243$

c $2^0 = 1$ **d** $64^{\frac{1}{3}} = 4$

e $3^{-3} = \dfrac{1}{27}$ **f** $2^6 = y$

g $x^0 = 1$ **h** $x^{2y} = 6$

3 a 4   **b** 11   **c** 3

4 a −1   **b** 3   **c** 2

d −2   **e** −4   **f** $\dfrac{3}{2}$

g $-\dfrac{3}{4}$ **h** −2

5 a 4   **b** $\dfrac{1}{4}$ **c** $\dfrac{11}{2}$

d −2   **e** −12   **f** $\dfrac{3}{2}$

g $\dfrac{8}{3}$ **h** 6

6 $f^{-1}(x) = 3^{x-3} - 1$

7 a 16   **b** −3, 1

8 a 7   **b** $\dfrac{1}{64}$ **c** 4

d $\dfrac{1}{10}$ **e** $4\sqrt{2}$ **f** 6

g $\dfrac{1}{256}$ **h** −10   **i** $\dfrac{1}{3}\sqrt{3}$

153

Exercise 2C

1 $\dfrac{3}{4}$

2   **a**   **i** $5\log x$ **ii** $5\log x$

    b   **i** $\log x \log y - \log y + 3\log x - 3$

        ii $(\log x)^2 + 4\log x + 4$

    c   **i** $\dfrac{1}{\log b} + \dfrac{1}{\log a}$ **ii** $\log a + 1$

3   **a**   **i** $x = 3^y$ **ii** $x = 16^y$

    b   **i** $x = a^{y+1}$ **ii** $x = a^{y^2}$

    c   **i** $x = \sqrt[3]{3y}$ **ii** $x = \sqrt{y}$

    d   **i** $x = e^{y-2}$ **ii** $x = e^2 y$

4   **a** $\log p + \log q + \log r$

    b $\log p + 2\log q + 3\log r$

    c $2 + \log p + 5\log r$

    d $\dfrac{1}{2}(\log p - 2\log q - \log r)$

    e $\log p + \log q - 2\log r$

    f $-(\log p + \log q + \log r)$

    g $\log p - \dfrac{1}{2}\log r$

    h $\log p + \log q + 7\log r - 1$

    i $\dfrac{1}{2}(1 + 10\log p - \log q + \log r)$

5   **a**   **i** 4 **ii** $\dfrac{1}{2}$

    b   **i** 6 **ii** $\dfrac{3}{2}$

6   **a**   **i** $7y$ **ii** $2x + y$

    b   **i** $x + 2y - z$ **ii** $2x - y - 3z$

    c   **i** $2 - y - 5z$ **ii** $1 + y + 2z$

    d   **i** $x - 4y$

        ii $2 + 2x + y + 2z$

7   **a** $2x + y$ **b** $2 + x - \dfrac{z}{2}$

Exercise 2D

1 $x = 111$

2 $x = -3$

3 $x = 10^{1.5} = 31.6$

4 $x = 9, \dfrac{1}{9}$

5 $x = 81, y = 25$

6   **a**   **i** $x = 1$ **ii** $x = 4$

    b   **i** $x = 9$ **ii** $x = 2$

    c   **i** $x = 8$ **ii** $x = 4$

7 $x = 4$ **8** $x = 8$

9 $x = \dfrac{5}{3}$ **10** $x = 2$

Exercise 2E

1   **a**   **i** $x = 2.45$ **ii** $x = 116$

    b   **i** $x = -1.83$ **ii** $x = 4.62$

    c   **i** $x = -1.71$ **ii** $x = 9.83$

    d   **i** $x = 1.11$ **ii** $x = -2.98$

2 $x = -0.232$

3 $x = 5 - \log_3 4$

4 $x = \dfrac{\log 5}{1 - \log 8}$

5 $x = \dfrac{\log 50}{\log 40}$

6   **a**   **i** $x = 1, \log_2 3$ or $\dfrac{\log 3}{\log 2}$

        ii $x = \log_3 2, \log_3 4$

    b   **i** $x = 2$ **ii** $x = \log_5 3$

    c   **i** $x = 1, \dfrac{1}{\log 5}$ **ii** $x = 2, \dfrac{\log 3}{\log 2}$

    d   **i** $x = 1, \sqrt{2}$ **ii** $x = 3, 9$

7 $x = 1, 3$

Exercise 2F

1   **a** $x > 1.89$ **b** $x < 1.43$

    c $x \leqslant -1.68$ **d** $x > 9.97$

    e $x > 8.54$ **f** $x < -2$

    g $x \geqslant -2$ **h** $x \leqslant -5.61$

    i $x \geqslant 3.77$

2 9.56

3 9.49 a.m Tuesday

4   Proof

Exercise 2G

1   **a** 7.39 **b** 1.65

    c 6.05 **d** 0.0498

2   **a** 0 **b** -0.693

    c   No real solution   **d** -2.30

3   **a** 4 **b** 2

    c 12 **d** 4

4   **a** 1 **b** 1

    c 4 **d** $\dfrac{1}{2}$

5   **a** 0 **b** 1.39

    c -1.70 **d** 3.07

6 **a** $\ln 11$ **b** $\frac{1}{4}\ln 7$

c $\frac{1}{2}(1 + \ln 8)$ **d** $2[\ln(2) - 3]$

7 **a** $x > \ln 9$

b $x \leqslant \frac{1}{4}(2 + \ln 3)$

c $x < -\frac{1}{3}(2 + \ln 2)$

8 **a** 7.39 **b** 0.135
c 2980 **d** −0.211
9 **a** 1.56 **b** 1.15
c 0.618 **d** 0.125
e 0.0560 **f** 0.763
10 **a** $y = 0.607x^{-5}$ **b** $y = 2.01x^2$
11 **a** $\ln 15, 0$ **b** $\ln 2, 2\ln 2$
c $\ln 5, 0$ **d** $0.5 - \ln 2$
12 **a** 4.91, 0.534 **b** 0.0375, 2.05

Exercise 2H

1 **a** $Y = mX + c$ $Y = y$, $X = x^2$, $m = c$, $c = d$
b $Y = mX + c$ $Y = y$, $X = \sqrt{x}$, $m = b$, $c = a$
c $Y = mX + c$ $Y = \frac{y}{x}$, $X = x$, $m = \frac{1}{b}$, $c = a$
d $Y = mX + c$ $Y = \log_{10} y$, $X = \log_{10} x$, $m = q$, $c = \log_{10} p$
e $Y = mX + c$ $Y = y$, $X = x$, $m = \ln b$, $c = \ln k$
f $Y = mX + c$, $Y = x$, $X = \frac{e^y}{x}$, $m = k$, $c = b$

2 $k = 0.18, n = 4.0$
3 $k = 7.2, a = 0.97$
4 **a** Proof **b** $a = 5.7, b = 2.6$
5 $a = 0.08, k = 0.24$
6 $a = 0.4, b = 1.6$
7 7.5, 0.5
8 $-\dfrac{\ln 3}{\ln 2}, \dfrac{\ln 3}{\ln 2}$
9 **a** Model 2: taking logs gives an equation of the form $y = 1.2 - 2.6x$
b $a = 16, k = 2.6$

End-of-chapter review exercise 2

1 $x = \dfrac{1}{3}$
2 $x = 2\ln 2, -\ln 2$
3 $x = \log_5 3$

4 **a**

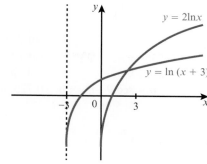

b $x = \dfrac{1 + \sqrt{13}}{2}$

5 Proof

6 $x = e^{\frac{4}{3}} = 3.79, y = e^{\frac{10}{3}} = 28.0$

7 $x = 1 \pm \sqrt{1 - e^y}$

8 $x = 3, 9$

9 $x < \dfrac{\log\left(\dfrac{4}{3}\right)}{\log 27}$

10 **a** $f^{-1}(x) = \dfrac{1}{2}(\ln(x - 1) + 3)$

b $f^{-1}(x)$ is the reflection of $f(x)$ in the line $y = x$

11 Stretch in the x direction stretch factor $\dfrac{1}{2}$ and translation $\begin{pmatrix} 0 \\ -3 \end{pmatrix}$ (in any order)

3 Trigonometry

Exercise 3A

1 **a** −0.675 **b** 1.494
c 1.133
2 **a** $\operatorname{cosec} x$ **b** $\cot x$
c $\sec x$ **d** $\sec^2 x$
e $\cot x$ **f** $-\operatorname{cosec} x$
3 **a** $\sqrt{2}$ **b** 1
c $-\sqrt{3}$ **d** $-\sqrt{2}$
e $-\dfrac{1}{3}\sqrt{3}$ **f** $\dfrac{2}{3}\sqrt{3}$
g 0 **h** $-\dfrac{2}{3}\sqrt{3}$
4 **a** $\dfrac{5}{4}$ **b** $\dfrac{4}{3}$
c $-\dfrac{1}{3}\sqrt{3}$ **d** $\dfrac{2}{3}\sqrt{3}$

5 $\pm 4\sqrt{3}, \pm\sqrt{2}, \pm\frac{1}{2}\sqrt{5}$

6 a $|\tan\phi|$ **b** $\sin\phi\cos\phi$
  c $\cot\phi$ **d** $|\sin\phi|$
  e $|\tan\phi|$ **f** $\cot^2\phi$

7 a $3\sec^2\theta - \sec\theta - 3$ **b** $0.723, \pi, 5.56$

8 $1.11, 2.82, 4.25, 5.96$

9 $\frac{1}{4}\pi, \frac{1}{2}\pi, \frac{3}{4}\pi, \frac{5}{4}\pi, \frac{3}{2}\pi, \frac{7}{4}\pi$

10 Proof

11 Proof

Exercise 3B

1 a $\frac{1}{2}\sin x + \frac{\sqrt{3}}{2}\cos x$

  b $\frac{\sqrt{2}}{2}\sin x - \frac{\sqrt{2}}{2}\cos x$

  c $-\frac{\sqrt{2}}{2}\sin x - \frac{\sqrt{2}}{2}\cos x$

  d $-\sin x$

2 a $\frac{4}{3}$ **b** $\frac{7}{25}$

  c $\frac{4}{5}$ **d** $\frac{117}{44}$

3 $-\frac{117}{125}, -\frac{3}{4}$

4 Proof

5 a $\frac{\tan\theta - 1}{\tan\theta + 1}$ **b** $-\frac{1}{2}, -\frac{1}{3}$

  c $2.68, 2.82$

6 a Proof   **b** $\frac{\pi}{3}$

7 Proof

8 $\pm 30°$

9 a Proof   **b** Proof   **c** Proof

10 $\frac{3}{11}$

Exercise 3C

1 a i $-\frac{7}{8}$ **ii** $\frac{1}{9}$

  b i $\frac{2\sqrt{2}}{3}$ **ii** $\frac{4}{5}$

  c i $\frac{4\sqrt{2}}{9}$ **ii** $\frac{24}{25}$

2 a $\cos(6A)$ **b** $2\sin 10x$
  c $3\cos b$ **d** $\frac{5}{2}\sin\left(\frac{2x}{3}\right)$

3 a $0, \pi, 2\pi$ **b** $90°$
  c $-\frac{\pi}{2}, \frac{\pi}{2}, 0.305, 2.84$ **d** $0°, 180°, 360°$

4 a Proof   **b** Proof
  c Proof   **d** Proof

5 $\pm\sqrt{2}-1, \sqrt{2}-1$

6 $-\frac{1}{3}\sqrt{5}, -\frac{4}{9}\sqrt{5}, -4\sqrt{5}$

7 Proof

8 a i Proof   **ii** Proof
  b $\frac{1-\cos x}{1+\cos x}$

9 a π **b** $\frac{1}{2}\pi, 3.99, 5.44$
  c $0, 0.869, 2.27, \pi, 4.01, 5.41, 2\pi$

10 a Proof
  b $(3x+1)(x-1)(3x+2)$
  c i Proof
    ii $90°, 199°, 222°, 318°, 341°$

Exercise 3D

1 Proof

2 a $\pm\frac{\sqrt{3}}{2}$
  b $\frac{\pi}{6}, \frac{5\pi}{6}$

3 a $4\cos^3 A - 3\cos A$
  b $\frac{3\tan A - \tan^3 A}{1 - 3\tan^2 A}$

4 a $8\cos^4\theta - 8\cos^2\theta + 1$
  b $8\sin^4\theta - 8\sin^2\theta + 1$

5 $\frac{2a-b}{4a}$

6 Proof

7 Proof

8 a Proof
  b $30°, 150°, 90°, 210°, 330°$

9 a Proof
  b $0°, 180°, 360°, 75.5°, 284°$

10 a Proof   **b** Proof
   c Proof   **d** Proof

Exercise 3E

1   **a** $2\sqrt{2}\sin(\theta - 45°)$ **b** $2\sin(\theta - 60°)$

2   **a** $2\sqrt{2}\cos\left(x + \dfrac{\pi}{6}\right)$

     b $5\sqrt{2}\cos\left(x + \dfrac{\pi}{4}\right)$

3   **a** $2\cos\left(x - \dfrac{\pi}{3}\right)$

     b   minimum: $\left(\dfrac{4\pi}{3}, -2\right)$, maximum: $\left(\dfrac{\pi}{3}, 2\right)$

4   1.57, 2.50

5 $\sqrt{61}\cos(\theta - 0.876)$

     a $\sqrt{61}$ when $\theta = 0.876$

     b $-\sqrt{61}$ when $\theta = 4.02$

6 $10\sin(x + 36.9°)$

     a   1   **b**   0

7   **a** $\sqrt{5}$, 26.6°, $-\sqrt{5}$, 206.6°

     b   12, 143.1°, 2, 323.1°

     c $\dfrac{1}{2 - \sqrt{2}}$, 225°, $\dfrac{1}{2 + \sqrt{2}}$, 45°

     d   1, 112.6°, $\dfrac{3}{29}$, 292.6°

8 $-\pi, -\dfrac{3\pi}{4}, 0, \dfrac{\pi}{4}, \pi$

9   **a** $\sqrt{12}\sin(x + 0.869)$

     b $-12 + 12\sqrt{3}$

10   **a** $\sqrt{10}$; 18.4°

     b   69.2°, 327.7°

End-of-chapter review exercise 3

1   **a**   **i** $-\dfrac{\pi}{6}, -\dfrac{5\pi}{6}$ **ii** $-\dfrac{\pi}{2}$

     b   **i** $\dfrac{\pi}{6}, -\dfrac{5\pi}{6}$ **ii** $\dfrac{\pi}{4}, -\dfrac{3\pi}{4}$

     c   **i**   0   **ii** $\dfrac{5\pi}{6}, -\dfrac{5\pi}{6}$

     d   **i** $\dfrac{\pi}{2}, -\dfrac{\pi}{2}$ **ii** $-\dfrac{\pi}{4}, \dfrac{3\pi}{4}$

2   Proof

3   **a**   Proof   **b**   1, 2

     c $\dfrac{\pi}{4}, \dfrac{5\pi}{4}$, 1.11, 4.25

4   **a** $13\sin(x + 1.18)$

     b   Vertical stretch with scale factor 13; translation 1.18 units to the left

5   **a** $\sqrt{58}\sin(x - 1.17)$

     b $y \in \left[-\sqrt{58}, \sqrt{58}\right]$

6   **a** $\sin\left(x + \dfrac{\pi}{4}\right)$, 1, $x = \dfrac{\pi}{4}$

     b $2\cos(x - 25°)$, 2, $x = 25°$

7   **a**   Proof   **b** $\dfrac{\pi}{4}, \dfrac{3\pi}{4}, \dfrac{5\pi}{4}, \dfrac{7\pi}{4}$

8   **a** $\dfrac{1}{6}\pi$ **b** $\dfrac{x + y}{1 - xy}$

9   **a**   Proof   **b** $\dfrac{1}{x}, 1 - 2x^2$

10   **a** $\dfrac{1}{2}\cos x - \dfrac{\sqrt{3}}{2}\sin x$

     b $-2\pi, -\pi, 0, \pi, 2\pi$

11   **a** $a = 1.2, p = \dfrac{2\pi}{3}$

     b   Amplitude = 0.9, period = 3

     c $y = \dfrac{3}{2}\sin\left(\dfrac{2\pi}{3}x + 0.927\right)$

     d   Amplitude = $\dfrac{3}{2}$, period = 3

     e   1.06

     f   0.0580, 0.557

12   **a** $a = 3, b = 5, c = -2$

     b   72°, 153°, 252°, 333°

4 Differentiation

Exercise 4A

1   **a**   **i** $3(x + 1)^3(x - 2)^4(3x - 1)$

         ii $(x - 3)^6(x + 5)^3(11x + 23)$

     b   **i** $(2x - 1)^3(1 - 3x)^2(-42x + 17)$

         ii $(1 - x)^4(4x + 1)(-28x + 3)$

2   **a** $\dfrac{3x + 2}{2\sqrt{x + 1}}$ **b** $\dfrac{3(2 - x)}{\sqrt{3 - x}}$

     c $\dfrac{2x(3 - 5x)}{\sqrt{3 - 4x}}$ **d** $-\dfrac{9x + 14}{\sqrt{2x + 5}}$

     e $\dfrac{(15x - 19)(3x + 5)}{2\sqrt{x - 2}}$

     f $\dfrac{(35x - 4)(5x - 4)^2}{2\sqrt{x}}$

3 $y = 64x - 48$ **4** $(-1, -1)$

5   36 cm², 4.24 cm   6 $x = 3, -\dfrac{1}{3}, \dfrac{7}{4}$

7   $V = 51.8$, $x = 6.4$

8   $a = 4$, $b = 5$

9   a $\dfrac{qa + pb}{p + q}$

    b

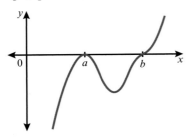

    c q is odd

10   a   Proof   b   Proof

Exercise 4B

1   a   i $\dfrac{2}{(x+1)^2}$ ii $\dfrac{-5}{(x-3)^2}$

    b   i $\dfrac{x(2x+1)^{-\frac{1}{2}} - (2x+1)^{\frac{1}{2}}}{x^2}$

       ii $\dfrac{2x(x-1)^{\frac{1}{2}} - \frac{1}{2}x^2(x-1)^{-\frac{1}{2}}}{x-1}$

    c   i $\dfrac{2(x^2 - x - 2)}{(x^2 + 2)^2}$

       ii $-\dfrac{x^2 + 2x + 4}{(1 + x)^2}$

2   a $\dfrac{x + 2}{2(x+1)^{\frac{3}{2}}}$

    b $\dfrac{10 - x}{2x^2\sqrt{x - 5}}$

    c $-\dfrac{3x + 4}{4x^2\sqrt{3x + 2}}$

3   $(0, 0), (1, 1)$

4   $a = -1$

5   $14y = 8x - 37$

6   $\left(2\left(\sqrt{2} - 1\right), 2\left(1 + \sqrt{2}\right)\right)$, $\left(-2\left(1 + \sqrt{2}\right), -2\left(\sqrt{2} - 1\right)\right)$

7   a $\dfrac{x^2 + 2x - 3}{(x + 1)^2}$

    b $-3 < x < -1, -1 < x < 1$

8   $x \in (0, 2), x \neq 1$

9   $a = 3, b = 4, p = \dfrac{3}{2}$

10   Proof

Exercise 4C

1   a $3e^{3x}$ b $\dfrac{3}{2}e^{\frac{x}{2}}$

    c $\dfrac{2e^{\sqrt{x}}}{\sqrt{x}}$ d $-\dfrac{2e^{\frac{2}{x}}}{x^2}$

    e $3e^{3x-2}$ f $6x(e^{3x^2+1})$

    g $-6e^{-x^3}x^2$ h $4e^{2x}(e^{2x} + 2)$

    i $-\dfrac{e^x}{(e^x + 2)^2}$ j $-\dfrac{6e^{4x}}{\sqrt{1 - 3e^{4x}}}$

    k $9e^{x^3}(e^{x^3} + 1)^2 x^2$ l $-\dfrac{e^x(4x + 1)}{\sqrt{1 - 4x}}$

    m $\dfrac{-e^x x^2 - 2e^x + 2x - 2e^{2x}}{(e^x + 1)^2}$

    n $\dfrac{1}{2}e^{5x-\sqrt{x}}\left(5 - \dfrac{1}{2\sqrt{x}}\right)$

    o $e^{3x}(-8e^x + 5e^{2x} + 3)$

2   $\dfrac{5}{2}$

3

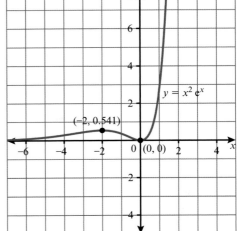

4   **a** $y = e(2x - 1)$, $y = -\dfrac{1}{e}$

     b $x = \dfrac{1}{2}\left(1 - \dfrac{1}{e^2}\right)$

5 $x = \ln 3$ **6** $y = 3x - \ln 4 + 2$

7 $y \geqslant 6 - 8\ln 2$ **8** $(6x^2 + 4x + 3)e^{2x}$

9 $x = -\dfrac{1}{2}, 2$

10   **a**   245 years   **b** -0.198 g/year

11   **a**   4.48 m²/min   **b**   7 minutes

12 $x + 9y = 81 + \ln 3$

Exercise 4D

1   **a** $\dfrac{1}{x}$ **b** $\dfrac{2}{2x - 1}$

     c $\dfrac{-2}{1 - 2x}$ **d** $\dfrac{2}{x}$

     e $\dfrac{b}{a + bx}$ **f** $\dfrac{-1}{x}$

     g $\dfrac{-3}{3x + 1}$ **h** $\dfrac{2}{2x + 1} - \dfrac{3}{3x - 1}$

     i $-\dfrac{6}{x}$ **j** $\dfrac{1}{x} + \dfrac{1}{x + 1}$

     k $\dfrac{2}{x} + \dfrac{1}{x - 1}$ **l** $\dfrac{1}{x - 1} + \dfrac{1}{x + 2}$

     m $\dfrac{1 - \ln 3x}{x^2}$ **n** $\dfrac{x - 2x \ln 2x}{x^4}$

2 $\left(e, \dfrac{1}{e}\right)$, local max

3   **a**   1, minimum

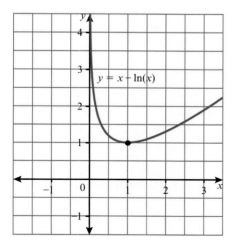

b $\dfrac{1}{2} - \ln 2$, minimum

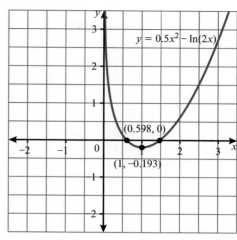

c   1, minimum

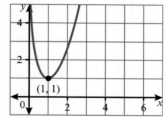

d   1, minimum

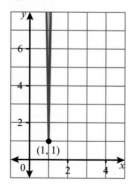

4 $9x - 6y = 9 \ln 3 - 4$

159

5 $x > 6, \dfrac{1}{x-2} + \dfrac{1}{x-6}$

   a $x > 6$

   b   no values of x

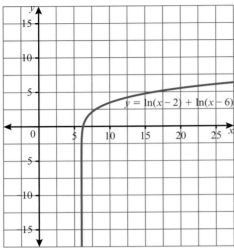

$y = \ln(x-2) + \ln(x-6)$

6   **a** $2x \ln x + x$ **b** $\dfrac{1 - 2\ln x}{x^3}$

   c $\dfrac{e^x(1 - 2x\,e^x)}{(x^2\,e^x + 1)^2}$ **d** $(1 + 2x^2)e^{x^2}$

7 $f^{-1}(x) = \dfrac{1}{2}\ln x$. The graph is a stretch of $y = \ln x$ by a factor of $\dfrac{1}{2}$ in the y direction.

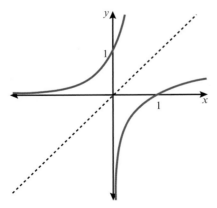

8 $\dfrac{y^2 - 4}{2y}$

9   Proof

10 $3 - \dfrac{1}{2\ln 3}$

11   **a**

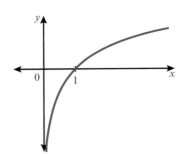

   b   e   **c** $0 < k < \dfrac{1}{e}$

Exercise 4E

1   **a** $-\cos x$ **b** $\sin x$

   c $4\cos 4x$ **d** $-6\sin 3x$

   e $\dfrac{1}{2}\pi\cos\dfrac{1}{2}\pi x$ **f** $-3\pi\sin 3\pi x$

   g $-2\sin(2x - 1)$

   h $15\cos\left(3x + \dfrac{1}{4}\pi\right)$

   i $5\cos 5x$ **j** $2\cos\left(\dfrac{1}{4}\pi - 2x\right)$

   k $2\cos 2x$ **l** $-\pi\sin\pi x$

2   **a** $2\sin x\cos x$ **b** $-2\cos x\sin x$

   c $-3\cos^2 x\sin x$ **d** $5\sin\dfrac{1}{2}x\cos\dfrac{1}{2}x$

   e $-8\cos^3 2x\sin 2x$ **f** $2x\cos x^2$

   g $-42\,x^2\sin 2x^3$

   h $\sin\left(\dfrac{1}{2}x - \dfrac{1}{3}\pi\right)\cos\left(\dfrac{1}{2}x - \dfrac{1}{3}\pi\right)$

   i $-6\pi\cos^2 2\pi x\sin 2\pi x$

   j $6x\sin^2 x^2\cos x^2$

   k 0 **l** $-\cos\dfrac{1}{2}x\sin\dfrac{1}{2}x$

3   Proof

   a $2\cot 2x$ **b** $-3\tan 3x$

   c $2\cot x$ **d** $-6\tan 2x$

4   **a** $\cos x\,e^{\sin x}$

   b $-3\sin 3x\,e^{\cos 3x}$

   c $10\sin x\cos x\,e^{\sin^2 x}$

5   **a** $\left(\dfrac{1}{4}\pi, \sqrt{2}\right)$, maximum;

       $\left(\dfrac{5}{4}\pi, -\sqrt{2}\right)$, minimum

   b (π, π), neither

c (0 2), maximum; $(\pi, -2)$, minimum

d $\left(\dfrac{1}{12}\pi, \dfrac{1}{2}\sqrt{3} + \dfrac{1}{12}\pi\right)$, maximum;

$\left(\dfrac{5}{12}\pi, -\dfrac{1}{2}\sqrt{3} + \dfrac{5}{12}\pi\right)$, minimum;

$\left(\dfrac{13}{12}\pi, \dfrac{1}{2}\sqrt{3} + \dfrac{13}{12}\pi\right)$, maximum;

$\left(\dfrac{17}{12}\pi, -\dfrac{1}{2}\sqrt{3} + \dfrac{17}{12}\pi\right)$, minimum

e $\left(\dfrac{1}{2}\pi, -3\right)$, minimum; $\left(\dfrac{7}{6}\pi, \dfrac{3}{2}\right)$, maximum;

$\left(\dfrac{3}{2}\pi, 1\right)$, minimum; $\left(\dfrac{13}{6}\pi, \dfrac{3}{2}\right)$, maximum

6 Tangent: $4x - y + 1 - \pi = 0$;
normal: $4x + 16y - \pi - 16 = 0$

7 $x = \dfrac{\pi}{3}, \dfrac{2\pi}{3}, \dfrac{4\pi}{3}, \dfrac{5\pi}{3}$

8 $\left(\dfrac{3\pi}{4}, -\dfrac{\sqrt{2}}{2}e^{-\frac{3\pi}{4}}\right)$

9 **a** 40 million litres

b $t = \dfrac{\pi}{2}$(1.6 days), $\dfrac{3\pi}{2}$(3.8 days)

10 **a** $\sec^2 x = \tan^2 x + 1$

b Proof

c $y - \dfrac{\pi}{3} = -\dfrac{4}{3}\left(x - \dfrac{1}{\sqrt{3}}\right)$

11 **a** $2 + \cos 2x - \sec^2 x$

b Proof

c Proof

Exercise 4F

1 **a** **i** $\dfrac{2}{3}$ **ii** $\dfrac{1}{2}$

   b **i** 0 **ii** $-\dfrac{1}{5}$

   c **i** -1 **ii** $\dfrac{5}{3}$

   d **i** -1 **ii** $-\dfrac{1}{2}$

2 **a** **i** $\dfrac{2x}{y^2}$ **ii** $-\dfrac{2x^3}{3y}$

   b **i** $\dfrac{y(8x - y)}{2x(y - 2x)}$ **ii** $\dfrac{y}{2y - x}$

   c **i** $\dfrac{1 - 2y}{2x - 4y - 1}$ **ii** $\dfrac{y}{2y - x}$

   d **i** $\dfrac{y(2x - e^y)}{xye^y - 4}$

     ii $\dfrac{\cos x - 3\sin y}{3x\cos y - 2\sin y}$

3 **a** $(3, 2), (-3, -2)$

   b $(\sqrt{2}, 4\sqrt{2}), (-\sqrt{2}, -4\sqrt{2})$

4 **a** Proof   **b** $3y - x - 8 = 0$

5 $x = 2$

6 $(3, 1), (-3, -1)$

7 $(2, e^4)$

8 **a** $y = 3x - 4$ **b** Proof   **c** $(1, -1)$

9 **a** $y + 3x - 4 = 0$ **b** $\left(\dfrac{8}{3}, -4\right)$

10 **a** $\dfrac{2x + 2y}{y - 2x}$ **b** Proof

Exercise 4G

1 **a** **i** $\dfrac{1}{3t}$ **ii** $-\dfrac{1}{10t}$

   b **i** $\dfrac{\sin\theta}{4\sin(2\theta)}$ **ii** $-\dfrac{3\cos\theta}{2\sin(2\theta)}$

   c **i** $\sin\theta$ **ii** $\dfrac{2}{3}\csc\theta$

2 **a** $y^2 = \dfrac{1}{x}$ **b** $y^2 = 12x$

   c $x^2 + y^2 = 4$

3 **a** $x + y = 1$, for $0 \leqslant x \leqslant 1$

   b $x^{\frac{2}{3}} + y^{\frac{2}{3}} = 1$

   c $x + y = 2$, excluding $(1, 1)$

   d $4x^3 = 27y^2$

4 $\dfrac{9}{4e}$

5 **a** $y = 16x - 255$ **b** $\left(-\dfrac{1}{16}, -256\right)$

6 Proof   **7** Proof

8 **a** $(2a + aq^2, 0)$ **b** Proof

9 $(33, 27)$

10 **a** $\dfrac{1 + \cos\theta}{2 - \sin\theta}$

   b $\tan^{-1}\dfrac{4}{3} \approx 0.927$

   c $1.80, 5.77$

End-of-chapter review exercise 4

1 $(3, 3e^{-3})$

2 **a** $g'(x) = 3 + \dfrac{1}{x} > 0$ **b** $-\dfrac{1}{9}$

3 **a** $(2, 4), (-2, -4)$ **b** Proof

c $(2, 4)$ local max; $(-2, -4)$ local min

4 **a** Left post (Left = 7.76 m, Right = 7.41 m)
b Proof

c $\sqrt[3]{2} + \dfrac{1}{\sqrt[3]{4}} = \dfrac{3\sqrt[3]{2}}{2}$

5 7

6 **a** $0, \dfrac{\pi}{3}, \pi, \dfrac{5\pi}{3}, 2\pi$

b $(0.568, 0.369), (2.21, -1.76),$
$(4.08, 1.76), (5.72, -0.369)$

c
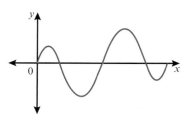

7 **a** $(6x - 6)e^{3x^2 - 6x}$
b $(1, e^{-3})$, minimum
c $x + 6y = 8$

8 Proof

9 **a** Proof **b** $\left(\dfrac{5\pi}{6}, 2\right)$

10 **a** $\dfrac{1}{y}\dfrac{dy}{dx}$

b $4\ln x - \ln(2 + 5x) - \dfrac{1}{2}\ln(x^2 + 1)$

c $\left(\dfrac{4}{x} - \dfrac{5}{2 + 5x} - \dfrac{x}{x^2 + 1}\right)\left(\dfrac{x^4}{(2 + 5x)\sqrt{x^2 + 1}}\right)$

5 Integration

Exercise 5A

1 **a** **i** $e^{3x} + c$ **ii** $\dfrac{1}{2}e^{2x+5} + c$

b **i** $6e^{\frac{2x-1}{3}} + c$ **ii** $2e^{\frac{1}{2}x} + c$

c **i** $2e^{-3x} + c$ **ii** $-\dfrac{1}{4}e^{-4x} + c$

d **i** $8e^{-\frac{x}{4}} + c$ **ii** $-\dfrac{3}{2}e^{-\frac{2}{3}x} + c$

2 **a** $x + \dfrac{1}{2}e^{2x} + c$ **b** $-\dfrac{1}{3}e^{-3x} - e^{-x} + c$

c $3e^{2x} + \dfrac{1}{3}e^{3x} + 9e^x + c$ **d** $\dfrac{e^{2x}}{2} - \dfrac{e^{4x}}{4} + c$

e $-x - \dfrac{9e^{-2x}}{2} + c$ **f** $-\dfrac{1}{12}e^{-12x} + c$

3 **a** $\dfrac{1}{4}(e^{20} - 1)$ **b** $\dfrac{1}{2}(e - 1)$

c $\dfrac{7}{12}$ **d** $\dfrac{e^{12} - 1}{3e^{11}}$

e $\dfrac{2}{3}\left(\dfrac{e^3 - 1}{e^5}\right)$ **f** $\dfrac{1}{2}(7 + 8e^2 + e^4)$

g $\dfrac{1}{6}(-7 + 3e^4 + 3e^8 + e^{12})$

h $3(e^{18} - 1)$ **i** $\dfrac{1}{5} - \dfrac{1}{5e^5}$

4 $y = 2e^{-x} + 3x + 1$

5 $-\dfrac{4}{3}e^{-3} - 3e^{-1} + \dfrac{13}{3}$

6 $2e - \dfrac{7}{2}$

7 **a** $-e^{-2a} - 3e^{-a} + 4$ **b** 4

8 1.86

9 **a** 8 **b** Proof

10 **a** $(0, 8)$
b **i** Proof **ii** $(\ln 5, 12)$
c $-16 + 16\ln 5$

Exercise 5B

1 **a** **i** $\ln|x + 4| + c$
ii $\ln|5x - 2| + c$

b **i** $\dfrac{2}{3}\ln|3x + 4| + c$
ii $-4\ln 2|x - 5| + c$

c **i** $\dfrac{3}{4}\ln|1 - 4x| + c$
ii $-\dfrac{1}{2}\ln|7 - 2x| + c$

d **i** $x + 3\ln|5 - x| + c$
ii $3x - \ln|3 - x| + c$

2 **a** $\ln\dfrac{7}{4}$ **b** $\dfrac{1}{3}\ln\dfrac{7}{4}$

c $\dfrac{\ln 5}{5}$ **d** $\dfrac{\ln 5}{2}$

e $-2\ln\dfrac{5}{3}$ **f** $\ln\dfrac{16}{9}$

3   **a** $1 - \ln 8$ **b** $-\dfrac{1}{2}\ln\dfrac{9}{8}$

      c $-\dfrac{3}{2} - \dfrac{\ln 3}{2}$

4   **a** $A = 2$ **b**   Proof

5   **a**   quotient $= 3x + 4$, remainder $= 4$

      b $\dfrac{17}{2} + 2\ln 3$

6 $k = 2$

7 $y = \dfrac{3}{2}\ln\left(\dfrac{1}{3}(2x + 1)\right)$

8 $y = 2\ln(4x - 3) + 2$

Exercise 5C

1   **a** 1 **b** $\dfrac{1}{2}\sqrt{2}$ **c** $\dfrac{1}{2}$

      d $-\dfrac{1}{6}\sqrt{2}$ **e** $\dfrac{1}{6}(\sqrt{3} - 1)$ **f** 0

      g $\sin 1$ **h** 1.51 **i** 4

2 $\dfrac{1}{5}$

3   **a** $\dfrac{1}{3}\tan 3x + c$

      b $\dfrac{3}{7}\tan(7x - 2) + c$

      c $\dfrac{1}{4}\tan(4x + 1) + c$

4   **a** $\dfrac{\sqrt{3}}{4}$ **b** $\dfrac{\pi}{3} - \dfrac{2}{3}\sqrt{3}$ **c** $\dfrac{1}{3}$

5   **a** $6\sec^2 3x$ **b** 2

6 $f(x) = \dfrac{x^3}{3} - 4\sin x + 3$

7 $y = 2\sin x + 3\cos x - 2\sqrt{2}$

8 $\dfrac{1}{2}$

9 $y = 2\sin 3x - 2\cos x + 2\pi - 1$

10 $A = (0, 0.75),\ B = \left(\dfrac{5\pi}{12}, 0\right);\ \dfrac{3}{4}\left(1 + \dfrac{\sqrt{3}}{2}\right)$

Exercise 5D

1   **a** $\dfrac{5}{2}x + \dfrac{5}{4}\sin 2x + c$

      b $1.5x + 1.5\sin x + c$

      c $\dfrac{1}{2}x - \dfrac{1}{16}\sin 8x + c$

      d $\dfrac{2}{3}\tan 3x - 2x + c$

      e $\dfrac{5}{2}\tan 2x - 5x + c$

      f $\dfrac{9}{8}x + \dfrac{3}{4}\sin 2x + \dfrac{3}{32}\sin 4x + c$

2   **a** $\dfrac{\pi}{3} - \dfrac{\sqrt{3}}{4}$ **b** $\dfrac{4\sqrt{3}}{3} - \dfrac{\pi}{3}$ **c** $\dfrac{3\sqrt{3}}{8} + \dfrac{\pi}{4}$

      d $\dfrac{\pi}{6}$ **e** $\dfrac{3\pi}{4}$ **f** $\dfrac{1}{6}(4 - \pi)$

3   **a** $\dfrac{5\sqrt{3}}{4} + \dfrac{\pi}{3}$ **b** $\dfrac{1}{4}(1 + \sqrt{3})$

      c $\dfrac{9}{4} - \sqrt{3} + \dfrac{5\pi}{3}$ **d** $\dfrac{1}{2} - \dfrac{\sqrt{3}}{2}$

      e $\dfrac{1}{8}(\pi + 18)$ **f** $\dfrac{\sqrt{3}}{2}$

4 $\dfrac{\pi}{2}$ **5** $\dfrac{\sqrt{3}}{4}$

6   **a** $A = \dfrac{3}{8}\ \ B = -\dfrac{1}{2}\ \ C = \dfrac{1}{8}$

      b $\dfrac{3\pi}{16}$

7   **a** $\dfrac{\pi}{2}$ **b** $\dfrac{3\pi^2}{8}$

8   **a**   Proof   **b**   Proof

9   **a**   Proof   **b** $\dfrac{\sqrt{2}}{2}$

10 $k = -\sqrt{3}$

Exercise 5E

1   **a**   **i** 0.886 **ii** 1.09

      b   **i** 1.48 **ii** 3.70

      c   **i** 3.38 **ii** 0.455

2   **a**

      b 3.86

      c   Concave curve: under-estimate

163

3 **a** 1.98
    b Use more trapezia; exact integration is possible

4 **a** $\sqrt{\dfrac{\pi}{2}}$ **b** 0.957
    c Concave curve: under-estimate

5 10.2 m

6 **a** $p = \pi^2$, $q = 4\pi^2$ **b** 22.3 m

7 **a** 3.90, under-estimate   **b** 5.52
    c $L = 3.90$, $U = 5.52$; use more triangles and trapezia

8 **a** 0.551
    b Over-estimate, since graph of $y = \sec x$ bends upwards.

9 25.5

10 **a** 1.9113
    b

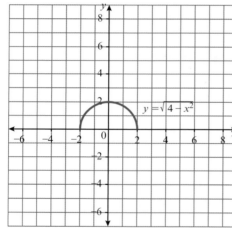

      $\dfrac{\pi}{3} + \dfrac{\sqrt{3}}{2}$

    c 0.1%

End-of-chapter review exercise 5

1 Proof   **2** $4 + \dfrac{1}{3}\ln\dfrac{11}{5}$

3 **a** 1650
    b Concave curve: under-estimate
    c By using more intervals

4 Proof

5 **a** $\dfrac{7}{2} - \dfrac{3}{2}e^{-2k} - 2e^{-k}$

    b $\dfrac{7}{2}$

6 Proof

7 **a** $A = 1$ **b** Proof

8 **a** Proof   **b** Proof

9 **a** Proof   **b** $2 - \dfrac{\pi}{4}$

10 $\dfrac{\pi(\pi + 2)}{2}$

6 Numerical solutions of equations

Exercise 6A

1 **a** −2   **b** 2
    c 1   **d** 6
    e −8   **f** 4

2 **a** 2 and 3   **b** 0 and 1
    c 1 and 2   **d** −2 and −1

3 **a** **i** Proof   **ii** Proof
    b **i** Proof   **ii** Proof

4 **a** **i** Proof   **ii** Proof
    b **i** Proof   **ii** Proof
    c **i** Proof   **ii** Proof
    d **i** Proof   **ii** Proof

5 **a** Proof   **b** Proof

6 **a** Proof   **b** $k = 2$

7 **a** Proof   **b** $n = 1$

8 **a** Proof   **b** Proof
    c $N = 12$

9 **a** Proof
    b **i** f(2) = −6, f(3) = 11
        ii f(x) is not continuous (has an asymptote) at $x = 2.5$

10 **a** **i**

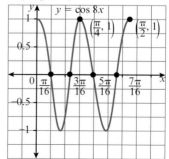

        ii Two

b i $g(0) = g\left(\dfrac{\pi}{4}\right) = 1$

ii $g(x)$ changes sign twice.

iii Proof using, for example,
$x = 0, \dfrac{\pi}{8}, \dfrac{\pi}{4}$

Exercise 6B

1 a i 3, 3.219, 3.305, 3.337, 3.349

ii 4, 2.982, 2.949, 2.948, 2.948

b i −1, 0, −0.250, −0.200, −0.211

ii 1, 0.540, 0.997, 0.546, 0.996

c i 0.5, 1.057, 0.938, 1.056, 0.940

ii 1, 1.364, 1.052, 1.329, 1.089

2 a i 0.70

ii 0.95

b i 4.51

ii 0.41

3 a i No **ii** No **iii** N/A

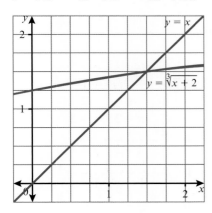

b i Yes **ii** Yes **iii** Greater root

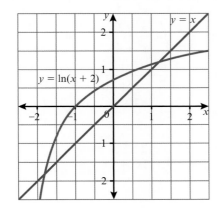

c i Yes **ii** Yes **iii** Smaller root

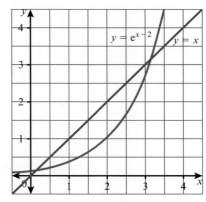

4 $0.9502, f(x) = x - \cos\left(\dfrac{x}{3}\right), 0.95$

5 Proof
1.6198, 1.8781, 1.6932, 1.8208, 1.7304,
1.7933; converging

6 a Proof

b 0.7895; it is converging to another root

7 Proof
$x_{n+1} = \sqrt[3]{e^{x_n} + 2}$ with $x_0 = 2$ converges to 2.27
in 11 steps,

$x_{n+1} = \dfrac{e^{x_n} + 2}{x_n^2}$ with $x_0 = 2$ converges to 2.27

in 3 steps

8 a Proof

b 3.11111, 3.10332, 3.10384, 3.10380; 3.104

9 a 9

b 5 steps, x_4 and x_5 are the same to
4 significant figures, 9.725

10 a i $a = 2, b = -\dfrac{1}{2}$

ii $a = 2, b = -6$

b i $a = 4, b = 1$

ii $a = 2, b = 1, c = 2$

c i $a = \dfrac{1}{2}, b = -\dfrac{5}{2}$

ii $c = \dfrac{1}{3}, d = \dfrac{2}{3}$

d i $a = 1, b = 2$

ii $a = 3, b = 1$

Exercise 6C

1 a Proof b 0.248

2 a Proof b 0.7105; 1.12

3 a Proof b 1.26

4 a $1 - e^{-a}$
   b Proof
   c 2.3

5 a $y - 2x = 1$
   b Proof
   c 0.70, 0.2

6 a 1 b 1.2684, 1.3106, 1.3106

End-of-chapter review exercise 6

1 a Proof b Proof c 2.77

2 a Two solutions

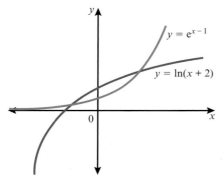

   b Proof
   c 1.13

3 a Proof
   b Proof
   c $x = \pi + \tan^{-1}\left(\dfrac{x}{2}\right)$; 4.275

4 a Proof
   b 2.61

5 a Proof
   b Proof
   c $a = \dfrac{1}{2}, b = 2$
   d 3.048

6 a i $(\pi - x, \sin x)$
      ii $(\pi - 2x)\sin x$
   b i Proof
      ii Proof
      iii Proof
   c i 0.710 ii 1.12

7 Further algebra

Exercise 7A

1 a $3 - \dfrac{3}{2x+1}$

   b $3 + \dfrac{7}{4x-2}$

   c $\dfrac{3x^2}{2} + \dfrac{3x}{4} + \dfrac{3}{8} - \dfrac{13}{8(2x-1)}$

   d $x + 1 - \dfrac{7x+2}{x^2+x+3}$

   e $4x + 3 - \dfrac{14x+8}{x^2+3}$

   f $x^2 - 1 - \dfrac{2}{x^2+2}$

2 $A = 1, B = 3, C = 3, D = -4$

3 $A = 2, B = 2, C = 5, D = 5, E = 4$

4 $A = 3, B = 1, C = -4, D = 1$

5 Quotient $x - 1$, remainder 3

6 $2 + \dfrac{3}{x+2}$

7 $a = -1$, quotient $= x + 1$

8 Proof

Exercise 7B

1 a i $\dfrac{1}{x} + \dfrac{1}{x-2} - \dfrac{2}{x-3}$

      ii $\dfrac{2}{x} - \dfrac{1}{x+2} - \dfrac{1}{x+1}$

   b i $\dfrac{5}{x-1} - \dfrac{2}{x+1} - \dfrac{3}{x+2}$

      ii $\dfrac{4}{x-3} - \dfrac{1}{x+4} - \dfrac{3}{x+1}$

2 a $\dfrac{1}{x-1} + \dfrac{1}{x^2+1}$ b $\dfrac{1}{x+1} - \dfrac{x}{x^2+4}$

   c $\dfrac{1}{x+3} + \dfrac{x-2}{x^2+4}$ d $\dfrac{4}{2x-3} - \dfrac{x-4}{x^2+1}$

   e $\dfrac{1}{3x+2} - \dfrac{1}{x^2+16}$ f $\dfrac{1}{1+4x} - \dfrac{1-4x}{4+x^2}$

   g $\dfrac{2}{1+2x} - \dfrac{2+x}{4+x^2}$ h $\dfrac{2}{x} - \dfrac{x}{x^2+9}$

   i $\dfrac{3}{x+4} - \dfrac{6x+1}{2x^2+7}$

3 **a** $1 - \dfrac{1}{x^2} + \dfrac{1}{x} - \dfrac{2}{x+1}$

  b $1 + \dfrac{1}{x} - \dfrac{x-1}{x^2+1}$

  c $1 - \dfrac{2}{x+4} + \dfrac{x-4}{x^2+1}$

  d $2 + \dfrac{2}{x-2} - \dfrac{3}{(x+2)^2}$

  e $3 + \dfrac{5}{x-2} - \dfrac{2}{x+2} - \dfrac{3}{2x-1}$

  f $-1 + \dfrac{2}{x} + \dfrac{1}{2x-5} + \dfrac{3}{2x+5}$

  g $1 + \dfrac{2}{x-1} - \dfrac{1}{x} - \dfrac{1}{x+1}$

  h $1 + \dfrac{3}{x^2} - \dfrac{4}{x+2}$

  i $3 - \dfrac{2}{x-1} + \dfrac{4}{4x^2+9}$

4 **a** Proof **b** $1 - \dfrac{3}{x-1} + \dfrac{3}{x-2}$

5 $\dfrac{1}{x-a} + \dfrac{1}{x-2a}$

6 **a** **i** $\dfrac{1}{x+1} - \dfrac{1}{(x+1)^2}$

    ii $\dfrac{1}{x-2} + \dfrac{2}{(x-2)^2}$

  b **i** $\dfrac{4}{x^2} - \dfrac{1}{x} + \dfrac{1}{x+4}$

    ii $\dfrac{1}{(x-1)} - \dfrac{1}{x} - \dfrac{1}{x^2}$

  c **i** $\dfrac{2}{x-1} + \dfrac{3}{(x+2)^2} - \dfrac{2}{x+2}$

    ii $\dfrac{1}{x-2} + \dfrac{6}{(x-2)^2} - \dfrac{1}{x+1}$

7 **a** Proof

  b $\dfrac{1}{x-1} + \dfrac{3-x}{(x-2)^2}$

8 $\dfrac{1}{x-a} + \dfrac{1}{(x-a)^2} - \dfrac{1}{x}$

9 **a** $\dfrac{3}{(2x+3)(x+2)}$

  b $\dfrac{6}{2x+3} - \dfrac{3}{x+2}$

10 **a** $R_T = \dfrac{R_1 R_2}{R_1 + R_2}$ **b** Proof

11 $-\dfrac{2}{3}$

Exercise 7C

1 **a** $1 - 3x + 6x^2$ **b** $1 - 5x + 15x^2$
  c $1 + 4x + 10x^2$ **d** $1 + 6x + 21x^2$

2 **a** 84 **b** -8
  c -270 **d** 256
  e $\dfrac{56}{27}$ **f** $-20a^3$
  g $20b^3$
  h $\dfrac{1}{6}n(n+1)(n+2)c^3$

3 **a** $1 + 2x - 2x^2$ **b** $1 - x + 2x^2$
  c $1 - 8x + 8x^2$ **d** $1 + \dfrac{1}{8}x + \dfrac{5}{128}x^2$

4 **a** $-\dfrac{1}{2}$ **b** $\dfrac{625}{16}$
  c $\dfrac{5}{24}$ **d** $-\dfrac{5}{2}$
  e 20 **f** $\frac{1}{8}\sqrt{2}$
  g $-\dfrac{1}{16}a^3$
  h $\dfrac{1}{48}n(n+2)(n+4)b^3$

5 **a** $1 - 4x + 12x^2$ **b** $|x| < \dfrac{1}{2}$

6 **a** Proof **b** $|x| < 9$
  c **i** $1 - \dfrac{x}{18} - \dfrac{x^2}{648}$
    ii $1 + \dfrac{x^2}{18} - \dfrac{x^4}{648}$
    iii $3 + \dfrac{x}{6} - \dfrac{x^2}{216}$
  d 3.1620

7 **a** $1 - 2x - 2x^2 - 4x^3$ **b** $|x| < \dfrac{1}{4}$
  c 9.79796 **d** 0.0776

8 4

9 -540 **10** $-\dfrac{1}{2}$

Exercise 7D

1 **a** $\dfrac{1}{3} + \dfrac{2}{27}x + \dfrac{2}{81}x^2 + \dfrac{20}{2187}x^3, \; |x| < \dfrac{9}{4}$

  b $4 + x - \dfrac{1}{16}x^2 + \dfrac{1}{96}x^3, \; |x| < \dfrac{8}{3}$

  c $\dfrac{1}{8} + \dfrac{3}{16}x + \dfrac{3}{16}x^2 + \dfrac{5}{32}x^3, \; |x| < 2$

  d $2 - \dfrac{1}{4}x - \dfrac{1}{64}x^2 - \dfrac{1}{512}x^3, \; |x| < 4$

e $\frac{1}{9} + \frac{4}{27}x + \frac{4}{27}x^2 + \frac{32}{243}x^3$, $|x| < \frac{3}{2}$

f $\frac{1}{2} - \frac{1}{4}x + \frac{1}{8}x^2 - \frac{1}{16}x^3$, $|x| < 2$

2 a $2 + 17x + 84x^2$

b $7 + \frac{1}{2}x + \frac{9}{8}x^2$

c $\frac{1}{16} - \frac{3}{64}x - \frac{5}{128}x^2$

3 $\frac{1}{2} - \frac{x}{16} + \frac{3x^2}{256}$; $|x| < 4$

4 a $2 + \frac{x}{12} - \frac{x^2}{288} + ...$ b 20.08

5 a $2 - \frac{4}{3}x - \frac{8}{9}x^2 - \frac{80}{81}x^3$, $|x| < \frac{1}{2}$

b $1 + \frac{1}{2}x + \frac{1}{4}x^2 + \frac{1}{8}x^3$, $|x| < 2$

c $\frac{1}{8} - \frac{3}{16}x + \frac{3}{16}x^2 - \frac{5}{32}x^3$, $|x| < 2$

d $2x - \frac{1}{4}x^4 + \frac{3}{64}x^7 - \frac{5}{512}x^{10}$, $|x| < \sqrt[3]{4}$

e $1 + 2x - 6x^2 + 28x^3$, $|x| < \frac{1}{8}$

f $\frac{4}{3} + \frac{16}{9}\sqrt{3}x + \frac{40}{9}x^2 + \frac{80}{27}\sqrt{3}x^3$, $|x| < \sqrt{3}$

6 $1 + 5x + \frac{27}{2}x^2$, $|x| < \frac{1}{2}$

7 $\frac{7}{32}$

8 Proof

9 $\frac{5}{2} + \frac{7}{4}x - \frac{3}{8}x^2 - \frac{17}{16}x^3$

10 $1 - \frac{1}{2}x + \frac{3}{8}x^2 + \frac{3}{16}x^3$

Exercise 7E

1 a $\frac{1}{1+x} + \frac{1}{1+2x}$

b $2 - 3x + 5x^2$ c $|x| < \frac{1}{2}$

2 a $\frac{1}{(x+1)^2} + \frac{2}{2-x} + \frac{2}{x+1}$

b $4 - \frac{7x}{2} + \frac{21x^2}{4}$ c $|x| < 1$

3 $1 - 3x + 7x^2$

4 $\frac{6}{1+4x} - \frac{3}{1+2x}$; $3 - 18x + 84x^2 - 360x^3$; $|x| < \frac{1}{4}$

5 a $\frac{1}{3-x} + \frac{1}{x+2} + \frac{2}{(x+2)^2}$

b $\frac{4}{3} - \frac{23}{36}x + \frac{29}{54}x^2$ c $|x| < 2$

6 a $A = 2$, $B = 1$

b i $2 - \frac{3}{2}x + \frac{17}{4}x^2$

ii The expansion is only valid for $|x| < 0.5$

End-of-chapter review exercise 7

1 $\frac{1}{x} + \frac{a}{x^2} + \frac{2}{x-a}$

2 Proof

3 a $1 - \frac{7}{2}x$

b $|x| < \frac{1}{12}$

c 3.86

4 No, as the expression is not defined for small x.

5 $1 - 2x + 3x^2 - 4x^3$

6 $1 - \frac{x^2}{2} - \frac{x^4}{8}$

7 $a = 1$, $b = 3$ or $a = 3$, $b = 1$

8 a $1 + x + \frac{2x^3}{3}$

b 1.44267

9 -270

10 $1 - x + x^3$

11 a $A = 1$, $B = -1$, $C = 1$; $|x| < 1$

b Proof

c $P = 1$, $Q = -1$, $R = 1$; $|x| > 1$

d 0.9901

e 0.019608

12 a $mc^2 + \frac{1}{2}mv^2 + \frac{3m}{8c^2}v^4 + ...$, $|v| < c$

b i 0.00373% ii 17.5%

c Proof

8 Further calculus

Exercise 8A

1
  a $\dfrac{6}{36x^2 + 1}$ **b** $\dfrac{2}{x^2 + 4}$

  c $\dfrac{6}{4x^2 + 9}$ **d** $\dfrac{3}{9x^2 - 12x + 5}$

  e $\dfrac{3x^2}{x^6 + 1}$ **f** $-\dfrac{3}{10x^2 - 2x + 1}$

2
  a $\dfrac{6x}{4x^2 + 1} + 3\tan^{-1} 2x$

  b $\dfrac{4x - (16x^2 + 1)\tan^{-1} 4x}{x^2(16x^2 + 1)}$

  c $e^{-x}\left(\dfrac{2}{4x^2 + 1} - \tan^{-1} 2x\right)$

  d $\dfrac{e^{\tan^{-1} x}}{x^2 + 1}$

  e $\dfrac{2}{x + x(\ln x)^2}$

  f $\dfrac{e^x(x^2 + 1)\tan^{-1} x - e^x}{(x^2 + 1)(\tan^{-1} x)^2}$

3 $y = \dfrac{x}{6} + \dfrac{\pi}{4} - \dfrac{1}{2}$

4 $y - \dfrac{\pi}{3} = -\dfrac{4}{3}\left(x - \dfrac{1}{\sqrt{3}}\right)$

5   Proof

Exercise 8B

1
  a $\dfrac{1}{8}\tan^{-1}\left(\dfrac{x}{2}\right) + c$

  b $\dfrac{1}{3}\tan^{-1}(3x) + c$

  c $\dfrac{1}{6}\tan^{-1}\left(\dfrac{x}{6}\right) + c$

  d $\dfrac{\sqrt{5}}{10}\tan^{-1}\left(\dfrac{2\sqrt{5}x}{5}\right) + c$

  e $\dfrac{\sqrt{3}}{9}\tan^{-1}(\sqrt{3}x) + c$

  f $\dfrac{\sqrt{2}}{6}\tan^{-1}\left(\dfrac{\sqrt{2}}{3}x\right) + c$

2
  a $\dfrac{\sqrt{3}\pi}{27}$

  b $\dfrac{\pi}{2}$

  c $\dfrac{\pi}{3}$

3   4.43

Exercise 8C

1
  a $\ln(1 + \sin x) + c$

  b $\dfrac{1}{3}\ln|1 + x^3| + c$

  c $\ln|\sin x| + c$

  d $\ln(4 + e^x) + c$

  e $-\dfrac{2}{3}\ln|5 - e^{3x}| + c$

  f $\dfrac{1}{3}\ln|\sec 3x| + c$

2
  a $\ln(e + 1)$

  b $\dfrac{1}{2}\ln 2$ **c** $\dfrac{1}{2}\ln\dfrac{4}{3}$

3
  a Proof

  b $\ln k = \ln 8$ so $k = 8$

4 $\dfrac{1}{3}\ln\dfrac{5}{2}$

5 $2\sqrt{3} - 2$, so $a = 2$, $b = 3$, $c = -2$

6
  a $\ln 2$ **b** $\sqrt{3}\pi - \dfrac{1}{3}\pi^2$

Exercise 8D

1
  a $2\ln|\sqrt{x} - 2| + c$

  b $-\dfrac{1}{3(3x + 4)} + c$

  c $2\cos\left(\dfrac{1}{3}\pi - \dfrac{1}{2}x\right) + c$

  d $\dfrac{1}{6}(x - 1)^6 + \dfrac{1}{7}(x - 1)^7 + c$

      $\equiv \dfrac{1}{42}(6x - 1)(x - 1)^6 + c$

  e $\ln(1 + e^x) + c$

  f $\dfrac{1}{2}\ln(3 + 4\sqrt{x}) + c$

  g $\dfrac{6}{5}x(x + 2)^{\frac{3}{2}} - \dfrac{8}{5}(x + 2)^{\frac{3}{2}} + c$

      $\equiv \dfrac{2}{5}(3x - 4)(x + 2)^{\frac{3}{2}} + c$

  h $6(x - 3)^{\frac{1}{2}} + \dfrac{2}{3}(x - 3)^{\frac{3}{2}} + c$

      $\equiv \dfrac{2}{3}(x + 6)\sqrt{x - 3} + c$

  i $\ln|\ln(x)| + c$

  j $\sin^{-1}\left(\dfrac{1}{2}x\right) + c$

2 a Proof   **b** $\tan^{-1} e^x + c$

3 a $\ln\left(\frac{1}{2}(1+e)\right)$ **b** $2\ln 2$

   c $\frac{7}{12}$ **d** $1\frac{1}{15}$

   e $\frac{1}{6}\pi$ **f** $109\frac{1}{15}$

   g 8π

   h $\frac{1}{2}\left(\tan^{-1} 3 - \tan^{-1}\frac{1}{2}\right) = \frac{1}{8}\pi$

   i $\frac{1}{2}$ **j** $\frac{1}{3}\sqrt{3}$

   k $3\ln\frac{4}{3}$

4 $\frac{1}{4}\pi - \frac{1}{2}$

5 a $\frac{1}{4}(x^2+1)^4 + c$ **b** $\frac{1}{3}(4+x^2)^{\frac{3}{2}} + c$

   c $\frac{1}{6}\sin^6 x + c$ **d** $\frac{1}{4}\tan^4 x + c$

   e $-\sqrt{1-x^4} + c$ **f** $-\frac{1}{8}\cos^4 2x + c$

6 a $\frac{\pi}{4}$ **b** $\frac{\pi}{6}$

   c π **d** $1 - \frac{\sqrt{2}}{2}$

   e $\frac{\pi}{2}$

7 a i 2732.8 **ii** 1.8

   b i $\frac{1}{6}$ **ii** $\frac{1}{3}$

   c i $9 - 8\ln 2$

      ii $-\frac{76}{15} - 12\ln 3 + 12\ln 5$

8 $\left(\frac{1}{4}\right)\tan(\ln(x^2)) + c$

9 $\frac{\pi}{12}$

10 $y = 3\ln|\sec x| + 4$

11 a $A = 1, B = 3$

   b $(4, 0.272)$

   c $\frac{4}{3}$

Exercise 8E

1 a i $3\ln|x-10| + 2\ln|x-3| + c$

     ii $2\ln|x+1| - \ln|x-3| + c$

   b i $\frac{1}{2}\ln|x-1| - \frac{1}{2}\ln|x+1| + c$

     ii $\frac{1}{2}\ln|x-1| + \frac{1}{2}\ln|x+1| + c$

   c i $3\ln|x-2| - \ln|1-x| + c$

     ii $-\ln|1-x| - 2\ln|1+x| + c$

   d i $5\ln|x+3| + \ln|x| - \frac{3}{x} + c$

     ii $2\ln|x-2| + 2\ln|x| + \frac{1}{x} + c$

   e i $\ln|x-1| - \frac{2}{x-1} - \ln|x+3| + c$

     ii $\ln|x+1| - \frac{1}{x+1} - \ln|x-2| + c$

2 a $\frac{1}{x-2} - \frac{1}{x+3}$ **b** $\ln\left|\frac{(x-2)}{(x+3)}\right| + c$

3 $-\ln 3$

4 a $\frac{1}{2-x} + \frac{2}{x+1}$

   b 8

5 $\ln\left(\frac{4}{9}\right) + \frac{1}{2}$

6 a $\frac{2}{x-1} - \frac{1}{x+2}$

   b $\ln\left(\frac{7}{4}\right)$

7 $\frac{e-1}{e+1}$

8 $\frac{1}{4}\pi^2 + 3\pi\ln 2 - 2\pi\ln 3$

9 a $\frac{1}{x-2} - \frac{x}{x^2+1}$ **b** Proof

Exercise 8F

1 a $\sin x - x\cos x + c$

   b $3(x-1)e^x + c$

   c $(x+3)e^x + c$

2 a $\frac{1}{4}(2x-1)e^{2x} + c$

   b $\frac{1}{4}x\sin 4x + \frac{1}{16}\cos 4x + c$

   c $\frac{1}{4}x^2(2\ln(2x) - 1) + c$

3 a $\frac{1}{36}x^6(6\ln(3x) - 1) + c$

   b $\frac{1}{4}(2x-1)e^{2x+1} + c$

   c $x(\ln(2x) - 1) + c$

4   **a** $\dfrac{1}{4}(e^2 + 1)$ **b** $\dfrac{1}{2}\sqrt{2}(4 - \pi)$

     c $\dfrac{ne^{n+1} + 1}{(n + 1)^2}$

5 $\dfrac{1}{2}(x^2 + 1)\tan^{-1}x - \dfrac{1}{2}x + c$

6 $1 - 3e^{-2}; \dfrac{1}{4}\pi(1 - 13e^{-4})$

7 $\dfrac{1}{9}\pi; \dfrac{1}{324}\pi^2(2\pi^2 - 3)$

8 $(e^3 - 1)\ln 2 + \dfrac{2}{3}e^3 + \dfrac{1}{3}$

9   **a**   3

     b $5\ln 5 - 2\ln 2 - 3$

End-of-chapter review exercise 8

1   **a**   Proof

     b $\sin^{-1}a$

     c $1 - \sqrt{1 - a^2}$

     d $a \arcsin a + \sqrt{1 - a^2} - 1$

2 $\ln 16 - \dfrac{15}{16}$

3   **a** $\left(\dfrac{\sqrt{2}}{2}, 1\right)$

     b   **i**   0 at A, $\dfrac{\pi}{2}$ at O **ii** $\dfrac{4}{3}$

4   **a** $x\cos^{-1}x - \sqrt{1 - x^2} + c$

     b $x\tan^{-1}x - \dfrac{1}{2}\ln(1 + x^2) + c$

     c $x((\ln x)^2 - 2\ln x + 2) + c$

5   **a**   Proof   **b** $\ln\dfrac{3}{2}$

6   **a** $\dfrac{1}{2}x^2 \ln x - \dfrac{1}{4}x^2 + c$ **b** $\ln 3$

7   **a** $\dfrac{4 - 3x}{2\sqrt{2 - x}}$

     b i and ii $-\dfrac{2}{15}(4 + 3x)(2 - x)^{\frac{3}{2}} + c$

8 $\dfrac{1}{3}\ln\dfrac{65}{2}$

9 $\dfrac{1}{4}$

10   **a** $\left(\dfrac{1}{2}\pi, \dfrac{1}{2}\pi\right)$ **b**   2

11 $2 + 2\ln 5 - 3\ln 3$

9 Vectors

Exercise 9A

1   **a** $\dfrac{1}{3}\begin{pmatrix} 2 \\ 2 \\ 1 \end{pmatrix}$ **b** $\dfrac{1}{5}\begin{pmatrix} 4 \\ -1 \\ 2\sqrt{2} \end{pmatrix}$

2 $-\dfrac{4}{3}$

3   **a**   **i** $\mathbf{a} + \dfrac{4}{3}\mathbf{b}$ **ii** $\mathbf{a} + \dfrac{1}{2}\mathbf{b}$

     b   **i** $-\dfrac{3}{2}\mathbf{a} + \mathbf{b}$ **ii** $-\dfrac{1}{2}\mathbf{b} + \dfrac{1}{2}\mathbf{a}$

     c   **i** $\dfrac{3}{2}\mathbf{a} - \mathbf{b}$ **ii** $-\dfrac{4}{3}\mathbf{b} + \dfrac{1}{2}\mathbf{a}$

4   **a**   Not collinear

     b   Not collinear

     c   Collinear, $AB : BC = 1 : 1 - 2a$

5 $AB : BC = 1 : 2$

6   **a** $C(10 - 8x, 1 + 6x)$

     b $x = \dfrac{6}{25}$

7   Proof

8   **a** $\dfrac{1}{2}(\mathbf{p} + \mathbf{q})$ **b**   Proof

9   Proof

10   Proof

11 $\pm\left(\dfrac{9}{\sqrt{97}}\mathbf{i} + \dfrac{4}{\sqrt{97}}\mathbf{j}\right)$

12   **a** $(4, -6)$

     b $\overrightarrow{OP} = \sqrt{65}, \overrightarrow{ON} = 2\sqrt{13}, \overrightarrow{PN} = \sqrt{13}$

Exercise 9B

1 $\dfrac{3}{2}$

2   **a** $-5\mathbf{i} + 4\mathbf{j} - 2\mathbf{k}$ **b**   Proof

3   **a**   Proof   **b** $3\mathbf{i} + 6\mathbf{j} + 19\mathbf{k}$

4 $\dfrac{\sqrt{474}}{5}$

5   **a** $\dfrac{3}{2}\mathbf{i} + \dfrac{3}{2}\mathbf{j} - 2\mathbf{k}$ **b** $\left(\dfrac{1}{2}, \dfrac{13}{2}, 0\right)$

6 $p = \dfrac{3}{8}, q = \dfrac{1}{8}$

7 $\mathbf{m} = \dfrac{q}{p + q}\mathbf{a} + \dfrac{p}{p + q}\mathbf{b}$

8   **a**   Proof   **b**   Proof

Exercise 9C

1 **a** and **d** are perpendicular, so are **b** and **c**.

2 **a** 45° **b** 167.3°
  c 180° **d** 136.7°
  e 7.0° **f** 90°

3 99.6° (or 80.4°)

4 $t = \dfrac{3}{2}$ or -2

5 76.4°

6 48.2°

7 -2; 132.5°

8 **a**

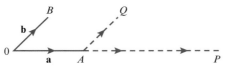

  b 14 **c** 30°

9 **a** $4\mathbf{j} + 3\mathbf{k}$; 5
  b Proof
  c The scalar product is non-zero.
  d 101°

Exercise 9D

1 $\mathbf{r} = \begin{pmatrix} 1 \\ 4 \\ 2 \end{pmatrix} + t\begin{pmatrix} -3 \\ -1 \\ 1 \end{pmatrix}$; $(-5, 2, 4)$

2 **a** $\mathbf{r} = \begin{pmatrix} 2 \\ -3 \end{pmatrix} + t\begin{pmatrix} 1 \\ 2 \end{pmatrix}$; $y = 2x - 7$

  b $\mathbf{r} = \begin{pmatrix} 4 \\ 1 \end{pmatrix} + t\begin{pmatrix} -3 \\ 2 \end{pmatrix}$; $2x + 3y = 11$

  c $\mathbf{r} = \begin{pmatrix} 5 \\ 7 \end{pmatrix} + t\begin{pmatrix} 1 \\ 0 \end{pmatrix}$; $y = 7$

  d $\mathbf{r} = t\begin{pmatrix} 2 \\ -1 \end{pmatrix}$; $x + 2y = 0$

  e $\mathbf{r} = \begin{pmatrix} a \\ b \end{pmatrix} + t\begin{pmatrix} 0 \\ 1 \end{pmatrix}$; $x = a$

  f $\mathbf{r} = \begin{pmatrix} \cos\alpha \\ \sin\alpha \end{pmatrix} + t\begin{pmatrix} -\sin\alpha \\ \cos\alpha \end{pmatrix}$;
    $x\cos\alpha + y\sin\alpha = 1$

3 **a** $\mathbf{r} = -\mathbf{i} + \mathbf{j} + t(3\mathbf{i} - 2\mathbf{j})$
  b $\mathbf{r} = 3\mathbf{i} - \mathbf{j} + s(\mathbf{i} + 5\mathbf{j})$

  c $\mathbf{r} = \begin{pmatrix} -3 \\ 4 \end{pmatrix} + s\begin{pmatrix} 2 \\ -3 \end{pmatrix}$

  d $\mathbf{r} = \begin{pmatrix} -2 \\ 2 \\ 1 \end{pmatrix} + t\begin{pmatrix} 1 \\ 0 \\ 0 \end{pmatrix}$

4 $k = 4$

5 $\left(\dfrac{19}{9}, \dfrac{28}{9}, \dfrac{41}{9}\right)$

6 **a** $\mathbf{r} = \begin{pmatrix} 11 \\ 7 \\ -3 \end{pmatrix} + t\begin{pmatrix} 2 \\ 2 \\ 0 \end{pmatrix}$

  b **i** $(2, -2, -3)$ **ii** $\sqrt{34}$

7 **a** $\mathbf{r} = 2\mathbf{i} - 5\mathbf{k} + t(3\mathbf{i} + 2\mathbf{j} - 6\mathbf{k})$
  b Proof

8 **a** $\begin{pmatrix} 1 \\ 1 \\ 9 \end{pmatrix}$

  b $x + 2y - 4z = 9$

  c $\begin{pmatrix} -1 \\ 3 \\ -1 \end{pmatrix}$

  d 61.9°

9 3

Exercise 9E

1 **a** $(-3, 1, 5)$
  b $(3, -5, 4)$

2 **a** Intersect at $(1, -1, 0)$
  b Parallel
  c Intersect at $(-7, -5, -4)$

3 43.1°

4 1 or -1

End-of-chapter review exercise 9

1 **a** $\mathbf{r} = \begin{pmatrix} 1 \\ 1 \end{pmatrix} + t\begin{pmatrix} 2 \\ -1 \end{pmatrix}$

  b $\left(\dfrac{13}{7}, \dfrac{4}{7}\right)$

2 **a** $a = -3, b = -7, p = -2, q = -1$
  b 78.9°

3 $(\cos 2\alpha, \sin 2\alpha)$; for all α, the intersection lies on the circle with $(-1, 0)$ and $(1, 0)$ at ends of a diameter

4 All $\dfrac{1}{4}(\mathbf{a} + \mathbf{b} + \mathbf{c} + \mathbf{d})$; the lines joining the midpoints of opposite edges of a tetrahedron meet and bisect one another.

5 $\mathbf{r} = \mathbf{i} + 3\mathbf{j} + \mathbf{k} + t(-6\mathbf{j} - 2\mathbf{k})$; $\dfrac{\sqrt{65}}{5}$

6 P does, Q does not

7 **a** $t = \dfrac{1}{5}$ or 1

b $\begin{pmatrix} -3 \\ 3 \\ 8 \end{pmatrix}$

c 82°

8 $\sqrt{17}$

9 **a** $r = \begin{pmatrix} 2 \\ -1 \\ -5 \end{pmatrix} + s\begin{pmatrix} -2 \\ 4 \\ 1 \end{pmatrix}$

b $x = 2$, $(-2, 7, -3)$

10 114°

10 Differential equations

Exercise 10A

1 **a** **i** $y = -\dfrac{3}{2}\cos 2x + c$

ii $y = 12\sin\left(\dfrac{x}{3}\right) + c$

b **i** $y = \dfrac{1}{3}e^{2x} + c$

ii $y = 8e^{\frac{x}{2}} + c$

c **i** $y = 3\tan x + c$

ii $y = \tan x - x + c$

d **i** $y = -\dfrac{1 + 2\ln x}{4x^2}$

ii $y = \sec x + c$

2 **a** **i** $y = \dfrac{4}{3}\sqrt{3x + 9} - 2$

ii $y = -2\sqrt{4 - x} + 3$

b **i** $y = \ln|x^2 + 1| - \ln 2$

ii $y = \dfrac{1}{4}x^2 + \dfrac{1}{2}\ln|x| + \dfrac{3}{4}$

c **i** $y = -2e^{-3x} + 2$

ii $y = -2e^{1-2x} + 2$

d **i** $y = \dfrac{1}{16}(4\sin^4(x) + 1)$

ii $y = \dfrac{1}{2}\sec^2 x + 4$

3 **a** **i** $\sin y = \dfrac{1}{2} - \cos x$

ii $\tan y = \tan x - \sqrt{3}$

b **i** $\ln|y| = \dfrac{1}{3}x^3$

ii $-\dfrac{1}{y} = \ln|x| - 1$

c **i** $e^{-2y} = -4e^x + 5$

ii $e^y = e^x + e^2 - 1$

4 **a** **i** $y = \pm\sqrt{x^3 + c}$

ii $y = -\dfrac{1}{x^2 + c}$

b **i** $y = \sin^{-1}(\ln|x| + c)$

ii $y = \tan^{-1}(\ln|x - 2| + c)$

c **i** $y = Ae^x(x - 1) - 3$

ii $y = \dfrac{A}{1 - x}$

5 $y = \dfrac{2cx^4 + 2}{1 - cx^4}$

6 $k = 3$

7 **a** When $t = 0$, $\dfrac{dN}{dt} = 0.8 > 0$; decreases from 5.7 years.

b $N = 2e^{0.8t - 0.07t^2}$

c 19665

d It will decay to zero.

8 $y = \arctan\left(\sin x + \dfrac{1}{2}\right)$

Exercise 10B

1 **a** **i** $\dfrac{dN}{dt} = 5N$ **ii** $\dfrac{dM}{dt} = 3M$

b **i** $\dfrac{dv}{dt} = \dfrac{kv}{\sqrt{t}}$ **ii** $\dfrac{dN}{dt} = k\sqrt{N}\sqrt[3]{t}$

c **i** $\dfrac{dr}{dt} = \dfrac{k}{2\pi\sqrt{r}}$ **ii** $\dfrac{dr}{dt} = -\dfrac{0.2}{\pi r^2}$

2 $\dfrac{dA}{dt} = -\dfrac{A}{100}$, $A = 15e^{-\frac{1}{100}t}$ kg

3 **a** $\dfrac{dA}{dt} = \dfrac{3200}{\sqrt{A}}$

b 12 seconds

4 **a** $\dfrac{dh}{dt} = 0$ when $h = 25$, so the tree stops growing.

b $\dfrac{dh}{dt} = 0.2\sqrt{25 - h}$, $t = -10\sqrt{25 - h} + 50$

c **i** 1.0 years   **ii** 10 years

d $h = t - 0.01t^2$ for $0 \leqslant t \leqslant 50$

5 **a** $\dfrac{dA}{dt} = -k\sqrt{A}$ **b** Proof

c $a = 20$ **d** 225

6 **a** $\dfrac{dx}{dt} = kx\,(15 - x)$ **b** 12 km

7 **a** $\dfrac{dh}{dt} = -0.016\sqrt{h}$ **b** 250 seconds

8 **a** Proof

b $\theta = 19 - 14e^{-0.3t}$; 11 minutes

9 **a** Decrease in size due to, for example, competition for food.

b $N = \dfrac{3e^{1.2t}}{1 + e^{1.2t}}$

c Proof; increases with the limit of 3000

End-of-chapter review exercise 10

1 **a** $y = \tan(\ln(x^2 + 1) + c)$

b $\sec y = c \sec x$, $c \neq 0$

2 **a** $y = \dfrac{(1 + x)}{2(2 - x)^2}$ **b** $2 \sin x \cos y = 1$

c $y = \sqrt{\dfrac{2}{x - 1}}$ **d** $y = 2 \sec x$

3 **a** $y = \dfrac{2(1 - kx^4)}{1 + kx^4}$

b $y = \ln(k + x \ln x)$

c $y^2 = 4\left(k + \tan\dfrac{1}{2}x\right)$

4 **a** $n = 5000\, e^{0.01(0.05t - 50 \sin 0.02t)}$

b 3150

5 **a** $N = \dfrac{1000}{1 + 499e^{-5t}}$

b 2.3×10^5

c The number of bacteria approaches 1 000 000.

6 **a** $4\pi r^2$

b $\dfrac{400}{\pi r^2(1 + t)^2}$

c $V = 1600\left(1 - \dfrac{1}{1 + t}\right)$

d **i** 7.0 cm   **ii** 0.021 cm s^{-1}

7 **a** Proof

b 34.7 months

c Not suitable, as it predicts indefinite growth.

d $N = 250\, e^{(0.04t + 0.191\sin(0.524\,t))}$

8 **a** $\dfrac{dv}{dx} = \dfrac{-8e^{-4x}}{v}$ **b** Proof

c $x = \dfrac{1}{2}\ln(4t + 1)$; $v = \dfrac{2}{4t + 1}$

9 **a** $\dfrac{dV}{dt} = Cx^2\dfrac{dx}{dt}$ **b** Proof

c $\dfrac{2}{5}x^{\frac{5}{2}} = -At + k$ **d** $\dfrac{32}{31}$

10 **a** $\ln n = 1 + \ln 5000 - e^{(-0.01t)}$

b $n \to 5000e \approx 13\,600$

11 **a** Proof   **b** 2.1 seconds

11 Complex numbers

Exercise 11A

1 **a** 13i   **b** $\dfrac{8}{13}$i

c $3i\sqrt{10}$ **d** 12i

2 **a** -30 **b** $-9 + 3i$

c -20 **d** $\dfrac{5}{6}$

3 **a** $\pm\dfrac{2i}{3}$ **b** $\pm\dfrac{2i}{\sqrt{3}}$ **c** $\pm\dfrac{5i}{4}$

Exercise 11B

1 **a** 4   **b** 6i   **c** 13

d 24i   **e** 24i   **f** -10

g 16   **h** -36

2 **a** $4 - i$ **b** $2 + 3i$

c $7 + 0i$ **d** $5 + 2i$

e $5 - 5i$ **f** $8 + 6i$

g $\dfrac{1}{5}(1 + 7i)$ **h** $\dfrac{1}{10}(1 - 7i)$

i $1 - 3i$ **j** $2 + 4i$

k $\dfrac{1}{2}(-1 - 3i)$ **l** $\dfrac{1}{5}(3 + i)$

3 $2x - y = 1$, $x + 2y = 3$, $x = 1$, $y = 1; 1 + i$

4   **a** $-2 - 5i$ **b** $\frac{1}{3}(7 - 2i)$

    c $\frac{1}{2}(-5 + i)$ **d** $\frac{1}{25}(7 + 24i)$

5   **a** $z = 2$, $w = i$
    b $z = 1 + i$, $w = 2i$

6   **a** $\pm 3i$ **b** $-2 \pm i$

    c $3 \pm 4i$ **d** $\frac{1}{2}(-1 \pm 5i)$

7   **a** $1 - 7i$
    b $-2 - i$
    c 5
    d $-3i$

8 $z = 3 + 4i$

9   **a** $x^2 - 2x + 5 = 0$
    b $x^2 - 6x + 25 = 0$
    c $x^2 + 2x + 6 = 0$

10 $x = 2$, $y = 1$

11   **a** $2 + i$ **b** $-2 \pm 3i$
    c i, $2 + i$ **d** $z = 2 + i$, $w = i$

Exercise 11C

1 $\frac{8}{13}(1 - 5i)$

2 $r(\cos\theta + i\sin\theta)$, where:

    a $r = 2$, $\theta = \frac{7}{12}\pi$

    b $r = 2$, $\theta = \frac{1}{12}\pi$

    c $r = 2$, $\theta = \frac{5}{6}\pi$

    d $r = 2$, $\theta = \frac{1}{12}\pi$

3   **a** $\cos\theta - i\sin\theta$ **b** $\cos\theta - i\sin\theta$

    c $r(\cos\theta - i\sin\theta)$ **d** $\frac{1}{r}(\cos\theta - i\sin\theta)$

4 $2\left(\cos\frac{1}{3}\pi + i\sin\frac{1}{3}\pi\right)$,

    $\sqrt{2}\left(\cos\left(\frac{-1}{4}\pi\right) + i\sin\left(-\frac{1}{4}\pi\right)\right)$;

    $-\sqrt{3} + i$

5

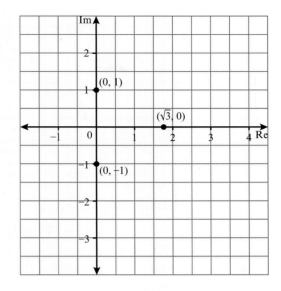

    a $-\frac{1}{6}\pi$

    b $\frac{1}{6}\pi$

    c $\frac{1}{3}\pi$

    d $\frac{1}{3}\pi$

6

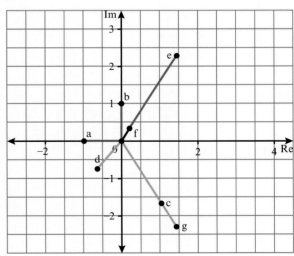

7 $e^{\cos\theta}$, $\sin\theta$

8

The graph shows points labelled:
- $-4.16 + 9.09i$ (e)
- $-5\sqrt{2} + 5\sqrt{2}i$ (b)
- $-3 + 0i$ (d)
- a $1 + \sqrt{3}i$
- $-0.99 - 0.41i$
- $0 - 5i$

a	$1 + \sqrt{3}i$	**b**	$-5\sqrt{2} + 5\sqrt{2}i$
c	$0 - 5i$	**d**	$-3 + 0i$
e	$-4.16 + 9.09i$	**f**	$-0.99 - 0.14i$

9 $r(\cos\theta + i\sin\theta)$ where:

a $r = 2.24,\ \theta = 1.11$

b $r = 5,\ \theta = -0.93$

c $r = 7.81,\ \theta = 2.27$

d $r = 10.63,\ \theta = -2.29$

e $r = 1,\ \theta = 0$

f $r = 2,\ \theta = \dfrac{1}{2}\pi$

g $r = 3,\ \theta = \pi$

h $r = 4,\ \theta = -\dfrac{1}{2}\pi$

i $r = 2,\ \theta = -\dfrac{1}{4}\pi$

j $r = 2,\ \theta = \dfrac{2}{3}\pi$

10 **a** $\sqrt{3} + i$ **b** $3 + 4i$

c $-3 + 4i,\ -9 + 4i$ **d** $\pm\dfrac{1}{2}\sqrt{2} + (2 \mp \dfrac{1}{2}\sqrt{2})i$

Exercise 11D

1 $z_1 = 3 - 2i,\ z_2 = -3 + 2i$

2 **a** $(z - 5i)(z + 5i)$

b $(3z - 1 - 2i)(3z - 1 + 2i)$

c $(2z + 3 - 2i)(2z + 3 + 2i)$

d $(z - 2)(z + 2)(z - 2i)(z + 2i)$

e $(z - 3)(z + 3)(z - i)(z + i)$

f $(z - 2)(z + 1 - 2i)(z + 1 + 2i)$

g $(z + 1)(z - 2 - i)(z - 2 + i)$

h $(z - 1)^2(z + 1 - i)(z + 1 + i)$

3 $(1 - i)(-1 + 2i)(-1 - 2i)$

4 $(-2 - i)(2 - i\sqrt{7})(2 + i\sqrt{7})$

5 Proof

6 **a** $\pm(2 + 2\sqrt{3}i)$

b $\pm(\sqrt{3} + i),\ \pm(1 - \sqrt{3}i)$

c -2^{10}

d 2^{60}

7 **a** $\pm 2\left(\cos\dfrac{1}{5}\pi + i\sin\dfrac{1}{5}\pi\right)$

b $\pm 3\left(\cos\dfrac{2}{7}\pi - i\sin\dfrac{2}{7}\pi\right)$

c $\pm(1 - i)$

d $\pm(2 + 5i)$

e $\pm(1.10\ldots + 0.455\ldots i)$

f $\pm(3 - 2i)$

8 **a** $e^{\frac{1}{3}\pi i},\ e^{\frac{4}{3}\pi i}$ **b** $\pm\sqrt{e}(\cos 1 + i\sin 1)$

Exercise 11E

1 **a** Circle centre $(0, 2)$ radius 7

b Circle centre $(-1, 3)$ radius 4

c Perpendicular bisector of the line joining $(0, 2)$ to $(2, 0)$, $y = x$

2 **a** $x^2 + (y - 4)^2 = 9$

b $(x - 1)^2 + (y - 4)^2 = 25$

c $y = 2$

d $y = x - 2$

3 **a**

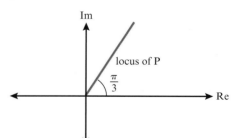

b

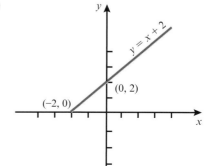

c

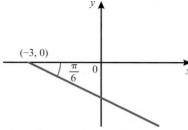

4 **a** $x^2 + y^2 = 26$
b $x = 1$
$(1, 5), (1, -5)$

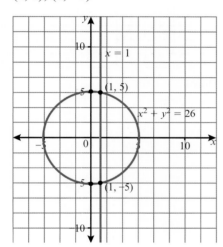

5

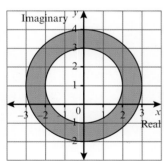

6 **a**

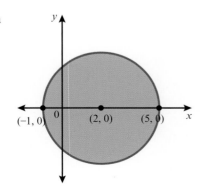

b

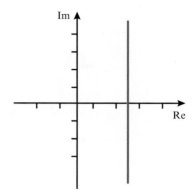

End-of-chapter review exercise 11

1 $1 - i, -6$

2 $k = \pm 2$

3 **a** $4, \dfrac{1}{3}\pi$ **b** $\pm(\sqrt{3} + i)$

c $1 - i(\sqrt{3} + \sqrt{2}), -1 + i(\sqrt{3} - \sqrt{2})$

4 **a** **i** $1, 0$ **ii** $1, \pi$
iii $1, 0$ **iv** $1, \pi$
v $1, 2\theta$ **vi** $1, 2\theta - 2\pi$
vii $1, 2\theta$ **viii** $1, 2\theta + 2\pi$

b **i** $2, 0$ **ii** 0, undefined
iii $2, 0$ **iv** 0, undefined
v $2\cos\theta, \theta$ **vi** $-2\cos\theta, \theta - \pi$
vii $2\cos\theta, \theta$ **viii** $-2\cos\theta, \theta + \pi$

5 **a** $c = 2 + 2i$ **b** $|c| = 2\sqrt{2}, \arg c = \dfrac{\pi}{4}$

6 **a** $1 + 2i, \dfrac{1}{2}$ **b** $w = 12$

7 **a** $z_1 = 3, z_2 = \dfrac{-3 + 3\sqrt{3}i}{2}, z_3 = \dfrac{-3 - 3\sqrt{3}i}{2}$

b $w_1 = 2i, w_2 = 1 - i$

8 **a** $6 + 3i$

b $\dfrac{17}{16}(6 + 3i)$

c $\dfrac{16}{15}(6 + 3i)$

9 **a** $\dfrac{\sqrt{3}}{2} - \dfrac{i}{2}$

b $z = 2\left(\cos\dfrac{\pi}{3} - i\sin\dfrac{\pi}{3}\right)$

c $8e^{\frac{-\pi i}{6}}$

d modulus $= \dfrac{1}{2}, \arg = \pi$

10 **a**

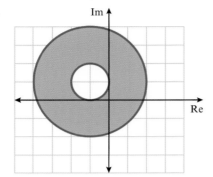

b

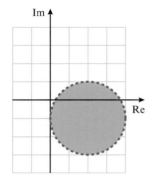

11 **a** The semicircle in the first quadrant of a circle with 3 and 4i at the ends of a diameter.

b The major arc of a circle with centre $(-1, 0)$ passing through i and $-$i.

12 **a** $(x + 1)^2 + (y - 1)^2 = 1$

b

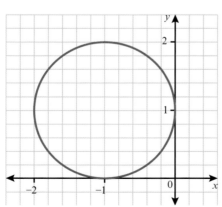

c **i** min $\sqrt{2} - 1$, max $\sqrt{2} + 1$
    ii min $\sqrt{5} - 1$, max $\sqrt{5} + 1$

13 **a** $a = 1$

b

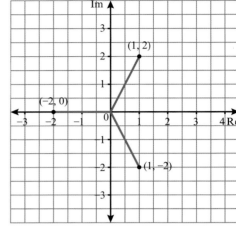

c Proof